SHOOT THE WORKS

SHOOT THE WORKS

by Judith Glashow,
Doris Goldstein
and Suzanne Mahler

Ziff-Davis Books New York

Library of Congress Catalogue Number: 80-50872
ISBN: 0-87165-058-4 (hardcover) 0-87165-059-2 (paperback)

Printed in the United States of America
First Printing 1980

Ziff-Davis Publishing Company
One Park Avenue
New York, New York 10016

Contents

Acknowledgment

We wish to thank Alan Appel for teaching us the techniques of photography.

SHOOT THE WORKS

1 Shoot the Works Now

You can protect your possessions with photographs. If a fire, theft or other disaster strikes even once in your lifetime, a photo record that substantiates your insurance claims, income tax deductions or property recovery claims can mean thousands of extra dollars in your pocket.

Experts agree that you can get much better recovery by keeping good records, which means a full inventory of everything you own, photos of as many items as possible, and receipts when available. Even if you are not insured, the same records that satisfy insurance company adjusters will satisfy the IRS and allow you to make deductions under a variety of circumstances that are listed later in this chapter.

Failure to keep good records is an invitation to disaster. If fire, flood, burglary or vandalism robbed you of your most valued possessions, could you actually prove you ever owned them? Could you list from memory every missing item? And would your unsupported list even be accepted? If the police called you in to identify stolen items, could you really describe them adequately?

The time to make a complete photo inventory is now. And that's what this book is all about. It tells you exactly what photographs to take and how to take them, detailing equipment and giving you all the necessary procedures that let you do the job right. Just follow the simple, step-by-step instructions. Photographic experience is not necessary. All it takes is the desire to protect yourself.

WHAT THE EXPERTS SAY

Photographs are now widely recognized as important means of documenting insurance, tax and other claims involving both personal and business property. Here's a small sampling of what those in a position to know have to say.

From the *Wall Street Journal:* "All insurance experts agree that policy holders can get much better settlements by keeping good reports. 'The single most important thing to do is take a full inventory of all your items,' says Gregory V. Martino, who specializes in personal-lines insurance at Continental Insurance Companies. Mr. Martino advises policy holders to retain receipts and to take photos of as many items as possible."

From Safeco's *Roof Lines:* "Photographic Record: You can photograph each room from various angles so that all contents will be included. Items not normally displayed can be arranged on a table and photographed. The photos can be slides or prints, even Polaroids, as long as they're clear and detailed." The Safeco article also recommends that you carry a cassette recorder from room to room, calling off the items in each. "Using a camera and tape recorder together can quickly provide you with a very thorough and detailed inventory and one you can easily update from time to time."

From a *People* magazine interview with John Marion, president of Sotheby Parke Bernet: "Once you've bought something, photograph it. Then sit down and make a complete record—whom you bought it from and what you paid, its history, a description of the item. If nothing else, you'll have a record so you can claim a tax loss if it's lost or stolen."

From a *McCall's* magazine feature entitled "One Picture Is Worth a Thousand . . . Dollars:" "What does photography have to do with insurance? According to Ron Vinsom of the Insurance Information Institute in New York, having pictures of your home and possessions could make it easier to file a claim in the event of fire or theft. . . . The pictures will show proof of ownership and remind you of everything you own or owned."

From a *Business Week* article entitled "Keeping Up With the Value of Your Insured Property:" "Use an inventory—with pictures. . . . The first step toward adequate coverage is to inventory everything owned by members of your household in the house and other buildings on your property. . . . Use a flash camera and plenty of color film for a visual record of your things."

From *The American Express, A Newsletter for Cardmembers:* "Homeowners are urged to keep detailed, accurate records of all possessions in the event of fire, burglary or damage. . . . Supplement information with pictures of each room, especially difficult-to-replace property like jewelry, antiques, original art."

We could go on quoting, but by now the pattern of advice should be clear. It all boils down to the same thing: make an inventory and take photos now, if you want full protection. On the other hand, none of the articles we have read to date really explain why you need a photo inventory, and they give only the sketchiest suggestions on how you might actually go about doing it. That is a big information gap, one which the book you have in hand fills. First, let's consider how and why photo protection works.

ONE PICTURE IS WORTH . . . ?

A few years ago a friend of ours who was vacationing in England was the victim of a hotel-room robbery in which she lost a valuable necklace inherited along with many other items from her grandmother. The loss was a shock because the necklace had personal value, and you just can't put a price on that. But by the time she returned to her home in the New York City area, she had discussed the matter with her husband and decided to put in a claim for insurance recovery, which would at least be partial compensation for her loss.

When she called her insurance agent to report the loss, he was sympathetic, explained the company claims procedure, and then added that she had to include proof of ownership with the claim. Did she have a bill of sale, he asked. No, it was inherited. Well then, had she ever had the piece appraised? No, she had no intention of selling it and had never considered an appraisal worthwhile. Was it listed and described on an inventory? No. How about a photo of it? Well, maybe, she would have to think about it.

At this point, she had run up against the classic stumbling block to claims recovery. Insurance industry standards require proof of ownership before a claim can be paid.

Fortunately, this story has a happy ending. Although she had never photographed the necklace itself, she did recall wearing it at her daughter's wedding, and sure enough, there in the wedding album she found a photo in which the necklace was clearly visible. A copy of the photo was accepted as proof of ownership and she collected.

Not everyone is so lucky. Consider the story of a couple who owned two homes, one in New York, the other in Florida. The day they left for Florida, their New York home was vandalized. They returned to New York to find their home a wreck, dishes broken, furniture slashed, clothing destroyed, stereo gone, jewelry missing. As soon as they recovered from the initial shock of seeing that the personal possessions they had collected with care and taste over the years had been wantonly destroyed, they made two phone calls: one to the police, the other to their insurance agent. Both the police and the insurance company representative asked for a list of missing and damaged items.

The damage was easy enough to pinpoint, but as they surveyed the wreckage, the realization dawned that they had no way of knowing exactly what was missing. Half their possessions were in Florida, there was no inventory for either household, and they would have to rely strictly on their own memories to make the list. It proved a nightmarish task. For two months they carried notebooks everywhere, and as items would come to mind they would jot them down—cuff links, dresses, silk shirts, power tools, paintings, crystal—the list went on and on. They would even wake in the middle of the night to write things down.

The claim was finally settled, although some uncertainty remained. The irony is that the difficulty could have been avoided if the couple had taken a complete photo inventory of both homes before the loss occurred.

Then there's the case of the husband and wife who had lived in the same home for more than 20 years while the neighborhood around them deteriorated. They stayed because the house was close to where the husband worked, and over the years, as his business prospered, they acquired a large collection of valuable antiques and other items. Meanwhile, their old neighbors had moved out and the new families coming in were considerably less well off financially.

Eventually, the couple's home was burglarized, and they put in a claim for loss. The insurance company, basing its decision on a statistical profile of the neighborhood which showed that it was now a low-income area, refused to accept the couple's estimate of the loss, stating that it was highly unlikely that a home in that neighborhood would contain so many valuable items.

They were fortunate, because they did not lose a great deal in that first burglary, but they also realized how vulnerable they were. On the recommendation of their insurance agent, they added home security devices and made a few unsuccessful attempts at inventorying their possessions, a task that proved to be more than they were ready to handle. Then they read a newspaper article about our Photo Protection Service and called us in. Now they have a complete photo inventory stored in a vault box. In the event of another serious loss, they will not be the victims of a statistical profile that undervalues their possessions.

Now consider what would happen if you were the victim of a theft and the police asked you to come down to headquarters and look at stolen property they had recovered. The following story, which appeared in the *New York Times* on March 2, 1978, paints a grim picture of the situation that will confront you.

Undoubtedly many of those victims failed to recover their jewelry simply because they were unable to describe it accurately. It is a fair bet that you have probably never taken

Police Invite Theft Victims to Glittering Loot Exhibit

By GREGORY JAYNES

A line of victims, all of whom went home sometime in the recent past to find something they had cherished gone, snaked across the waxed floors of Police Headquarters in New York yesterday on its way to a table made brilliant by precious, stolen possessions.

The victims were there because the police had notified them that more than $1 million in recovered jewelry would be on display in the auditorium at headquarters yesterday, today and tomorrow. Pearls and rubies, gold watches, a silk purse and a diamond sow—over 1,200 items looking very much like the best of the diamond district—shone bright from a block-long table beneath a piece of plastic.

"Some people say it's $2 million worth," said Lieut. Martin Kennedy of the Public Morals Division. "Some people say it's $1 million. It's six figures, there's no doubt about it, right? It's all real. The pearls are pearls. The gold is 14 and 18 karat."

A Row-by-Row Examination

The first wave of several hundred people was let into the auditorium at 11 yesterday morning. They were told to take seats. Then police let them go forward row by row, a maneuver that meant those on the tail of the line had to wait as long as two hours, most frequently to find nothing there that belonged to them.

When a familiar item did turn up, an officer quickly removed it from the identifier's view. Then commenced the meticulous process of description.

"I'm sorry, madam," said a jeweler who was there at the behest of police, "that is not the setting I'm looking at." He was squinting through a loupe. "I wish I could say you could take it home," the jeweler commiserated. "It's not mine, you know."

If a description proved satisfactory, the item was tagged and put back on display. The victim was given a voucher. That is because, before the event ends tomorrow, there may be others who come as close to giving acceptable details of the same item. In that case the victims will be invited back, and a jewelry expert will have to decide who pockets what.

Victim Recalls Burglary

"It was a year Feb. 1 that we were hit," said Frank DeRupo, whose wife, Fortunata, was inching along the table, bent double at the waist, peering at every gem. Mr. DeRupo said that as near as he could tell, the burglars had entered his house in Brooklyn at about noon and had taken away about $15,000 worth of jewelry, a pair of sneakers and a pillow case.

"When I walk down the street, like when I'm walking my dog," Mr. DeRupo said, "if I see a strange car, I take down the license. If nothing happens, I throw it away. But these people in my neighborhood, broad daylight, they don't see nothing.

"It takes the security out of your house. You end up putting bars on the front, bars on the back." "I live in a jail."

Before the day ended, Mrs. DeRupo had identified, and received a voucher for, a cameo and a pendant. She did not find a present she had given her husband a few years ago, a diamond-studded white gold ring bearing the inscription "Frank, Love Tina, 25th Anniversary."

A Heart-Breaking Experience

"My wife, look at her," Mr. DeRupo said. "She's heart-broken. She comes here hoping, she's going to leave crying." And she did.

All of the jewelry presently on display was seized Feb. 16 when the Public Morals Division raided the Brand Polishing Company, at 82 Bowery. The proprietor, Morris Brand, was arrested and charged with criminally receiving stolen goods.

All of the jewelry that is not identified to the satisfaction of police will be returned to the Brand Polishing Company. "If we can't prove it belongs to someone else," a sergeant explained, "how can we prove it doesn't belong to the fellow we took it from?"

the time to study your jewelry through a high-powered magnifying glass (loupe), and even if you had you might not be able to describe the pieces well in a stressful situation like this.

Now, imagine yourself in some future line-up of victims and consider how much easier everything would be for you if you were equipped with photos of everything you lost. Instead of trying to describe a setting from memory while a jeweler peered at it through a loupe, you would simply hand him a full color slide of the piece and let the jeweler make the comparison. In the event that someone else were to adequately identify the same piece, it's a fair bet that the claimant with the photo would walk out with the item.

INFLATION

The way prices are escalating, particularly in all areas of Americana collectibles—everything from grandfather clocks and mission furniture to paintings and prints to carnival glass and wooden duck decoys—many of the things you have around the house may be worth much more than when you purchased them. And let's not forget the incredible value of gold, silver, stamps, and coins.

If you lose one of these things, the original bill of sale is not an accurate estimate of its true value. For example, you may have taken a fancy to an Art Nouveau lamp years ago and purchased it for $100 or so. But a Tiffany lamp that sold for $100 several years ago may today sell for seven or eight times that amount. So what is your piece really worth now?

The way to document collectibles is through photography. With photos in hand, you have clear visual documentation of an item's appearance and condition, and if you are following the advice given in this book you will also have a close-up of the maker's mark. These photos can be essential for assessing actual value in the event the piece is lost or damaged.

If you are thinking of having some items appraised, but you don't want to go to the expense of bringing an appraiser to your home or the uncertainty of sending the piece itself to an appraiser, then consider having an appraisal made on the basis of photos. For many items this route can save you both time and money.

Another important effect of inflation is the escalating cost of replacing lost or damaged items that are in everyday use in your home —lamps, furniture, stereo systems, color TVs and clothing are only a few of the items that fall into this category. Some insurance companies now offer a special type of coverage called *cost replacement value insurance.* The terms vary widely, with limitations, but the basic idea is simple. A TV set you bought three years ago for $500 costs $590 to replace today. If it were stolen or destroyed, your standard homeowner policy would provide about $413 coverage, minus the policy's deductible, because it covers only the depreciated value of the contents of your home. But if you had a full value contents endorsement, the company would pay for a new TV set of similar kind and quality (minus the deductible, of course).

If property is damaged, rather than destroyed or stolen, then some replacement value policies will pay the cost of repair, without deduction for depreciation, if the predamage usefulness and appearance can be restored.

It is up to the policy holder to document the value, usefulness and appearance of the item. The best way for you to do that is to have a bill of sale with a description of the item plus a photograph that establishes its condition.

RECOVERY AND PHOTO PROTECTION

Many people buy insurance without really understanding what they are purchasing. That is probably why so many policy holders do not have an adequate inventory, and why insurance executives continue to insist that most people are underinsured.

If you sustain a loss of personal property, there are two major factors that affect recovery. First, the type of insurance you carry; second, the quality of the records you have kept to substantiate losses.

Under a typical homeowner policy, personal property is automatically covered up to 50 percent of coverage on the structure, but there are many exclusions and limitations that affect coverage on certain types of property and limit the recoverable amount on these items to a pittance. For example, you get a total of $500 for all furs and jewelry stolen in a single robbery. Another $500 limit applies to securities, passports, deeds, travel tickets, and stamp collections. In many states, homeowner policies group jewelry along with cash, gold, silver, platinum and banknotes under a $100 limit. Some policies also have a $1000 limit for silverware and guns.

If you rent an apartment, then personal property, theft and personal liability protection is usually provided by a tenant (renter) policy, which usually does not include damage to the building structure itself. The exclusions and limitations on these policies are similar to those found in homeowner policies.

To get additional protection, you can buy a personal property floater policy or add a rider to a homeowner or renter policy to cover personal property, which usually requires an item-by-item list, or schedule, and appraisal by a recognized authority to certify the valuations.

Getting an appraisal is not as difficult as you might think. Many items can be evaluated by checking their current price in local stores or in a mail order catalog. Antiques can usually be appraised by a reputable local dealer. Unusual items such as a Sumerian artifact can often be appraised on the basis of one or two good photographs sent to an expert.

The first step toward adequate coverage is to take a complete inventory of everything you own. The best method, described in detail in this book, is a photographic inventory on color slide film accompanied by a written inventory that lists each item, keyed to its photo, and including a brief description, serial numbers, original cost, date of acquisition, and estimated current value.

Once you add up the total valuations, you will know whether the 50 percent coverage is adequate and whether you should arrange to cover certain items on a separate schedule. You may be surprised to learn how much your personal property is worth.

The inventory is the key. It tells you how much insurance you should carry, and in the event of loss it will make recovery virtually certain.

When you have a loss covered by insurance, you have a right to collect. That is the service you have paid for, and reputable insurance companies are set up to make fast, fair payment on legitimate claims. It's their business. But it is up to you, the policy holder, to document the loss.

Your best documentation is a good, up-to-date photographic inventory kept in a bank vault or fireproof safe. If the inventory was made by a professional service, you also have a third source of reference to verify the ownership of the insured items.

In the event of a dispute over the amount to be recovered, a variety of appeals procedures, which your insurance claims agent can outline for you, are available. But if you have done your inventory right, you will probably never have to go that route.

INCOME TAX DEDUCTIONS

Casualty and theft losses are usually deductible in the year they happen. The situation is slightly different for losses due to theft, which you can deduct the year you discover the loss, even if it occurred earlier. For tax purposes, the IRS defines theft as burglary, robbery and embezzlement. A casualty is the destruction of property from an event of a sudden, unexpected or unusual character.

Here is an IRS checklist of deductible casualties:

Auto accident (if not willful negligence)
Drought
Earthquake
Explosion
Fire
Flood
Freeze
Hurricane
Lightning
Mine cave-in

Shifting earth
Shipwreck
Soil erosion (if from sudden causes)
Sonic boom
Storms
Vandalism
Wind

According to the IRS, "Your deduction is generally the difference in value of the property before and after the casualty. But, the loss can't be more than your cost or other basis. After determining the amount of loss, you then reduce the deduction by any insurance recovered. That amount must also be reduced by $100. (The $100 floor applies to each casualty.)"

As usual, the tax preparation information supplied by the IRS is more concerned with explaining how you should fill out the forms than it is in helping you evaluate your loss. But if you get audited, you have to come up with proof. In practice, the documentation that satisfies an insurance claims adjuster should also satisfy an IRS agent.

To get this tax break, you must have a good inventory. In the event of a major loss, it could mean thousands of extra dollars in your pocket, depending on your tax bracket. This applies equally to personal and business property losses.

PHOTO DOCUMENTATION FOR ESTATE PLANNING

Photos do more than provide a record for insurance, tax and theft recovery. In the event of the death of the owner, they become a record of valuable items in the estate.

In most cases, a complete photo inventory need not accompany a will. You may need no photos at all. Or you may want to photograph only selected items of unusual monetary or sentimental value that are being willed to specific individuals. We cannot provide a general formula. Estate planning is a purely individual matter and is something you should discuss with your attorney at the time you make or revise a will.

HOW GOOD SHOULD THE PHOTOS BE?

A good photo inventory picture should be a sharp, detailed, full color image of your subject. It must serve as a clear source of reference, which is why the subject of lighting comes up so often in the following chapters. But it does not have to be pretty. Photos that would bring the barbed criticisms of camera club "experts" and photo instructors fluttering down like dry leaves around your head can be A+ inventory shots.

The sole purpose of inventory photos is to record maximum information about your possessions. Technically, these are very easy shots to make and anyone can do them. It does not require a knowledge of photography or its technical jargon. In fact, if you have an automatic 35mm SLR camera that lets you see through the lens and figures the exposure for you—the type so widely advertised on TV by Minolta, Canon, Pentax, Nikon, Olympus, and others—and if you follow the suggestions we make in this book, you should be able to do a perfectly adequate job without ever having shot a roll of film before in your life.

If you are an experienced photographer with a lot of photo courses under your belt, then your main problem will be to divest yourself of the aesthetic criteria that are so important to other types of photography and to pay attention to the job at hand, in which the standards are strictly practical. These standards are laid out clearly in Chapters 3 and 4.

2 Equipment

You do not need special equipment to make a photo inventory. Any camera you have, even a pocket camera, will let you do at least a partial inventory. However, there is a limit to how much you can do with a simple pocket or instant camera. In this chapter, we discuss the equipment that we have found lets us make the most complete, information-filled inventory possible. Then we give you the pros and cons of some other commonly used cameras and lighting set-ups. If you don't have an ideal equipment mix, we recommend that you make do with what you have. It's better to get some sort of photo inventory done now than to put it off for months while you shop for better equipment.

THE IDEAL SET-UP

The best way to make a photo inventory is to use a 35mm SLR (single-lens reflex) camera with normal and wide-angle lenses. Load the camera with Ektachrome 160 tungsten slide film and use two 250-watt ECA or 500-watt ECT (3200 K) floods in aluminum reflectors as your main light source. Use a tripod and cable release to keep the camera steady. For close-up shots, you may also need an extension tube, macro lens or No. 4 close-up attachment lens. Other accessories, such as light stands, colored cloth for use as background material, and a No. 85B filter so that you can use Ektachrome 160 in daylight are also useful. A ruler is essential for use as a scale indicator.

Although simple, this is a carefully rationalized equipment system, and it is unlikely that you will have every item on the list. In fact, recent camera industry sales data indicates that millions of photographers now own an automatic SLR with a normal lens and no accessories at all. If you fall in that group, you may want to buy some inexpensive flood lights and a tripod, or you may prefer to get an inexpensive automatic or dedicated flash unit. Our equipment list provides flexibility and delivers quality results, but feel free to make any substitutions with which you feel comfortable.

THE CAMERA

A 35mm SLR, preferably one with automatic exposure control, is far and away the best camera to use when you want to make a thorough photo inventory. With an automatic SLR, what you see is generally what you get. When you load it with color slide film, you get a detailed, full-color record. The slides are easy to review using a standard slide projector or slide viewer. Color is reasonably faithful to the original subject, and if

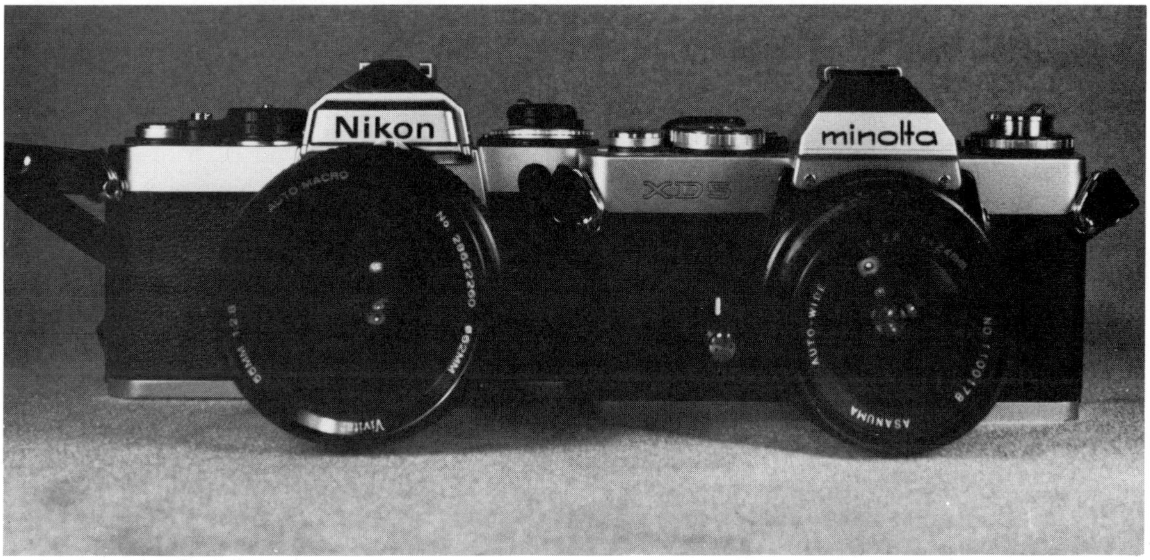

The ideal camera for making a photo inventory is an automatic SLR (single-lens reflex) with interchangeable lenses.

you have handled your camera correctly, the detail will be more than adequate.

Many appraisers and insurance agents suggest that amateurs make instant Polaroid or Kodak PR-10 shots, because instant cameras are so easy to use. On the other hand, instant prints do not contain the detail of a color slide, only some instant cameras make close-ups, and the film is expensive. Instant prints are acceptable if you plan to make 10 or 20 shots to document a handful of selected items. But instant camera/film systems are designed in fact for photographing people. When you try to use them to photograph rooms and objects, you find that color quality is only fair, and detail rendition is poor. What's more, the flash, which is a must for indoor instant shots, produces big glare spots on the smooth surface of paintings, china and silver, and the light from the flash is uneven. Optimum camera-to-subject distance is about eight feet. Anything closer will be too light and anything further away too dark.

Like instant cameras, simple pocket cameras are also designed to make snapshots of people, and they do the job well, but most of these cameras do not have good lenses and they give you no control over exposure. If you must use a simple Instamatic (127) or pocket (110) camera, then load it with Kodacolor 400 and use flood lights indoors.

SLR pocket cameras, such as those made by Pentax and Minolta, give you all the flexibility of a 35mm SLR. If you are among the lucky few who own a camera of this type, use it just as you would its larger-format 35mm compadre. The only difference is that you will have to use a daylight-type slide film, such as Ektachrome 64 or Kodachrome 64, or a color print film, such as Kodacolor 400, because tungsten film is not available in 110 cartridges.

A 35mm rangefinder camera will also do the job for you; however, most of the models sold today do not let you focus closer than about three or four feet. This means that you will have some trouble getting a clear shot of china markings, coins, and other tiny subjects. Of course, you can always put a supplementary close-up lens on the camera and measure the distance between lens and subject with a tape measure, as we explain in Chapter 4.

Cameras that use 120 roll film, such as the famous Hasselblad, Bronica, Mamiya and Rolleiflex models, provide top quality images, but you need a special projector to show the slides. If you decide to do the inventory on color print film using one of these cameras, then you have the added expense of having prints made. That's why we recommend the 35mm SLR over roll film cameras for photo inventory work.

High-quality, ultra-miniature cameras such as the Minox B or C models will also do the job for you. But if you already own one of those cameras, then you know all about the problems of working with the tiny negatives they produce.

You can also get away with using one of the fleamarket specials, such as an ancient Kodak Brownie. But honestly, you are better off buying a new camera or borrowing an SLR from a friend or relative.

If you have always wanted to try a 35mm SLR, but haven't wanted to make the investment, then you might consider renting one from your local camera store. Have the salesman show you how to load it and make sure you get one that features automatic exposure. Armed with ten minutes of instruction on how to handle the camera and the information in this book, you should be able to make a perfectly adequate photo inventory—even if you've never made a serious photo in your life.

LENSES

You can do the job with the normal lens that comes with your camera, but when it comes time to make shots of entire rooms or

You can get away with using nothing more than a normal lens, but it helps if you also have a wide-angle lens, such as a 28mm or 24mm lens for a 35mm camera.

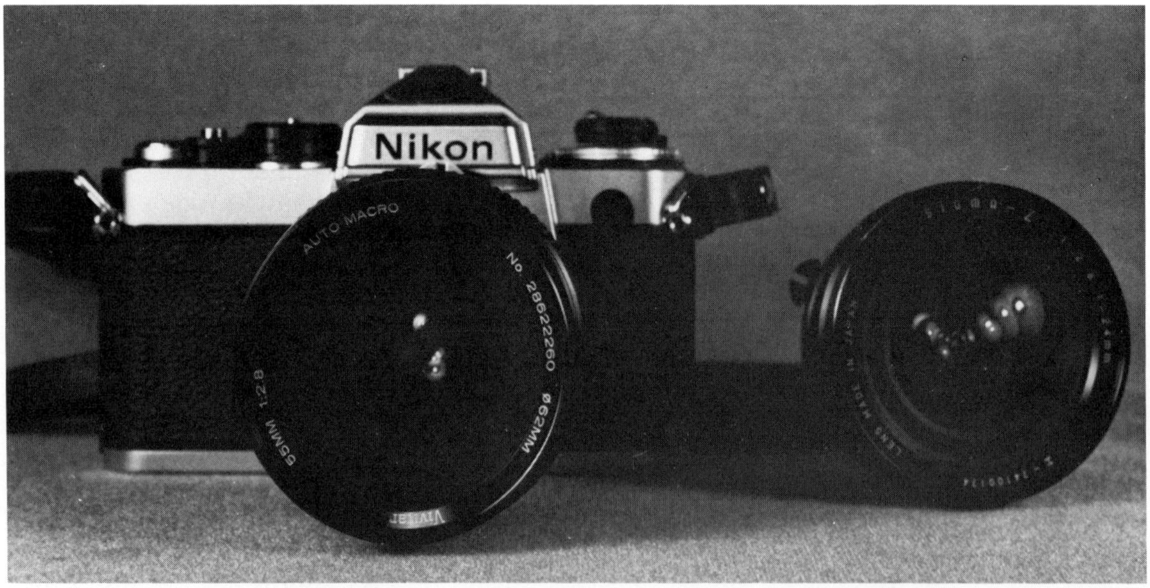

large furniture groupings, then a wide-angle really helps. We have found through a process of trial and error that a 24mm lens on a 35mm SLR is the easiest to work with, although a 28mm wide-angle also performs well.

Avoid the fish-eye lenses. They produce a distorted view that is inappropriate for a photo inventory.

If you do not have a wide-angle lens, or if you are using a fixed-lens camera, then you will have to make two or more overlapping shots to cover the same area that you could get in one shot with a wide-angle.

As professionals, we decided to replace one of our normal lenses with a 55mm macro lens that focuses from infinity to ultra-close-up and will give us images that are actually life-size on the slide. But there is no need for you to go that route, as you'll see when you read the section on close-up equipment.

You do not need a telephoto lens to make

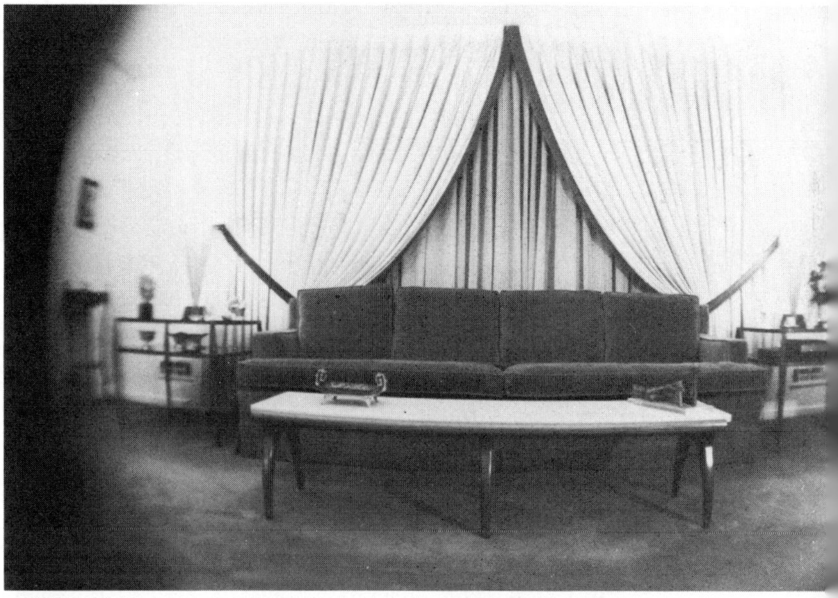

Do not use a fish-eye lens for inventory photos. The spherical perspective characteristic of these lenses produces curved lines that defeat the documentary function of the photos.

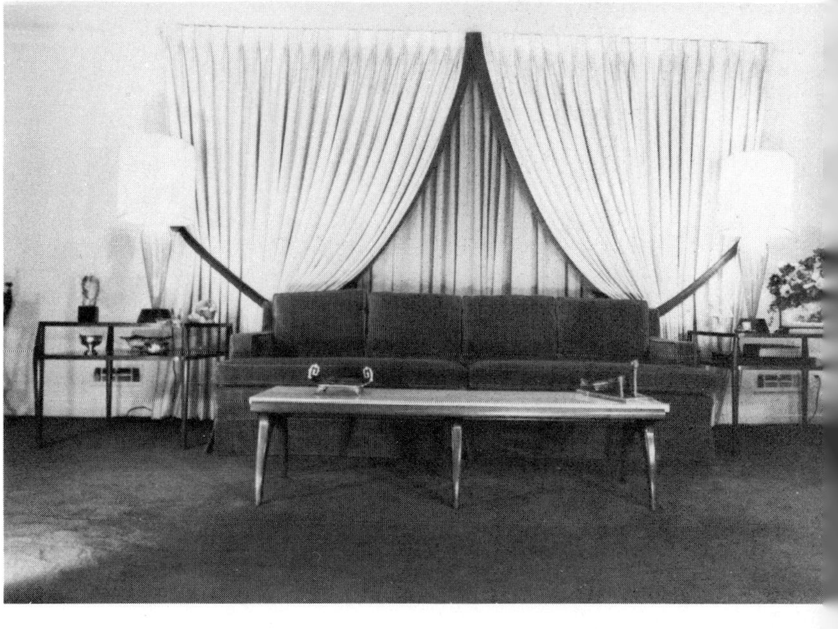

A 24mm wide-angle lens on a 35mm camera keeps straight lines straight.

a photo inventory. On the other hand, if you own a close-focusing ("macro") zoom, then it may come in handy for close-ups.

LIGHTS

With all the ballyhoo over electronic flash, many photographers are under the impression that photographic lightbulbs are rapidly going the way of the snail darter, if not the dodo. Professionals know better. Lightbulbs designed for photography, whether of the expensive tungsten-halogen type or the classic screw-base design, produce a continuous light that is easy to adjust and easy to meter.

If you load your camera with Ektachrome 160 tungsten, then 250-watt ECA and 500-watt ECT photo lamps will give you perfect color balance. If you use Kodachrome 40 film, then 250-watt No. 1 and 500-watt No. 2 photofloods will give you faithful color rendition.

Since a photo inventory is usually made indoors, where artificial lights are a necessity, it just makes good sense to use an indoor film and the lights that go with it. What's more, standard screw-base photo lamps are inexpensive. They screw into any socket that accepts a household lightbulb and if you stick with the lower powered 250-watt types, you can use them with inexpensive aluminum reflectors that screw onto a socket that has a clamp or lightstand adapter attached. These lights are available at most camera specialty stores.

Lights with a spring clamp can be attached to any convenient shelf or chair back. If you need more height, you can tie a stick to the back of a kitchen chair or use a small stepladder. Don't bother buying lightstands unless you plan to be doing a lot more with them than making a photo inventory. If you do buy lightstands, you also need the stand adapter that allows you to attach the light to the stand. The cheapest type is a sleeve with a stud on the end for a small metal ball and a set screw

Inexpensive aluminum-reflector clamp lights plus 250-watt or 500-watt photographic floods are all the lighting capability you need to make a complete photo inventory.

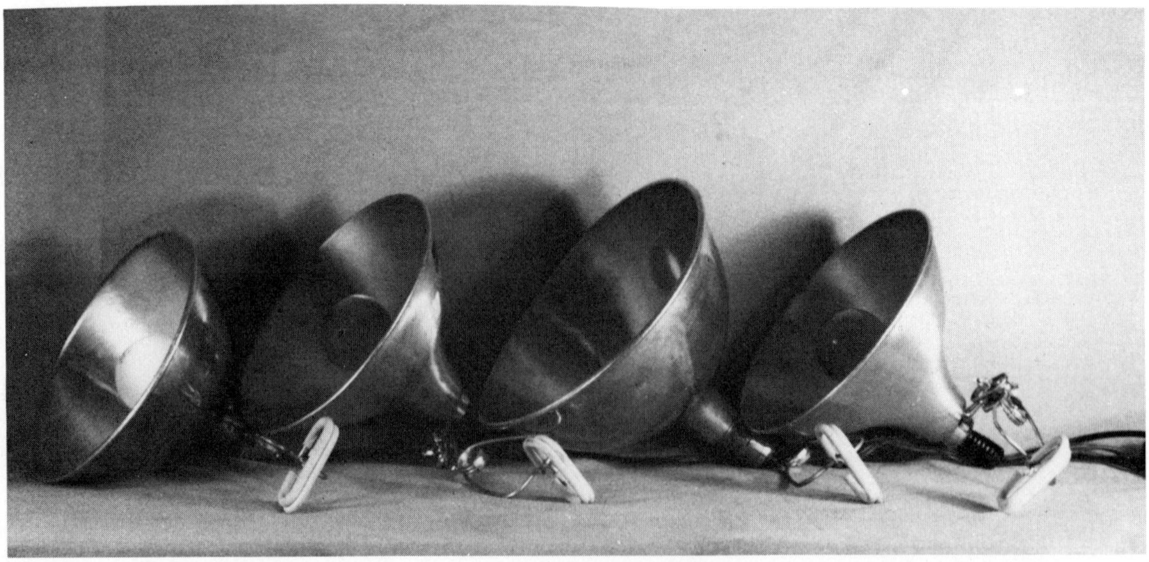

in the sleeve so that you can stop the light from rotating.

More expensive lights for standard photo lamps, such as the ventilated lamps with ceramic sockets, may have a stand adapter already attached.

For professional use, there is a large variety of lighting kits available that include lights, stands, and a case to carry them in. These kits are advertised in magazines aimed at professional photographers, such as *The Rangefinder* or *Photomethods,* and are also included in the *Popular Photography Directory and Buying Guide,* which is available at most photo stores.

If you would prefer to use electronic flash, then plan to load your camera with a daylight slide film such as Kodachrome 64, Ektachrome 64, Ektachrome 200, Agfachrome 100, or Fujichrome RD-100. The advantage to electronic flash is the speed of the light. It's so fast it eliminates any possibility of blur due to camera motion, which means that you won't need a tripod for most of your shots. Just walk around your rooms and flash away.

The disadvantage of electronic flash is that you can't see what the light is doing. If you use the flash mounted on the hot shoe of your camera, you will get a very flat light with harsh shadows. Smooth surfaces, such as glass, silver, and most paintings, will have white glare spots that obliterate detail. And in long shots of furniture groupings and rooms, there will be a noticeable fall-off in light intensity from foreground to background, with some objects too light to see clearly and others too dark. In Chapter 5 we have included a number of techniques that will let you electronic flash aficionados get around some of these problems.

If you feel you must use a portable flash, then we recommend that you use an automatic or dedicated unit that calculates the exposure for you. These units work quite well, and ensure that the majority of your shots come out properly exposed.

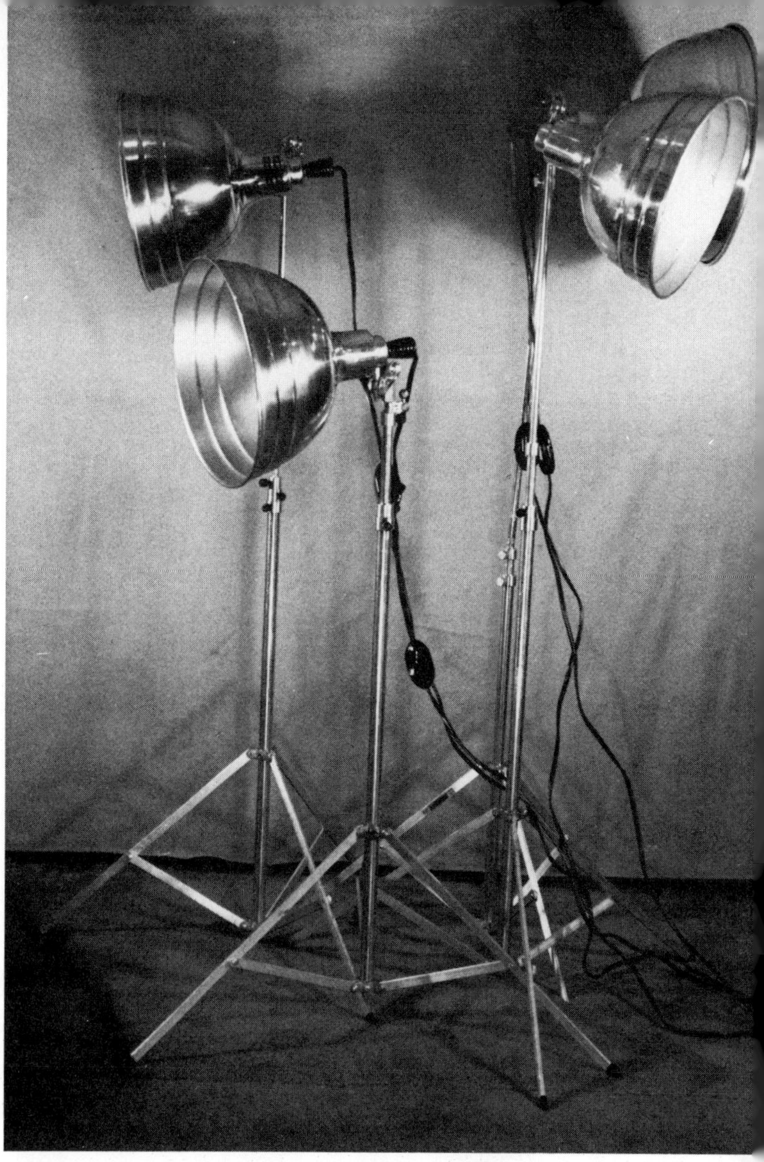

Light stands are convenient, but unnecessary if you have clamp lights.

As an additional point of information, there are units designed for professional use that have built-in modeling lights which allow the photographer to preview the effects of the flash, but a four-light electronic flash set-up of this type is well beyond the pocketbook of the amateur. The professional with such a set-up is better off leaving it in his or her studio and using flood lights for inventory work.

DIFFUSERS

A diffuser is used to scatter light and make it softer. You can purchase diffusers for your reflectors, or simply do without. We use diffusers on our lights because they help reduce glare spots on china, silver, chrome and other polished surfaces. They also soften shadows, which improves detail rendition with some subjects.

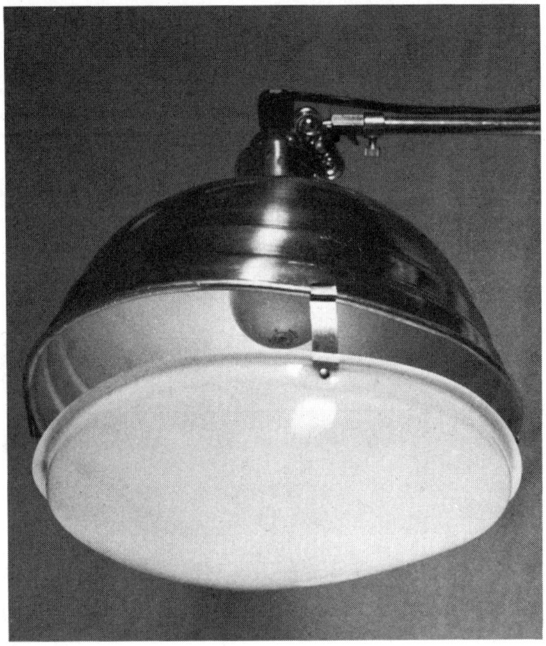

Diffusers that clamp onto your reflectors help soften the light and reduce glare spots. They are nice to have, but not essential.

FILM

We recommend that you make your photo inventory on color slide film. Although you may feel more comfortable with color prints, slides are superior for a number of reasons.

First, slides offer consistent color quality that is a reasonably accurate reproduction of the colors in the original subject. You do not have this advantage with color prints, because color is modified by a printing machine according to a computerized program designed to yield good prints of average portrait subjects.

Second, when you get the slides back from the processing lab, they will be numbered in sequence. This numbering system is a big help in organizing the inventory. (If you have your slides developed by a custom lab, be sure to tell them you want the slides numbered. Some labs use unnumbered mounts.)

Third, slides are considerably less expensive than prints. When you consider that the typical photo inventory will contain anywhere from 70 to several hundred shots, the cost factor becomes significant.

Fourth, slides take up less room than prints in a bank vault box. You can keep them in the box in which they come from the processor or put them into see-through vinyl pages with pockets for 20 slides per page.

Fifth, slides contain a richness of detail that will be missing from all but the most expensive color prints.

We use Ektachrome 160 tungsten film, which has an ASA (ISO) speed of 160 and is balanced for use with 3200 K ECA and ECT flood lights. For the occasional outdoor shot in daylight, we put a No. 85B conversion filter over the lens. Kodachrome 40, designed for use with 3400 K photofloods, is also a good choice, but if you use it outdoors with a No. 85 conversion filter, the effective speed will be around ASA 20, which we find inconveniently slow.

If you use electronic flash, then stay with a standard daylight-type film such as Ektachrome 64, Fujichrome RD-100, Agfachrome 100, or Ektachrome 200.

If you happen to be using a non-adjustable pocket or Instamatic camera, then try Kodacolor 400 color print film. With these very limited cameras, the high-speed color print film gives you an extra edge because of its

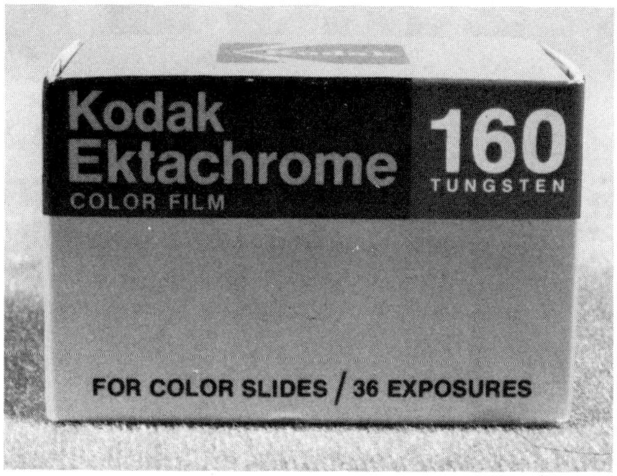

Ektachrome 160 tungsten color-slide film is the ideal choice for use with 250-watt ECA or 500-watt ECT flood lights. The combination results in nearly perfect color in every shot.

wide exposure latitude and special sensitizing characteristics, which let it respond well with most light sources. This is the only case in which we recommend print film.

As for you instant film buffs, all we can say is, consider the cost. On a shot by shot basis, it's more than twice as expensive as color slide film. What's more, unless you have a close-focusing SX-70 camera, or a sophisticated medium-format camera with a Polaroid back, you are not going to be able to take close-ups of china marks, coins, jewelry, and so on. And finally, consider the size of the image you get. Those instant prints are great for family albums, but they can't compare with the clarity and detail that you get from a color slide when you project it or look at it through an 8X magnifier.

TRIPOD

If you work with floodlights, you will need a tripod for the camera. It's the only way to get sharp photos at slow shutter speeds. If you have an SLR with a built-in self timer, use the timer to trigger the shutter. Otherwise, use a cable release. Either way, you eliminate the possibility of blur due to vibrations caused by pushing the shutter button with your finger.

Even if you decide to go with electronic flash, you will need a tripod for ultra close-ups where accurate focus is critical.

You do not need an expensive tripod. Any tripod will do so long as it's solid and the legs don't bend when you press down on it. If

When you use flood lights, a tripod or camera stand is essential. It allows you to use slow shutter speeds and small f/*stops (*f/11 *or* f/16*) for maximum sharpness.*

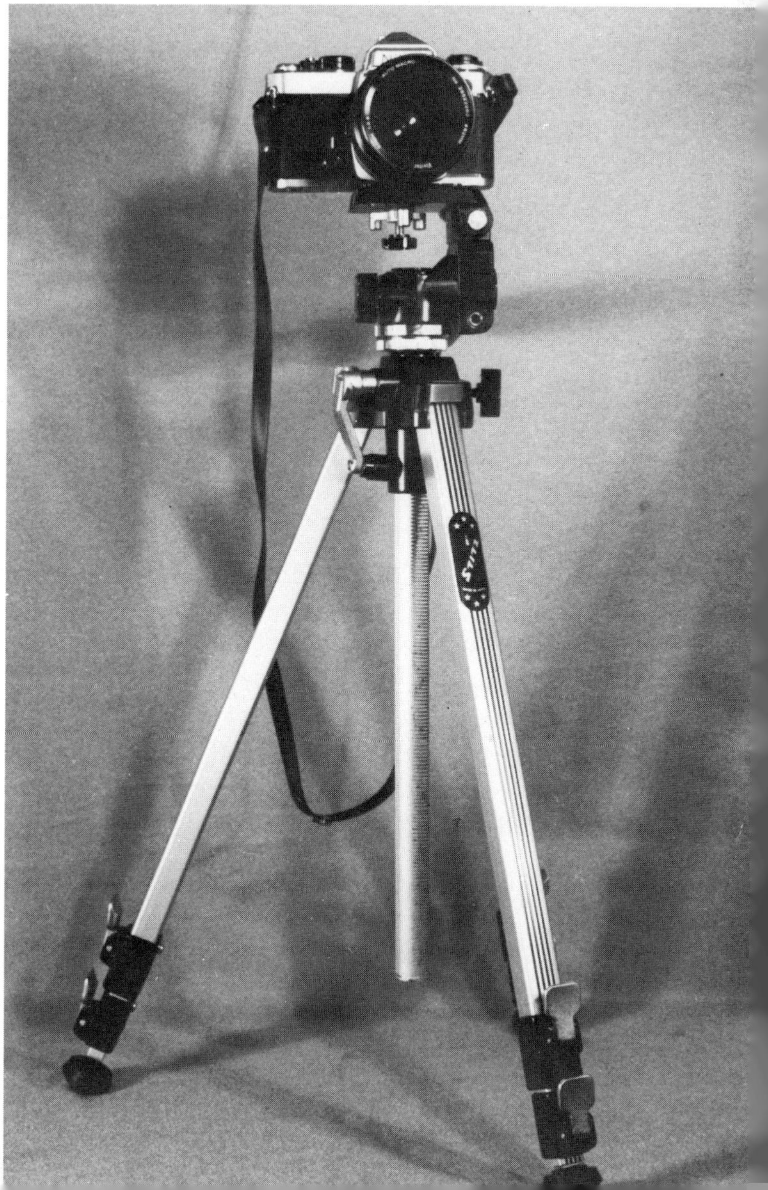

you're handy, you can probably build a camera stand out of scrap wood in a few minutes. The tripod socket on the bottom of most 35mm SLRs accepts a ¼" × 20 threaded stud, which you can purchase in the form of a carriage bolt for a few cents in any well-stocked hardware store.

If you buy or borrow a second-hand tripod, make sure it has a head. Most tripods have a head that screws onto a stud projecting from the top of the center column. The tripod head provides a safe platform for your camera. On the other hand, the stud that holds the head on the tripod is usually too long for the tripod socket on the base of the camera, although it is frequently the same diameter. If you screw your camera down hard onto that head stud, you could damage the camera base.

CLOSE-UP EQUIPMENT

The normal lens on a modern SLR will usually focus close enough to fill the frame with a sheet of typewriter paper. This is more than adequate for most of the items you will be photographing for your inventory. But if you are photographing a coin or stamp collection, then you'll need to get closer. If your interest in close-up photography does not go beyond getting a complete photo inventory of your own property and taking the occasional snapshot of a wildflower, then you can get by with an inexpensive accessory close-up lens that attaches to the accessory mount on the front of your lens. You can also use one of these close-up attachments to get close-ups using both rangefinder and fixed-focus cameras.

Close-up lenses are usually given numbers to indicate their strength in optical units called *diopters.* The higher the number, the stronger the lens. If you have an SLR camera, you can skip the +1, which doesn't provide enough extra magnification to make a difference so far as inventory photos are concerned. The +1 is useful only if you have a rangefinder or fixed-focus camera that won't let you get closer than three or four feet from your subject.

If you want to buy just one close-up lens to use with an SLR, then we recommend a +3 or +4. With your camera lens focused to 3½ feet, the lens will be 10 inches from the subject when you use a +3 and 8 inches from the subject with a +4. At that distance, the +3 will fill the frame with an area 5⅛" × 7½" and the +4 will cover a 4" × 6" area. Although not ideal, this coverage is adequate for most coins and stamps. You can get stronger lenses, but they are hard to find. Alternatively, you can buy several of different strengths and use them together to get greater magnification.

Close-up lenses require no exposure compensation, which makes them easy to work

Close-up lenses such as this +2 give you a magnified image without the need for exposure compensation. The small arrow engraved on the rim should be pointing toward the subject.

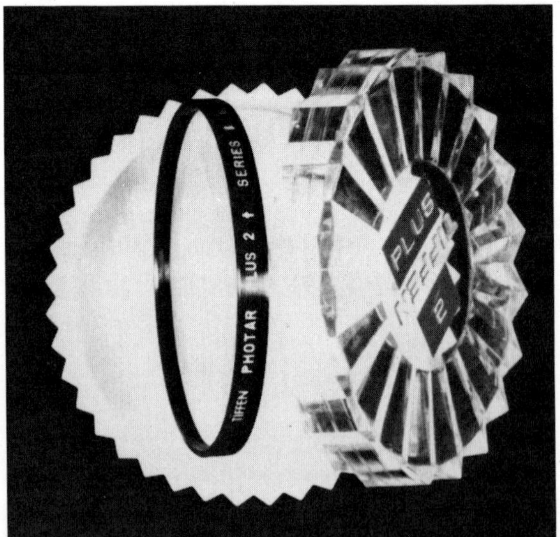

with. If you have an SLR, you can focus normally, and the image is as bright as ever, which is not the case with the extension tubes and bellows that we describe next. With rangefinder and fixed-focus cameras, you have to measure the distance between lens and subject, as explained in the chapter on close-ups.

Another way to get a large image of a tiny subject is to put some sort of extension device between the lens and the camera. For images up to life-size on the negative, you can use extension tubes, which are available in a wide range of lengths. For larger-than-life images on the film, the usual practice is to use a bellows extension. Extension tubes may be useful, but it is unlikely that you would ever need a bellows to take an inventory photo.

When you use an extension tube, you must either use through-the-lens metering or increase exposure to compensate for the loss of

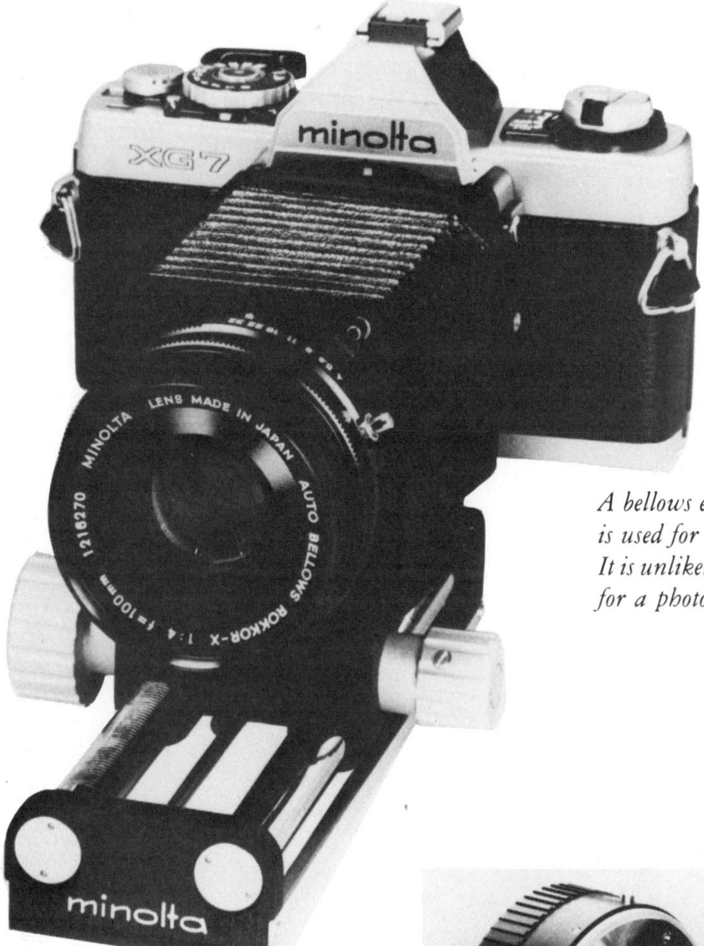

A bellows extension that fits between lens and camera body is used for images that are life-size and larger on the film. It is unlikely that you would need this kind of magnification for a photo inventory.

Extension tubes that fit between the lens and the camera body yield high-quality images, but they are comparatively difficult to use.

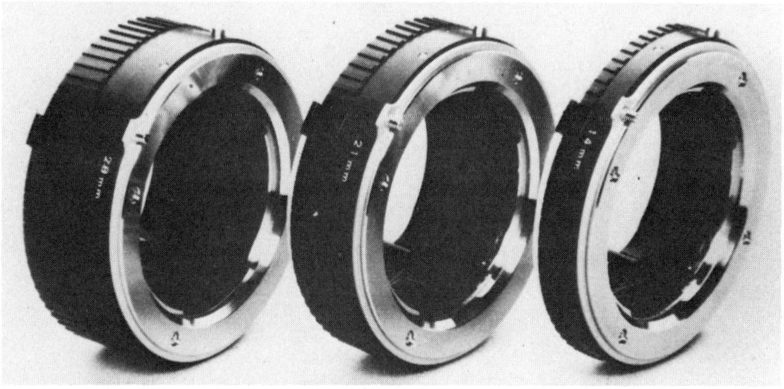

light intensity as it travels down the tube. If you already own a set of extension tubes, then you may find a use for them in photographing small objects in your inventory, but don't run out and buy a set just for this one job. By and large, extension tubes are a nuisance to use.

The ideal close-up device is a true macro lens, one designed specifically for close-up photography. The typical 50mm macro lens, which is the most useful for photo inventory work, has two parts. The lens alone, when mounted on the camera, will cover the entire range from infinity focus down to images that are about one-half life-size on the film. The second part of the lens is actually an extension tube. With this tube in place, you can get images from one-half life-size to life-size on the film. The macro lens is a professional tool, so we do not recommend it for amateur use. Unless you have some special need for ultra-high-quality close-up images, stick with a close-up lens attachment such as the +4.

FILTERS

If you use a film that is color-balanced for floodlights, then you should have a conversion filter so that you can get correct color when you want to use the film outdoors in daylight. Unfiltered daylight will give your slides a blue cast. For Ektachrome 160 tungsten, use an 85B filter in daylight; for Kodachrome 40, use an 85 filter. If you are calculating exposure with a hand-held light meter, then increase the exposure by two-thirds *f/*stop, or a full stop if you prefer, to compensate for light absorbed by the filter. For example, if your meter reads *f/*8, you should open up to *f/*5.6. If you use through-the-lens metering, the meter should compensate automatically for the filter.

When you use a daylight film, such as Ektachrome 400, with floodlights, you will get a reddish-yellow cast unless you add blue to the light by using a conversion filter on the lens. For 3200 K ECA and ECT bulbs, use an 80A filter. For 3400 K No. 1 and No. 2 photofloods, use an 80B filter. If you want to get correct color using daylight film and 100-watt lightbulbs as your main light source, use an 80A plus an 82B light balancing filter over your lens. When you use through-the-lens metering, the meter will compensate for the light absorbed by the filter. If your meter does not read through the lens, then you will

Among the other items that you will find useful are a cable release, a No. 85B filter so that you can use Ektachrome 160 film in daylight, a polarizing filter, and a ruler for use as a scale indicator.

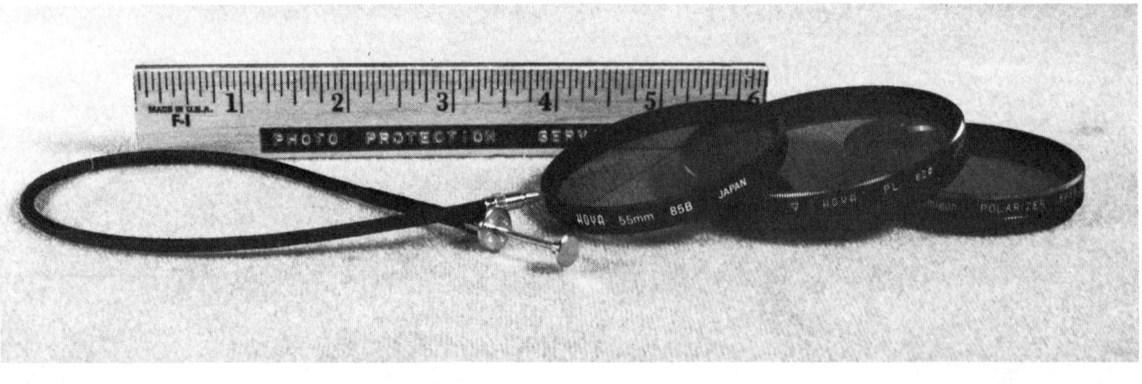

have to increase exposure by two *f/* stops to compensate for an 80A or 80B filter. The 80A + 82B combination requires a 2⅔ *f/* stop exposure increase.

A polarizing filter helps to reduce glare on smooth, nonmetallic surfaces at an angle to the camera. The effect is to dampen some of the glare spots on china and glass.

BACKGROUNDS

When you make your close-ups of individual pieces—china, silverware, and so on—you should set them against a plain background. Velour works best, but any plain colored blanket will do. Paper does not make a particularly good background because the surface is shiny and produces glare spots. Backgrounds are easy to improvise with materials you find around the house, and there are a number of suggestions in Chapter 4 that will help you.

THE SCALE INDICATOR

A 6- or 12-inch ruler is essential. A good many of your photos will include the ruler, or at least the end of it, to show the size of the objects pictured. Without the ruler, there is no way of telling how large the original is just by looking at the photo. A painting, for example, could be three inches square or five feet square, but without that scale indicator, there would be no way to know.

We have found that a plain, wooden ruler works best. Both plastic and metal rulers are less satisfactory because their smooth surfaces reflect glare from the lights, and wherever there is a white spot of glare in the photo, the graduations on the ruler are illegible.

PROCRASTINATION

Don't let lack of equipment stop you from getting started on your inventory. Just photograph whatever you can with the equipment you have or can borrow. If you decide that the results don't give you adequate information, you can always try again later with better equipment. Meanwhile, you have partial protection and will have a better idea of the value of your own property, which can be of considerable benefit in planning your future needs.

Here you can see how the ruler is used. Without it you would have no way of knowing how large the marble head and pedestal actually are.

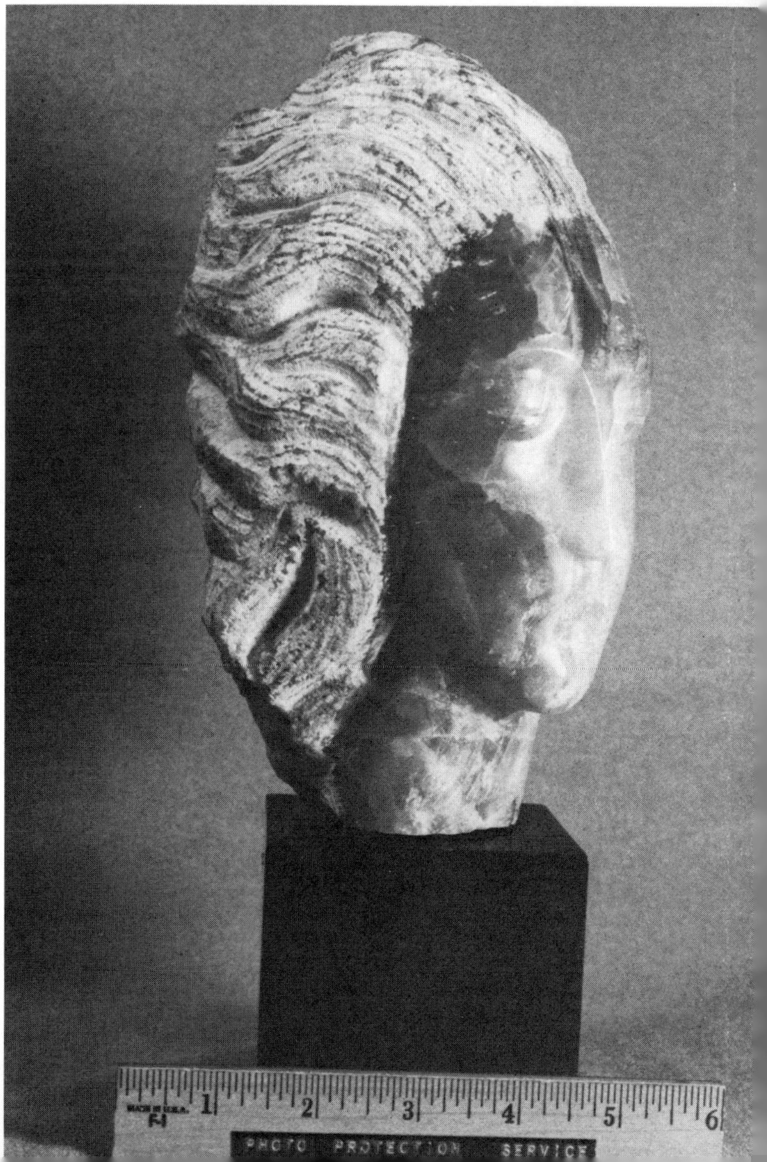

3 Getting Started

When you first consider the task of making a photo inventory, the job may seem overwhelming. You are going to take anywhere from 70 to several hundred separate photos, and the total will probably be on the high rather than the low side. In photographing your own property, you will be confronted not only by those things you can see but by your own jumbled memory of things put away in drawers, closets and trunks—a lifetime's accumulation. But with a little planning you can make the job simple and straightforward.

The trick is to organize your task room by room. You will probably start with the living room, which is the key room in the house, then move on to the kitchen, bedroom and other rooms, then to the garage, and finally outdoors. If you are doing the job for yourself, then you can do the work over a period of days or weeks, finishing one room and moving on to the next, evening by evening.

In each room, make three types of photo. First, take overall views of the room. If you have a wide-angle lens, you can cover each room in two or three shots. If you don't, then you will have to take the room in several overlapping sections.

Next, move in and take shots of groupings of objects and individual shots of large items. The techniques used to make these overviews and large-object shots are detailed in this chapter.

Finally, you will need to take close-ups. Some close-ups can be made on the spot, without moving the objects. Others will require placing valuable items on a special background. The techniques involved are covered in the following chapter on close-ups, which you should also read before you start to make your photo inventory.

THE INVENTORY SHEET

The only way to do the job right is to make a written inventory that will be keyed by number to the photos. In Chapter 6 you will find an example of the standard inventory sheet used by Photo Protection Services, along with detailed instructions on how to fill it out. We mention it here only because you may want to fill in part of the inventory sheet as you photograph, rather than wait till you get the slides back from the processing lab.

If you set aside a day to do the complete job, then you can probably keep track of things without the aid of the inventory sheet. Later, when you get the slides from the lab, you can fill out the written portion of the inventory. We have found that this is the easiest system. But if you decide to do it this way, approach the job in a methodical fashion, organizing it into segments and completing one segment before moving on to the next. For example, you might begin with the living room, taking your overall views first, then moving in for medium shots of groupings and individual close-ups of objects that will remain in place. Proceed to photograph each room in the house in the same way. Then set up a table-top background as explained in the following chapter and begin bringing small objects to the background, starting with those in the living room and moving methodically through the house.

If you are doing the job in segments over several evenings, then you are probably better off making the identification portions of the inventory as you go. That way you will have a record of what you have photographed and will be able to refer to it each time you pick up the work. It will help you keep on course. Without it, you could end up photographing some items twice and forgetting others entirely.

If you choose this number-as-you-go system, there is no need to fill in the entire sheet. All you really want at this point is a record of the subjects you have already photographed. Just fill in the roll and shot number in the left hand column and a brief description of the subject, such as "living room overall," "knickknack shelf," or "wall with African art."

Assign a letter to each roll of film—A, B, C and so on. When you get the slides back from the lab, a quick look through the box will tell you which roll it is. Or if you prefer, the last shot on each roll can simply be a close-up of a sheet of paper on which you write a six-inch high letter to identify the roll.

If you make only one shot of each subject, beginning with No. 1 on the frame counter of your camera; then the numbers stamped on the slide mounts should correspond exactly with the numbers on the inventory sheet. If you occasionally make duplicate shots, possibly at different exposures to make sure of a tricky subject, you will have to renumber the slides by hand when you get them back. This is not a difficult chore. Either way, every slide will be identified so that it exactly matches the number on the inventory sheet. For example, if you are using 36-exposure rolls of film, then your numbers would run A1 through A36, B1 through B36, and so on.

LIGHTING AND EXPOSURE TECHNIQUES

In this section, we are discussing exposure with photographic floodlights, so keep that in mind as you read through it. Exposure with flash presents some special problems. If you haven't yet decided which light source to use, then compare the different exposure problems involved by also reading the sections on flash in Chapter 5. The comparison may help you make up your mind.

If you are using floodlights, then for this and all succeeding shots, mount your camera on a tripod. If your lighting is bright enough, you might get away with a hand-held photo, but indoors, hand-held shots usually mean wide *f*/stops, in the neighborhood of *f*/1.4 to *f*/4, and when you have a choice, you should shoot at small stops of *f*/11, *f*/16 or even *f*/22. The reason you want small *f*/stops is that these stops provide the greatest sharpness in depth, from near to far, and when you do a photo inventory, sharpness is paramount. To use a small *f*/stop, you will probably need to use a slow shutter speed to get correct exposure, and this means a tripod-mounted camera. Trying to hand-hold a camera at shutter speeds slower than 1/125 sec. inevitably leads to slight blurring of fine detail due to body vibrations.

Getting the right exposure, the one that

will give you maximum color and detail, is easy with modern equipment. The light meter built-in to most 35mm SLRs, and hand-held light meters in general, are precision tools that make the job a snap.

We use the built-in light meter in our cameras in two ways. First, we rely on it to give us the right exposure of scenes that our experience tells us do not present any special problems. Second, we use it as a tool to help us adjust our lights when we have unusually dark or light objects in the scene.

If you are looking for the easiest way out, let your automatic camera do all the work for you. Since the meter is reading approximately what the lens sees, the results will always be in the ballpark, although occasionally some shots will be a bit over- or underexposed. If you are photographing your own property, these improperly exposed shots are nothing to worry about. When you get the slides back from the processing lab, you can always set to one side the shots that didn't come out and retake them, giving a little more or less exposure than the meter indicates. If you happen to have a fully automatic camera that doesn't permit manual exposure adjustment, then set the ASA speed to the next higher number to get less exposure and to the next lower number to get more exposure. Just remember to set the ASA back to the correct speed of the film when you have finished making your "adjusted exposure" shots.

We have found that there are only two situations that constantly come up in photo inventory work that require special handling. The first is the presence of a very large window without drapes. The second is the presence of a large piece of dark furniture such as a piano or wooden dining table in an otherwise light-colored room.

If you are working in the daytime in a room where there is a large window area and no curtains, take your exposure reading with the light to your back. Do not include the window area in your exposure reading or you will end up with a good picture of the outdoors and a very dark room. If you are making an overall shot that must include the window area, set the exposure manually. If your camera only gives automatic exposures, wait till dark to take the picture.

Now here's the trick that will let you get good shots of very dark furniture in a light room. First, set up your lights as you think you want them and focus the camera. Next, without touching the focus, pick up the camera and walk over to the darkest object that you want to record faithfully and make a note of the exposure the camera gives you. Then walk over to the lightest object in the scene and see what exposure the camera gives you of that.

Do not base your readings on light walls and other broad areas without detail. The idea is to get optimum exposure for the detailed areas with color and let everything else fall where it will.

If the difference between lightest and darkest is more than three *f/*stops, you are going to have to throw more light on your darkest subject. To do this, take one of your floods and shine it directly on the dark piece. When you have gotten a meter reading that brings the darkest and lightest objects within three *f/*stops of each other, set your *f/*stop midway between the two. For example, if a dark couch reads 1/15 sec. at *f/*16 and a pale blue shag rug reads 1/125 sec. at *f/*16, then the correct exposure for the scene would be 1/60 sec. with the aperture set halfway between *f/*11 and *f/*16. The results should be perfect exposure.

The use of the meter as a tool for placing your lights is simple and effective. Naturally you can do the same thing with a hand-held meter, but we find that the meters built in to today's cameras are equally reliable.

Remember that photo lights are extremely hot, and inexpensive aluminum reflectors do not radiate heat well. If your lights do not have a wooden or plastic handle attached so that you can adjust them without touching the reflector, then we suggest you wear a glove or use a pot holder to make fine adjustments in the angle of the reflector. If you touch a hot reflector with your bare hands, you can get a nasty burn.

THE LIVING ROOM

The living room frequently contains some of the most valuable objects a family owns, and the procedure you follow here can be used, in slightly modified form, for other rooms in the house.

Your first step is to take two or three overall views of the room so that you have a record of everything in its day-to-day setting—the furniture placed as it usually is, lamps and bric-a-brac in customary locations, paintings on the walls, drapes over the windows, and so on.

Lighting: You may need several lights to get adequate illumination throughout the area being pictured. Use two lights, one to either side of the camera, for general illumination. If the ceiling is low and white or very light colored, you can direct them at the ceiling to provide broad, diffuse light. If the ceiling is dark, distant, or brightly colored, aim the lights directly into the room. Place additional lights just out of view of the lens or hide them between pieces of furniture to give extra illumination to dark subjects such as pianos, wood cabinets or leather-covered

This is an overall shot of a living room, taken with a wide-angle lens. If you use only a normal lens, you will need two or three overlapping shots to get the same coverage. The dark area to the right is a dining alcove, which would be covered in a separate view.

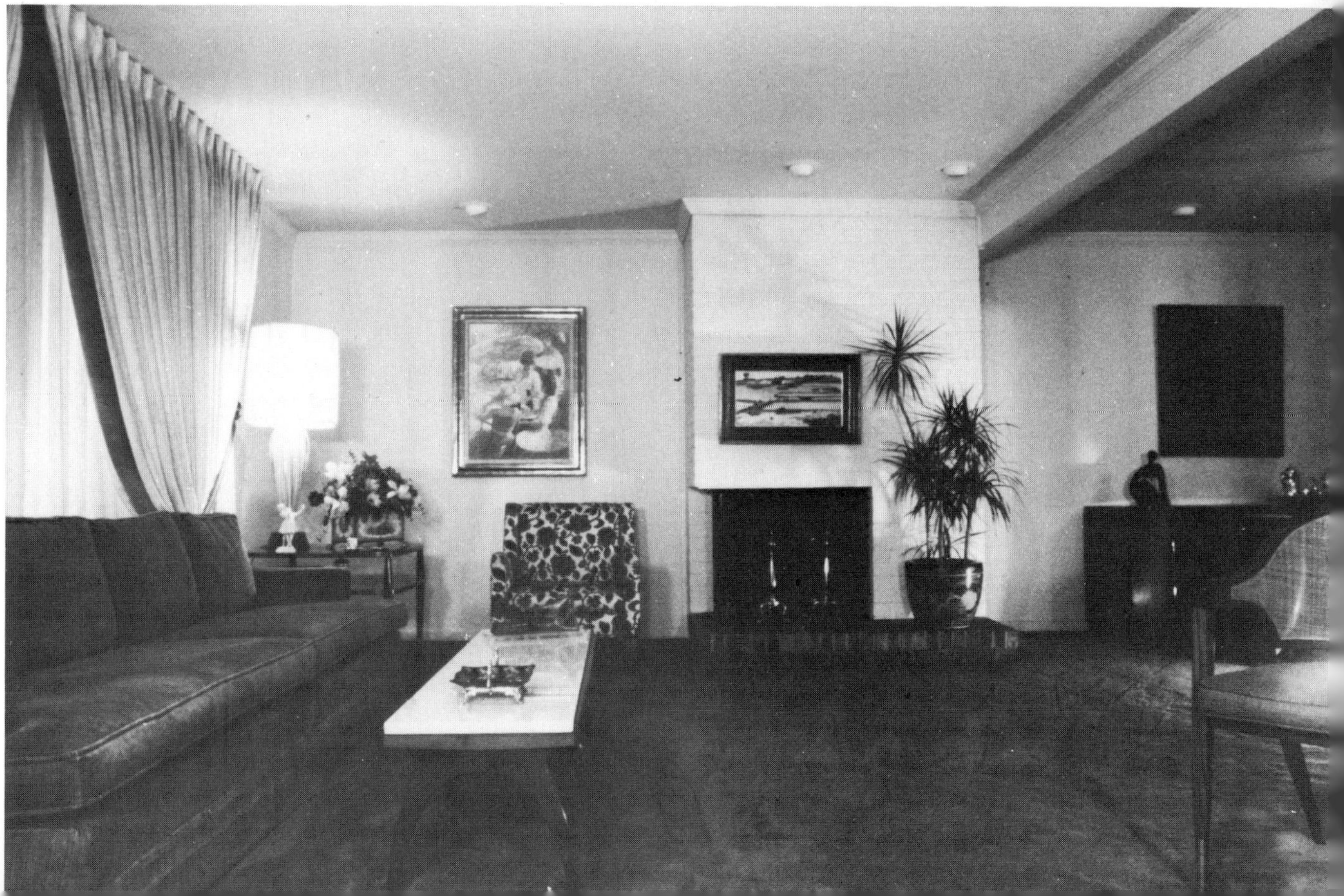

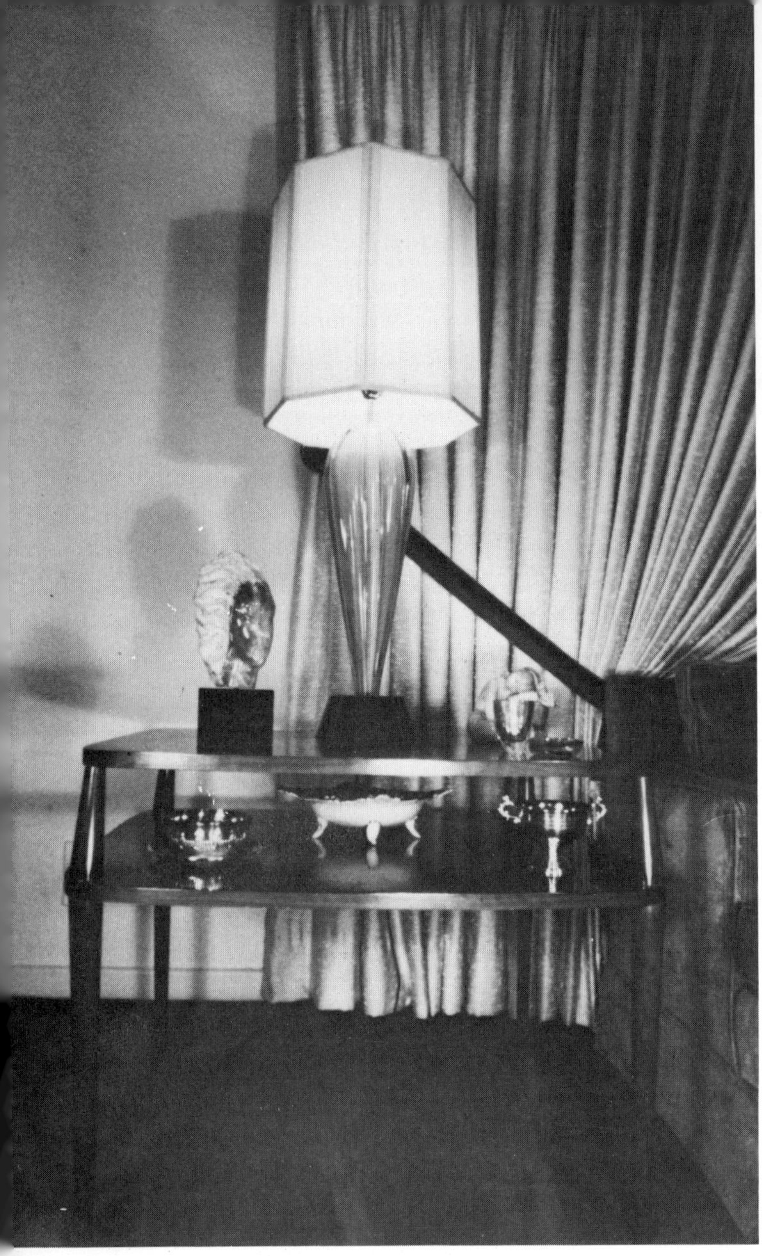

The next step is to photograph furniture groupings. This is a small-group shot of a table in the living room.

chairs. You can place the extra lights on stands, clamp them to convenient shelves or lay them on the floor.

If you are photographing during the daytime, you will get better color if you draw the shades or curtains on all windows and depend strictly on your floods for illumination with Ektachrome 160 tungsten or Kodachrome 40 film.

For a more natural effect, turn on the lights in your table and floor lamps. Try it two ways, one with the room lights off, one with them on, and see which you like best. Since room lights that appear in the scene influence exposure and cause automatic cameras to underex-

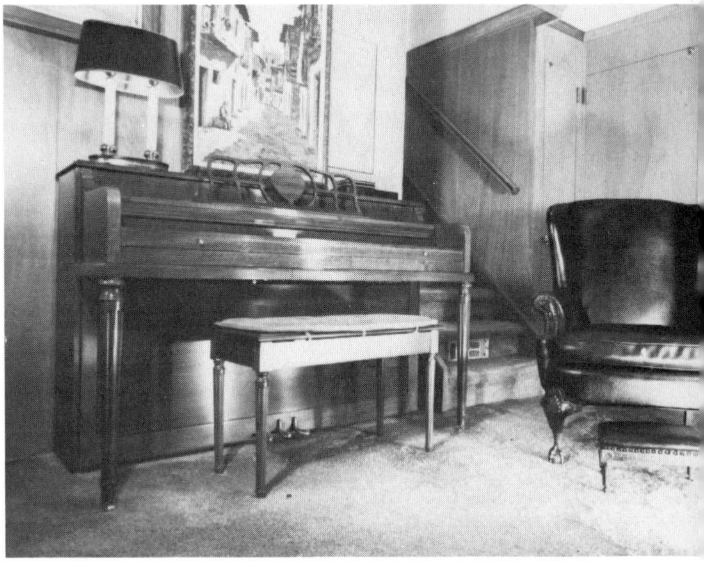

Light pointing directly at the piano and leather chair in this picture produced glare and loss of detail. Modifying the lighting will solve this problem.

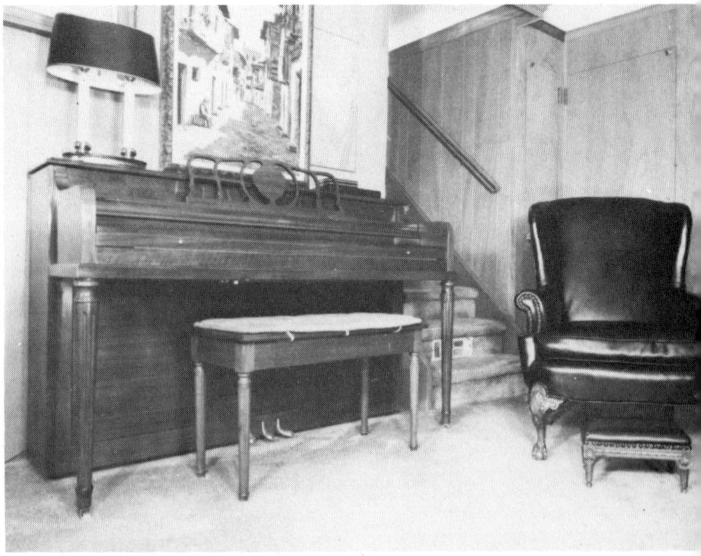

By directing the light toward the ceiling for a bounce-lighting effect, the glare was significantly reduced in this picture.

pose slightly, you might want to open up one-half stop from your metered exposure to compensate, but if you prefer not to fool with it, then don't. Slight underexposure won't hurt much.

If you have two large, dark pieces of furniture, placed one in front of the other, a walnut table partially blocking the view of a grand piano, for example, they will tend to blend together in the overall photo. You can separate them visually by placing a light between them, in this example behind the table and angled so that it shines on the grand piano. The light fixture itself should be out of view of the lens, hidden by the table. Its beam will lighten the piano and create the necessary separation.

FURNITURE GROUPINGS AND WALLS

The next step is to take medium-long shots of furniture groupings and walls on which pictures, tapestries and other items are displayed. The number of shots and camera placement will depend on what you have in the room. If you study the accompanying photos, you can get a better idea of the type of things these medium shots would normally include.

For example, a conversation area consisting of a couch, two overstuffed chairs, a couple of end tables and a coffee table would all be covered in a single shot. Later, you would return to this area for more detailed shots, but at this point in the inventory process you are looking for natural groupings of objects.

A wall with a collection of masks, paintings, or other items would also be taken as a unit. Unless the collection contains items of unusual value, a shot of this type might be all that is required. When you project the slide, you will be able to recognize each mask,

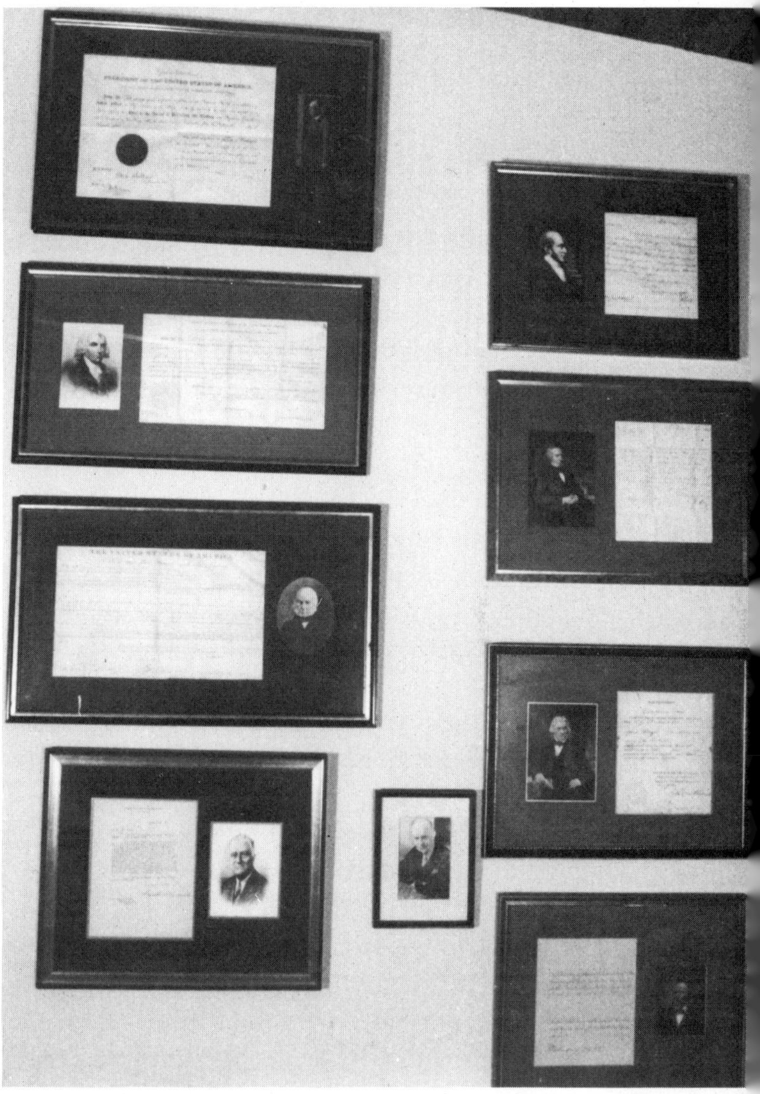

The document collection hanging on this wall was first photographed as a group. Then the photographer moved in to make close-ups of individual documents that were considered particularly important. It was not necessary to remove the documents from the wall.

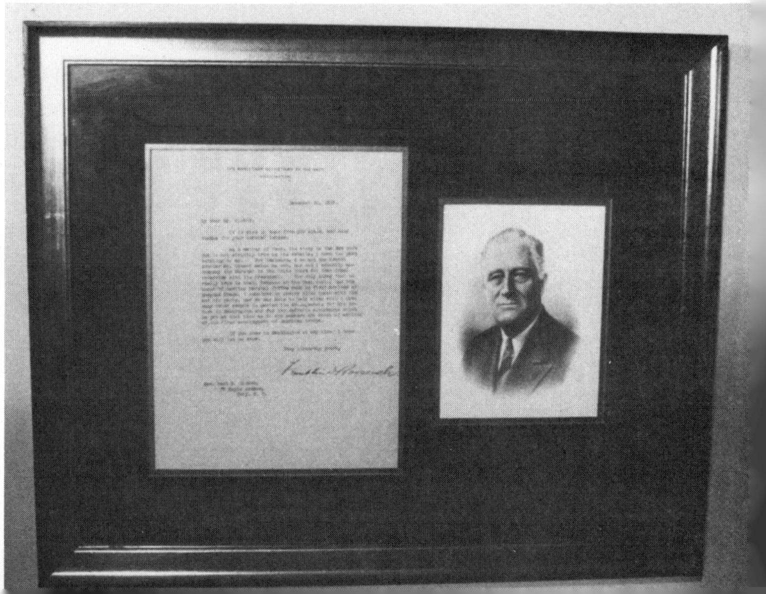

painting, or whatever and count the number of items displayed.

In addition to giving you a numerical count of items visible in a room setting, the medium-long shots focus attention on the settings in which the various pieces are displayed. Visually this reinforces the concept of ownership, because it shows where the pieces belong in their day-to-day existence. These shots also show the condition of larger pieces of furniture, rugs, and so on.

MOVING IN

Once you have made your overall views and taken medium-long shots of furniture groupings and walls, begin moving in to record detail. As you make individual shots of wall pieces, adjust your lights so that they provide even illumination and watch out for reflections of the lights in picture glass. If you have two lights, one on either side of a painting at a 45° angle to the picture glass, then minor adjustments of the lights should eliminate any major glare spots. Finally, don't forget your scale indicator. Use a bit of masking tape to hold your ruler in place next to the piece and include the ruler in the shot.

On-camera electronic flash presents a problem when you photograph items behind glass because the light bounces back directly into the camera lens, creating a huge glare spot that obliterates the center of the subject. The best way around this problem is to use the bounce flash techniques that are described in Chapter 5.

In the case of valuable paintings, you may want to move in even closer and make a separate shot of the signature alone. In this situation you would end up with two photos, one showing the entire painting, the second an ultra-close-up of the signature. Use any of the techniques described in the next chapter to make the close-up.

Tapestries should always be photographed twice. The first shot should show the entire piece. The second should be a close-up of the back of the tapestry to show how the threads were knotted and woven. The back of a tapestry is like a signature, and the way the threads have been tied can be an important factor in assessing its value.

Tables with lamps, porcelain figures, small pieces of sculpture and so on should be taken as a unit with all the pieces in place. Later, you can take the more valuable small items to a background set-up and photograph them individually.

If the room contains a large number of items and you have an assistant, you can isolate the free-standing pieces from a complex background by having an assistant hold up a plain, solid-color blanket or sheet behind the subject. For example, you may have an Art Nouveau lamp placed on a table and a number of paintings on the wall behind it. To get a photo of the lamp alone, have your assistant stand behind it and hold up the background cloth. That will give you a clear record of the lamp without any confusing background detail, and you won't have to move the lamp to find a better background.

Large pieces of sculpture should also be photographed in place. If there is a complex background behind it, have an assistant hold up a sheet or blanket as a background. If there is a plain wall behind it, you are in luck. To accurately photograph sculpture, you may need two or more shots. One will show the entire piece. Another might be a close-up of the sculptor's name, if it happens to be carved into the piece. In addition, the pedestal on which the piece stands may also be valuable, so don't neglect to get a shot of that as well. You might also take a photo to show the back of the piece to document its condition, although this is not always necessary.

If you have a cabinet full of china, photo-

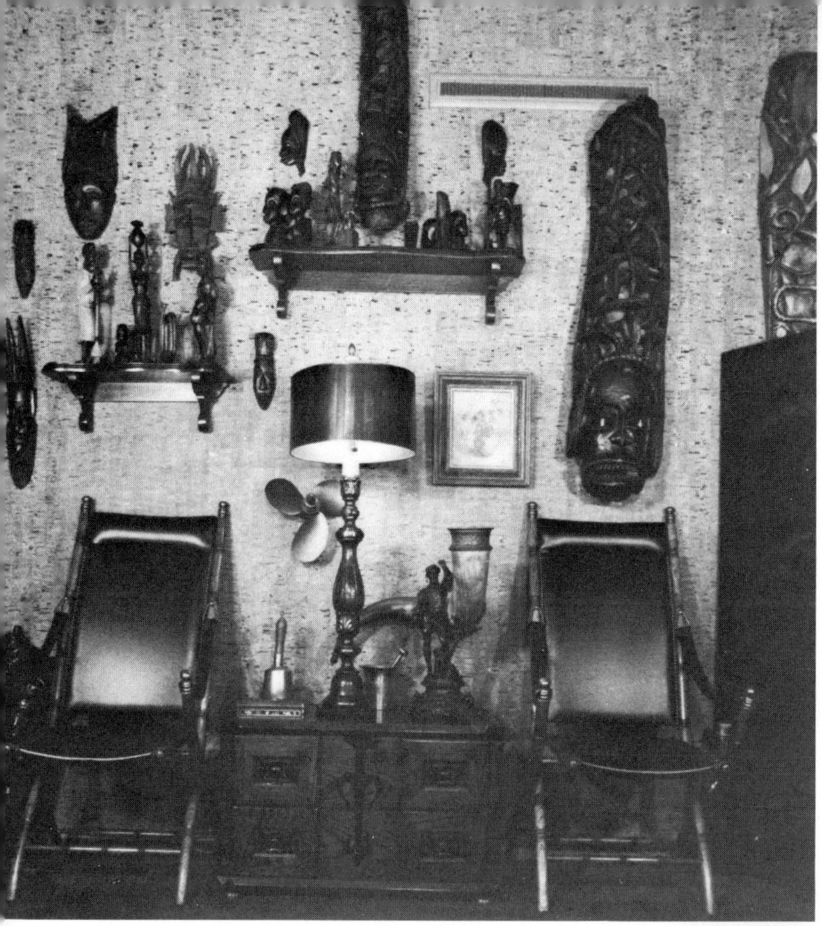

This collection of Africana was first covered with an overall shot of the wall. Then the photographer moved in and took three small-group photos that permit easy identification of the items in the collection. Because none of the items were considered particularly valuable, individual photos were not taken.

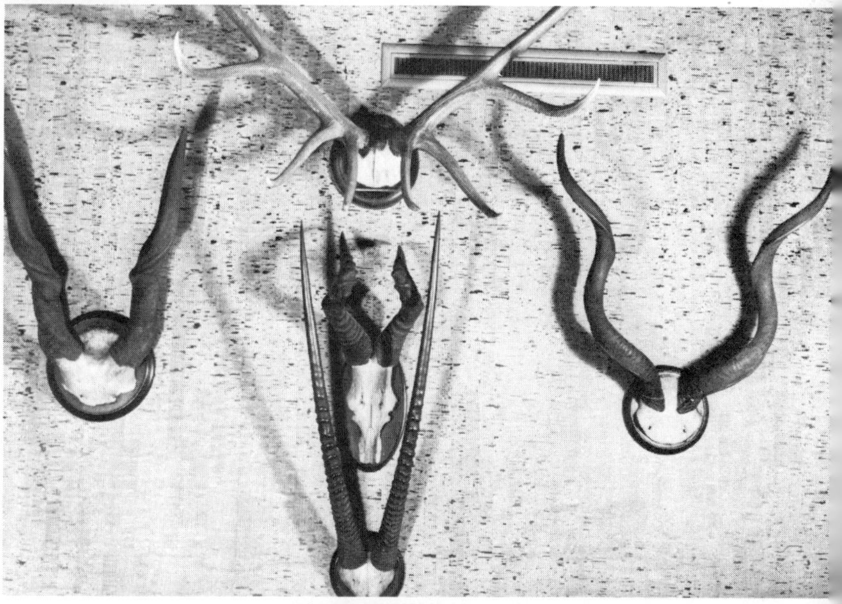

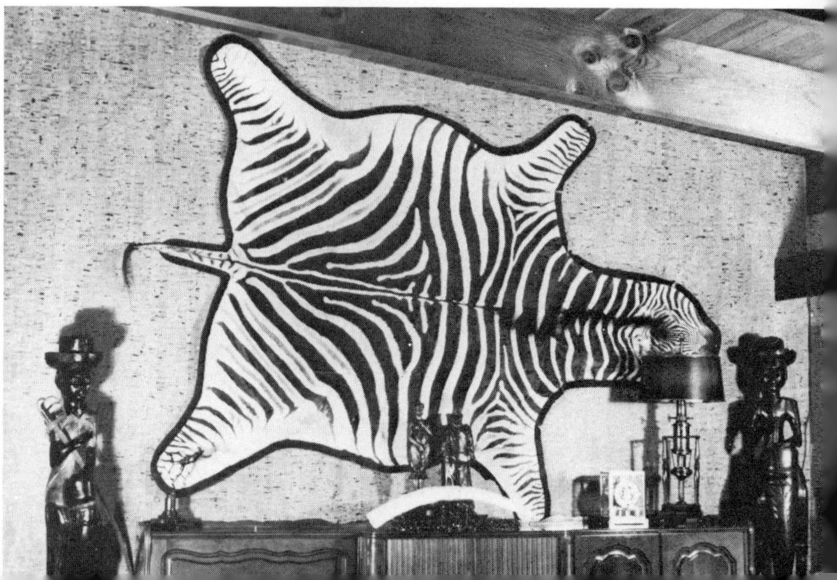

graph the cabinet first. Open glass-fronted breakfronts so that you get a clear record of the interior. Next, adjust your lights so that the interior of the cabinet is illuminated. You will find that properly lighting a cabinet may require three or four lights, two to light the outside, one placed on either side of the camera, and two directed into the interior, one on a stand just behind your camera and the other on the floor or a small stand just out of view of the camera lens.

When you begin bringing subjects to the table-top background described later, you will get individual photos of whatever the cabinet contains, so at this point the one full view of the cabinet and its contents will do.

If you have fine linen and silverware stored in a sideboard, you can remove the linen and spread it out on a couch or chair to photograph. There is no need to remove everything—just those items you consider of special value. If you have a box of silverware, set it on the floor, open it, and photograph it. Later, you can bring the contents to your background set-up and photograph them as described in the next chapter.

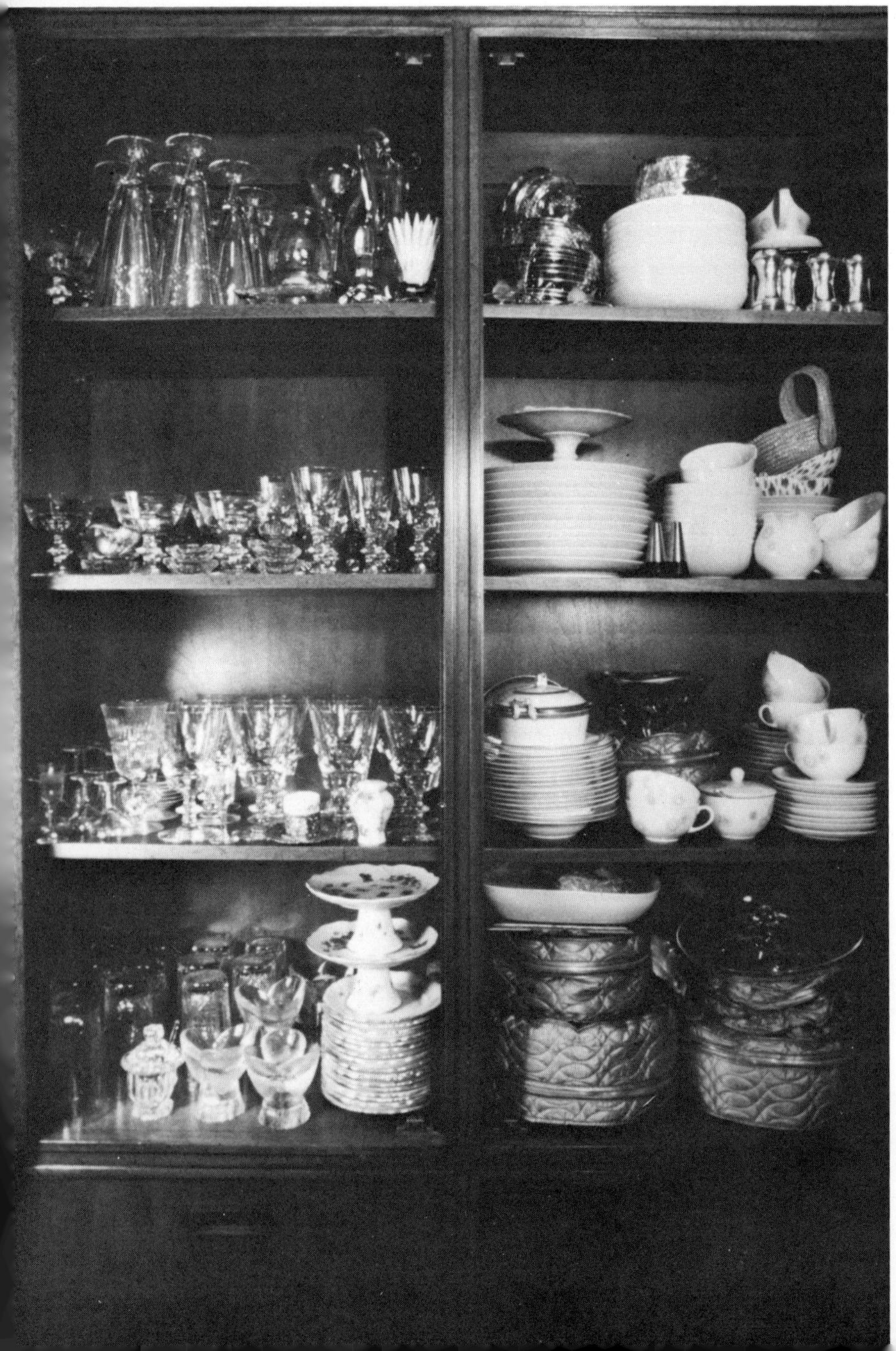

Lighting a breakfront is tricky. You should adjust your lights so that they illuminate the interior. Items in this cabinet were later photographed in a table-top set-up, but at this point, the photographer was concerned only with recording the larger pieces in the room, the pieces that could not be moved, and showing where collectibles were normally kept.

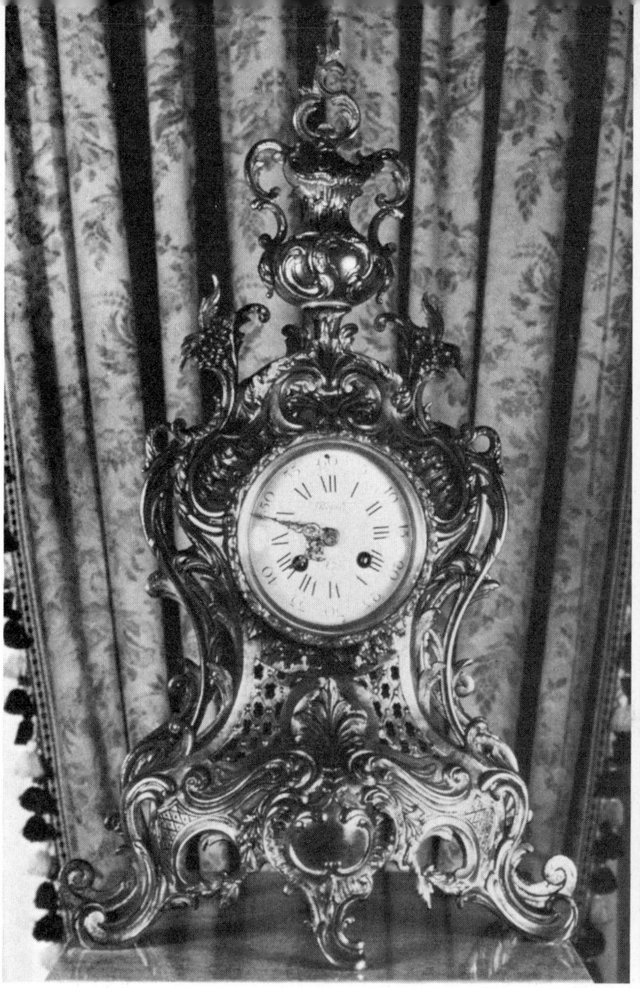

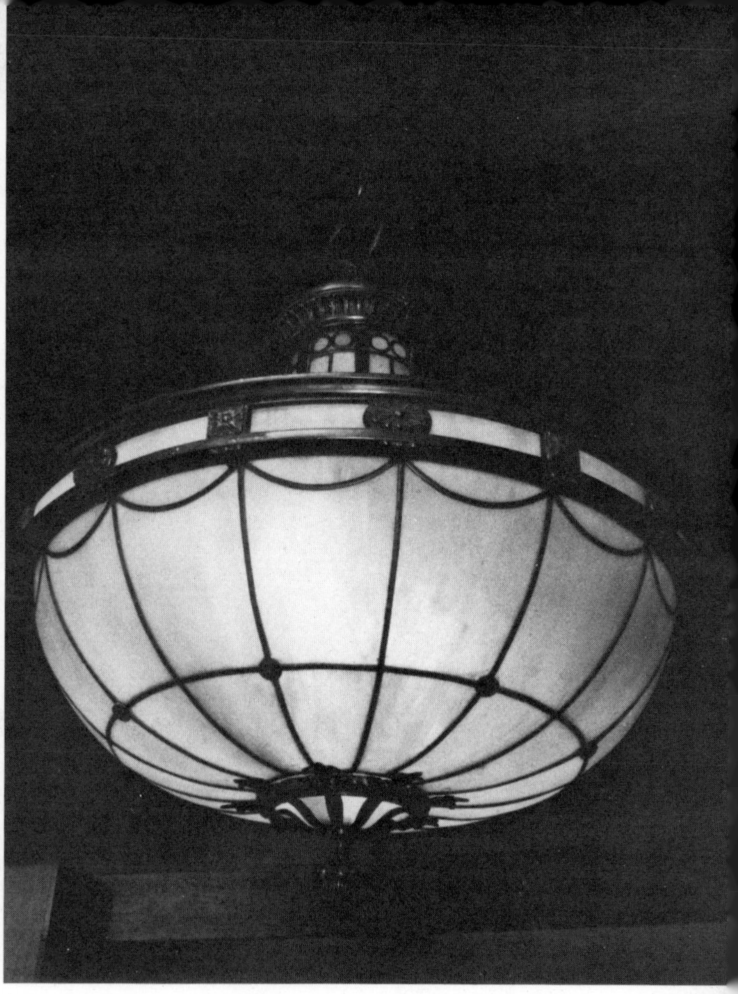

As you move around a room, take individual shots of the large objects that you consider of special interest. Among the items that receive this individual attention would be ornate clocks, an antique fireplace screen, or a Tiffany lamp.

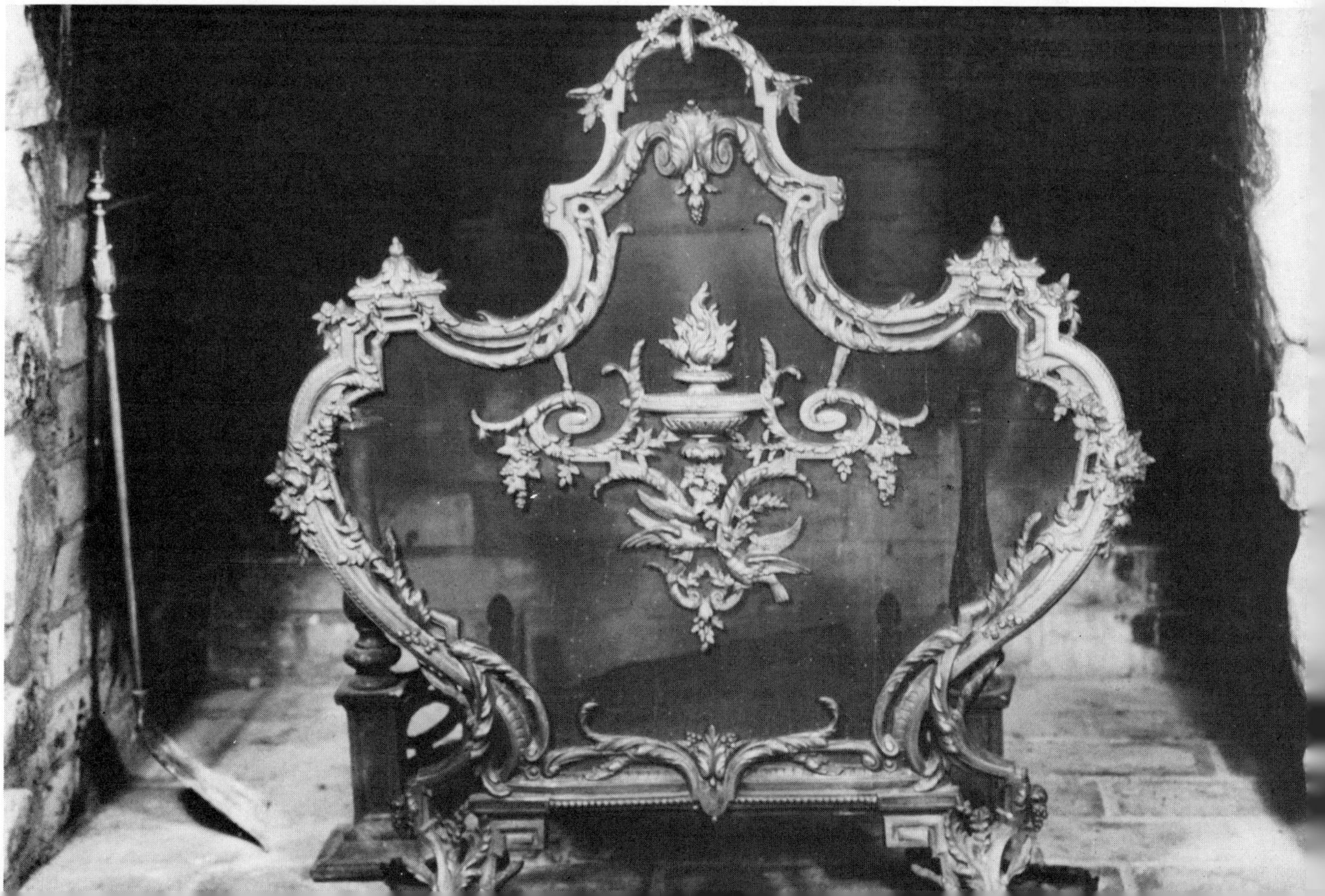

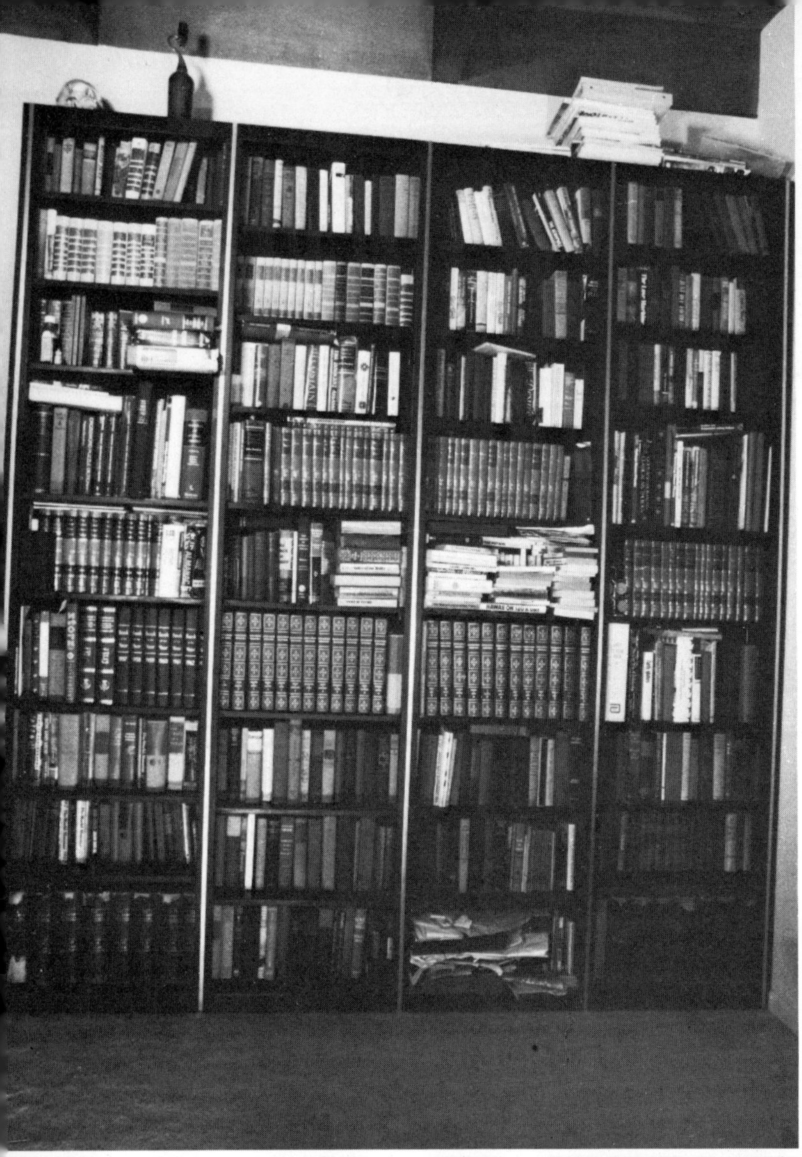

A bookcase can be photographed as a unit. If it contains books of special interest, such as a set of handbound volumes, then those books should be taken as a small group to make them more easily identifiable.

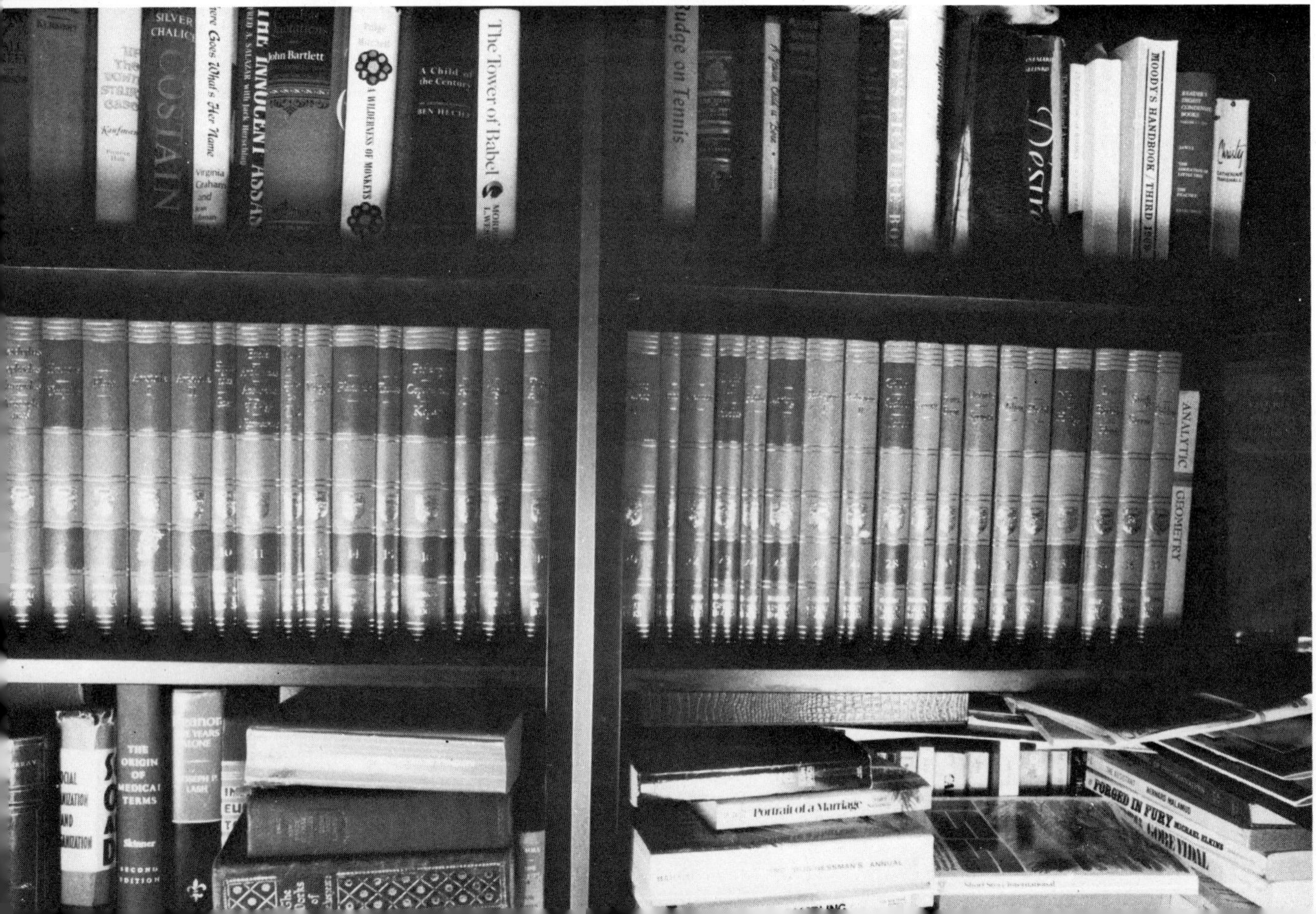

THE KITCHEN

Take two overall views of the kitchen, one with all the cabinet doors and drawers closed, the other with doors and drawers open. If you have a wide-angle lens, you may be able to take the entire kitchen in one view, or at the most two, one from either corner of the room, which would give you a total of four shots. If you are using a camera with only a normal lens, then you may have to take several views to cover the entire room.

There is no need to take individual shots of appliances, everyday dishes, or stainless forks, knives, and so on. The overviews are adequate to show the contents of the kitchen.

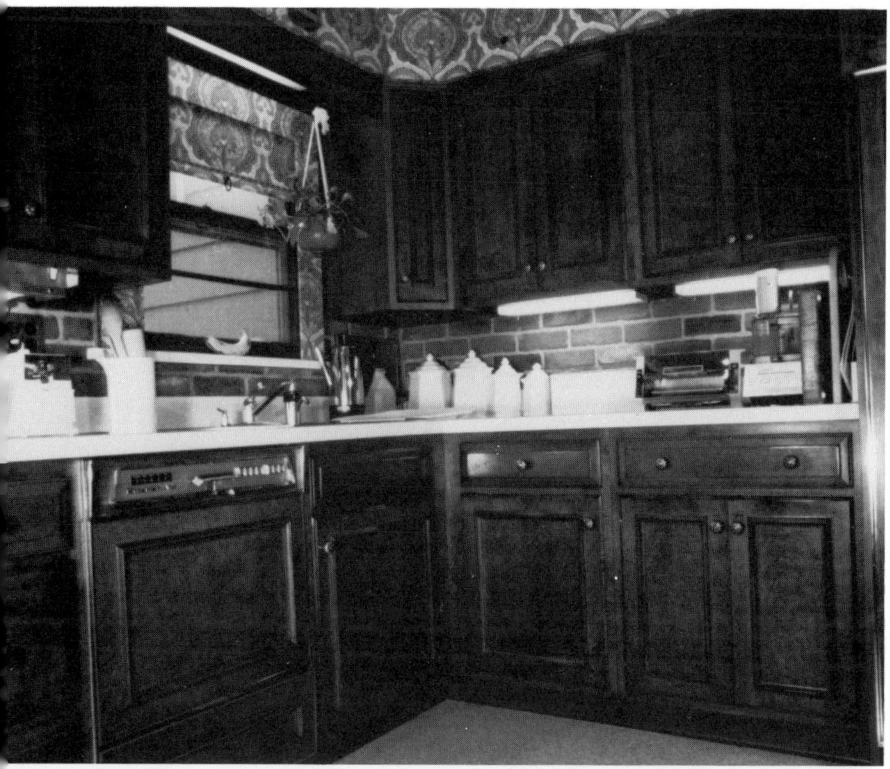

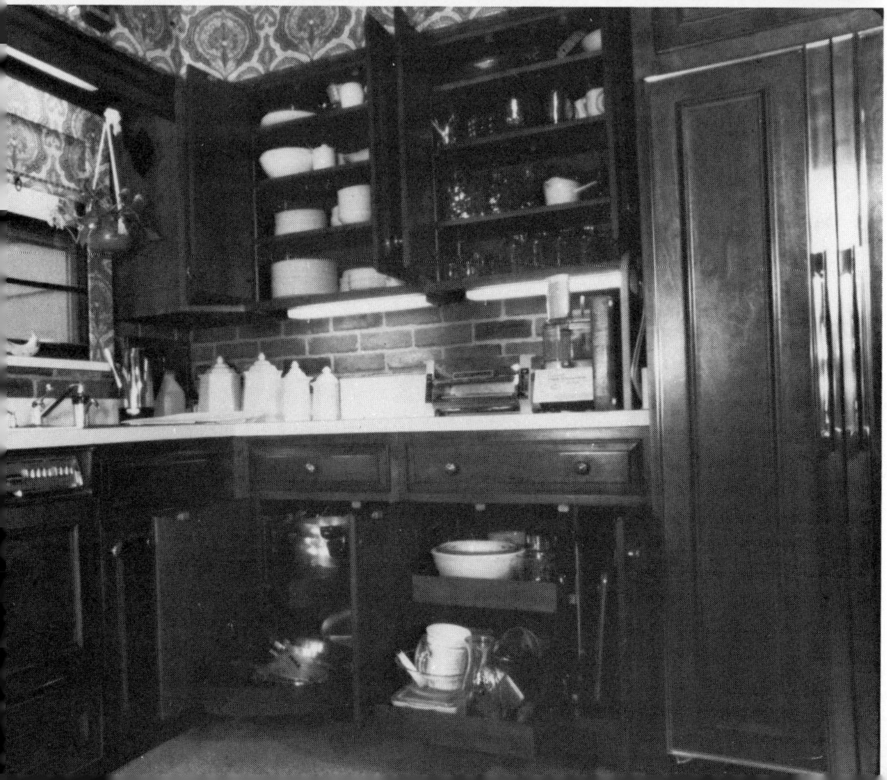

If you have a wide-angle lens, you can document a kitchen in two slides, the first with cabinets closed, the second with cabinets open to show contents. To get the same coverage with a normal lens, take overlapping views.

BEDROOMS

A view of the bedroom from the doorway is often sufficient. At most, two views, one from each corner, will show everything in the room. If you have unusually valuable pieces in the bedroom, treat them as you did pieces in the living area, photographing them individually.

Don't neglect your clothes closets. Take a photo of each closet so that you can identify the items in it. One or two shots should do it. Photograph furs individually by laying them out on the bed, which makes an excellent background. If you have a jewelry box, set it on the floor, open it, and photograph it. Later you can make close-ups of individual pieces.

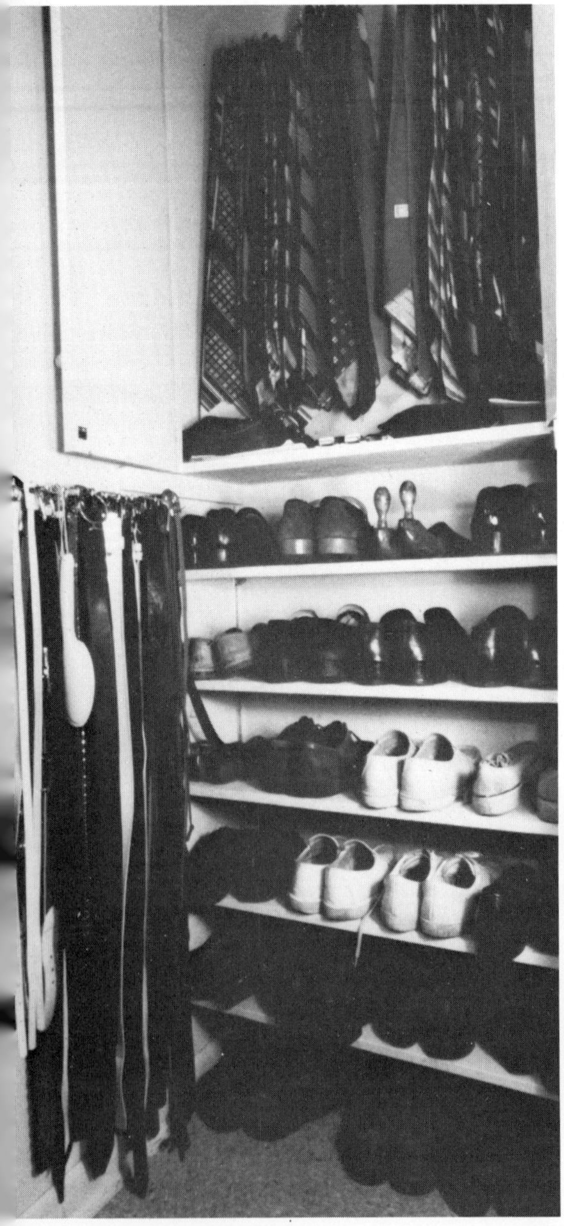

Don't neglect closets. There is no need to take individual shots of every suit and dress you own, but you should take group shots with suits, shoes, coats and so on in place, arranged neatly so that they can be counted easily.

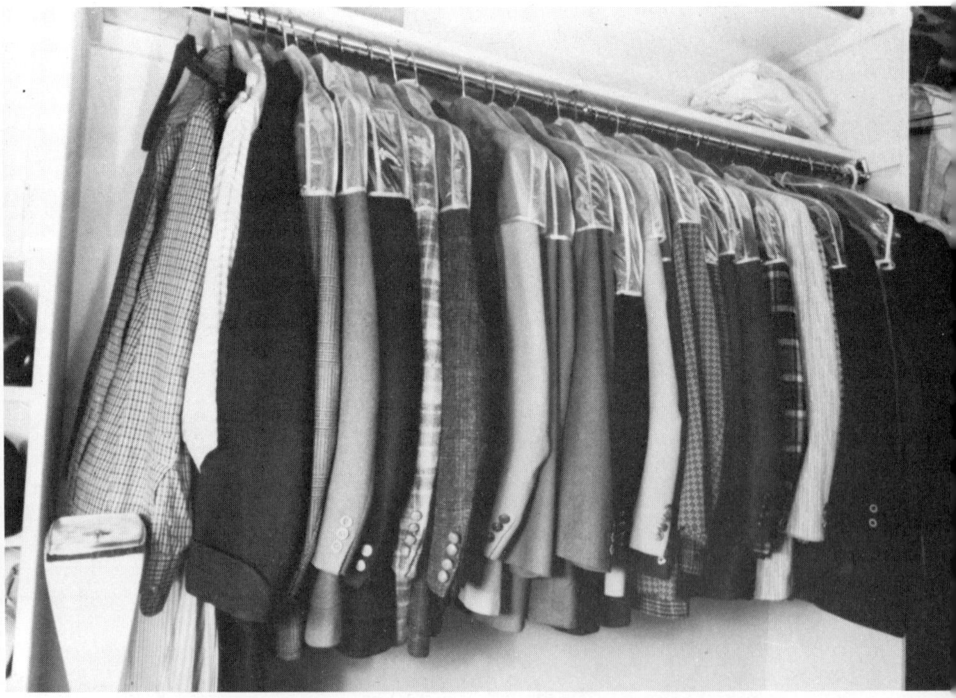

CHILDREN'S ROOMS

One shot from the doorway should do it, unless the room contains a stereo, TV, typewriter, computer, or expensive sporting equipment, in which case you should also take individual shots of the valuable items.

WORKSHOPS

Take an overall view of the workshop. If tools are in cabinets, open the doors so that the contents can be identified. If you have an unusually large collection of specialized tools, you can lay them out on your workbench or on the floor and photograph them as a group.

THE GARAGE

Don't neglect to take an overall view of the garage, which is where bicycles, lawn mowers, tractors, and sporting gear such as skis and snowmobiles are usually kept. It's surprising how equipment piles up in a garage, and while we take it for granted, if you had to go out and replace some of those items tomorrow, the replacement cost could be mind-boggling. For example, a lawn tractor purchased 10 years ago for $800 could cost you from $2000 to $3000 to replace today.

LANDSCAPING

After you have finished photographing each room in your house, take some shots outside. Valuable trees and plantings are subject to windstorms, fire, flood and other disasters and if damage occurs, you may be able to recover through your insurance or IRS deductions.

Workshop tools are best photographed in a simple group shot.

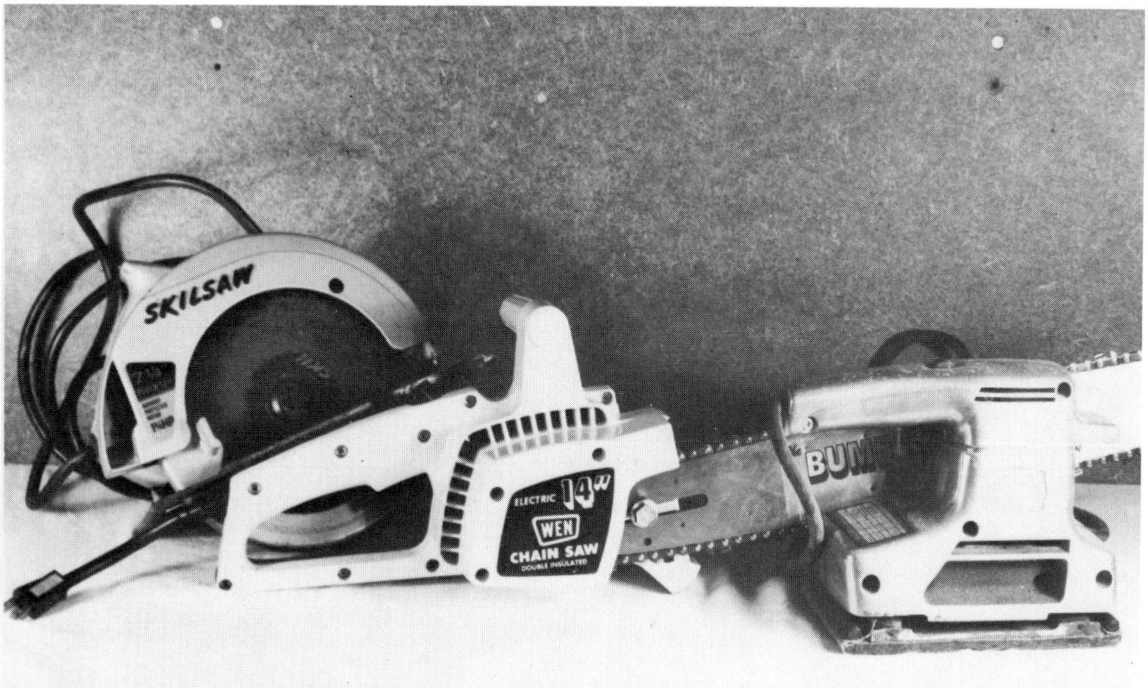

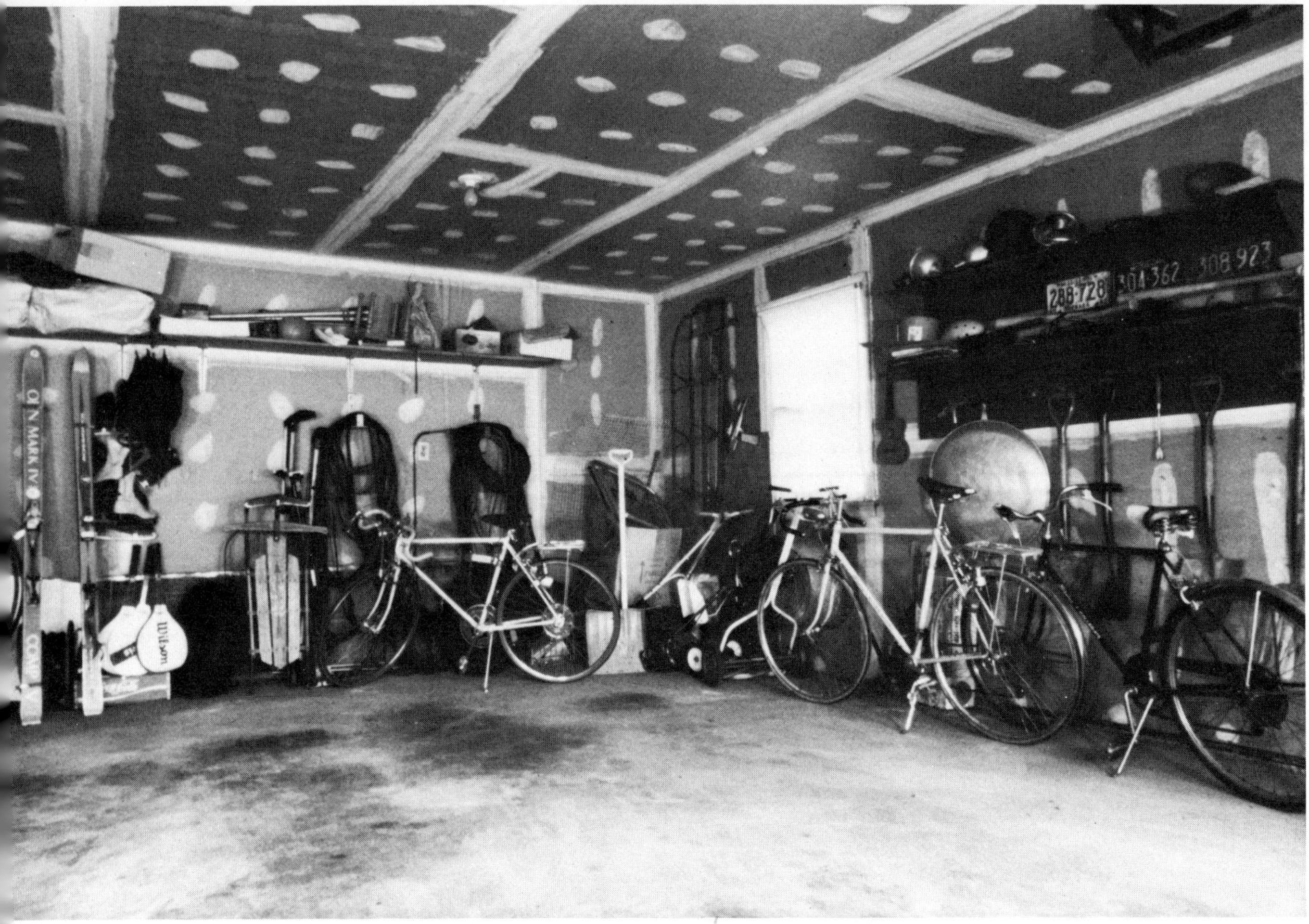

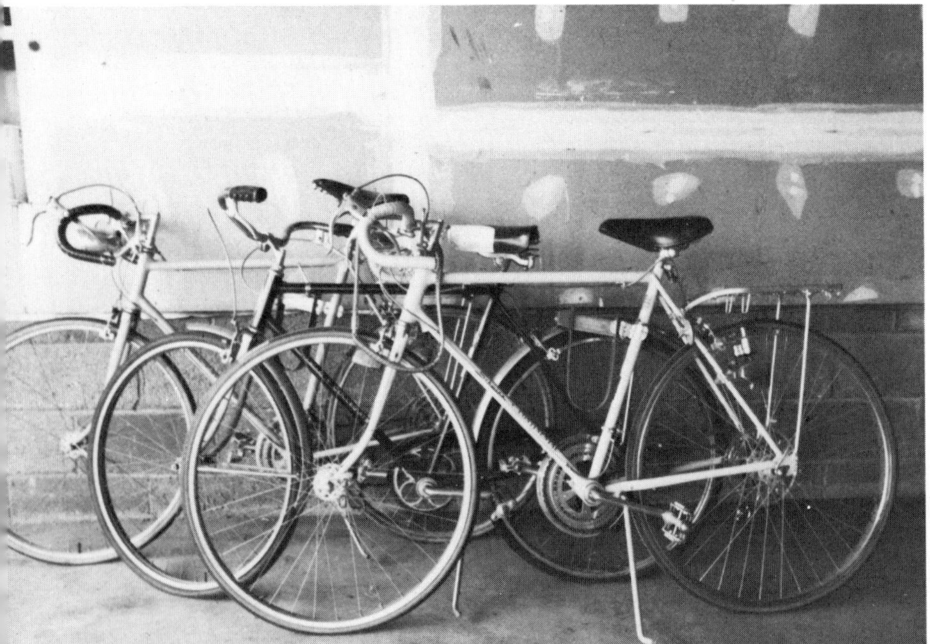

One photograph is usually enough to document a garage and its contents. If you have valuable sporting equipment or tools, though, additional shots of these items are in order.

OUTDOOR FURNITURE

Porch, pool and patio furniture and accessories are valuable. There is no need to photograph them individually, but be sure to include them in a couple of long shots.

These two photos provide complete documentation of a patio and deck area with its furniture.

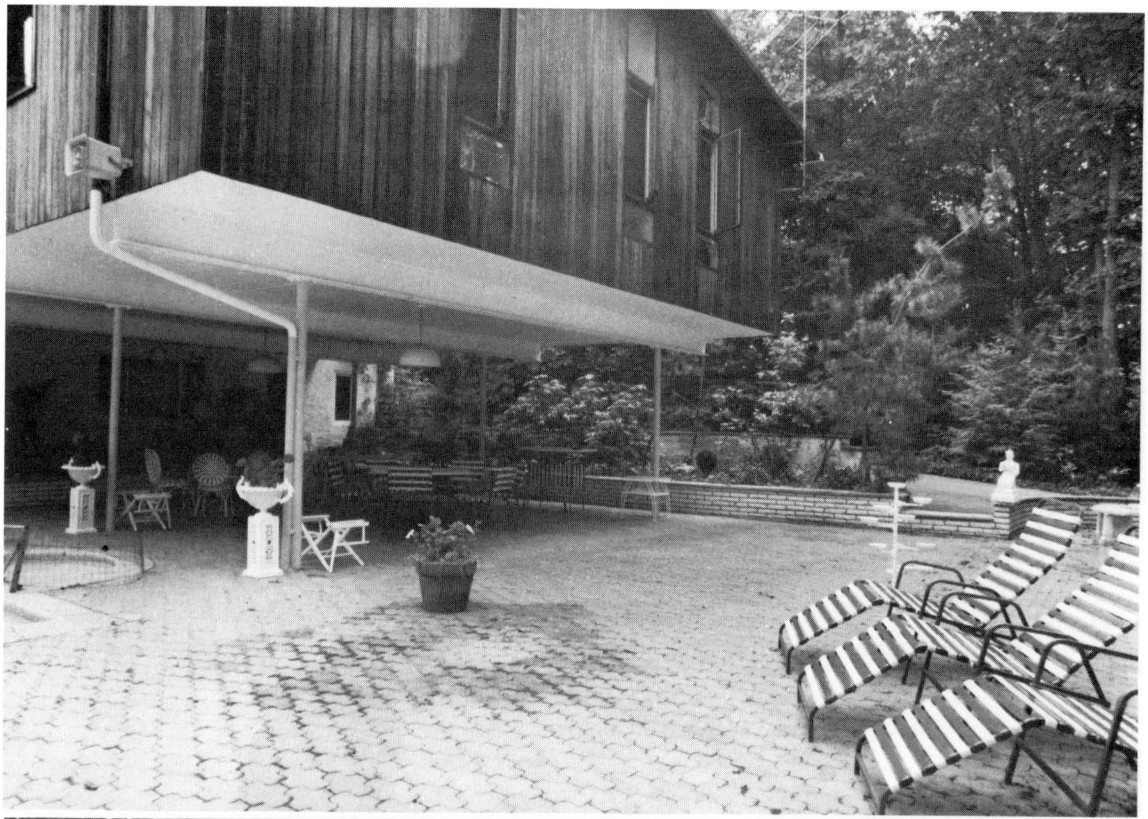

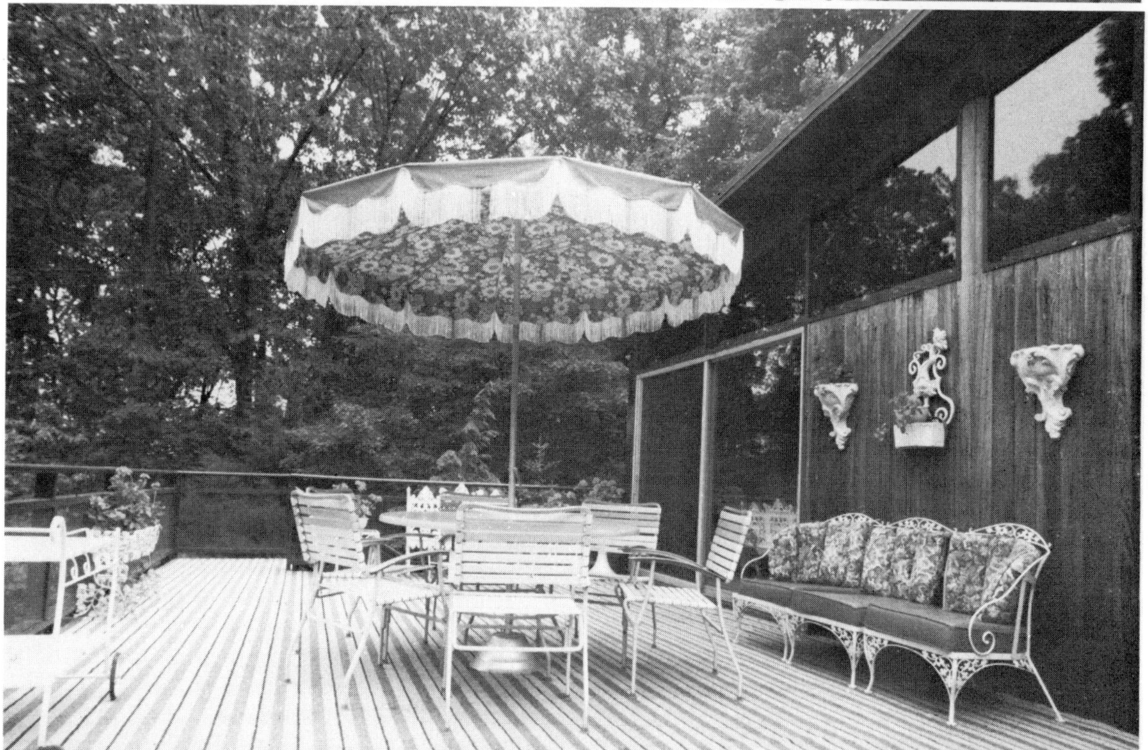

BUSINESS PROPERTY

Making a photo inventory of items used in the conduct of a business is essentially no different from making a household inventory. Overviews of the various rooms show the location of typewriters, computers, desks, and other office furniture. Individual shots of specialized machines and tools document their existence and condition.

Unless your business is collectibles, or you have a large plant, making a photo inventory of your business property may not involve more than 15 or 20 shots. If you are a retailer or distributor, there is no need to photo-inventory stock. Your usual records should already have that problem well in hand.

If your business is antiques, fine art, or jewelry, you have a special problem, and if you are not already doing so, you should be making one or more shots of every unusually valuable piece that passes through your hands. Use the same techniques that are described in this book for photographing individual items. The only exception is a jewelry business, where you might want to maintain a permanent copy set-up, in which case, investigate the feasibility of a Polaroid MP-4 copy system. It will give you high-quality, larger-than-life images that are easy to file.

The same principles used for a household inventory apply to business property. In this photo, three important business machines fit easily into one shot.

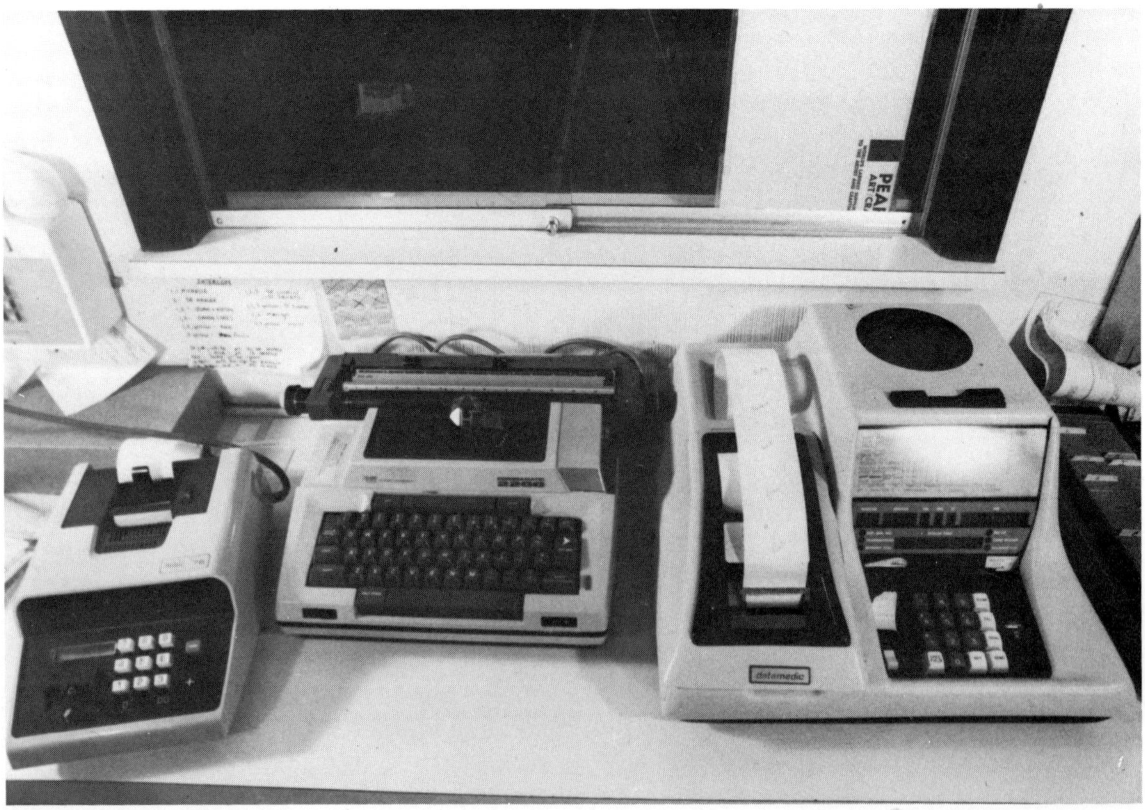

4 Close-Ups of Small Objects

Once you have finished photographing the large objects that remain in place—large paintings, furniture, lamps and so on—you are ready to begin the next phase of the inventory, which is to photograph small items that can be brought to a table where you have a background-and-lighting set-up. Items to be photographed against a prearranged background include china, silverware, porcelain, crystal, stamps, coins, jewelry, handguns, documents, and other small collectibles.

THE BACKGROUND SET-UP

Begin the small-object phase of the inventory by clearing a table top for use as a set. Next, set up a background board on the table. The background board can be a sheet of scrap plywood, Masonite, the side of a large cardboard box, a suitcase, or even a table pad. The functions of the background board are to hold up a piece of cloth that will serve as the background for the items to be photographed and to support items that need to be leaned against it. Alternatively, you can tack your background cloth to a wall and move your table under it.

For the background cloth we use 44″ × 72″ swatches of velour in green or red for color photos, but many materials around your own house will work equally well. For example, solid-color blankets are ideal, as are solid-color bed sheets. For very small items such as jewels and coins, you can use a velour shirt.

We avoid the use of paper as a background because it has a sheen that is hard to control. Felt also has a shine to it, though not as much as paper.

Set up the background board about eighteen inches from the end of the table. If the table has a good surface, put something under the board to protect the table. A towel will do. Next, drape the background cloth over the board and table. You now have a simple set into which you can place the items to be inventoried. Now set up two lights, one on each side of your table-top set. They should be at equal distances from the background board and at least four to five feet away. If you get them closer, you will have problems with uneven light distribution. The lights should shine down into your set at an angle. If you place them about three feet above the level of the table, you should get good coverage.

If you have decided to use a portable electronic flash mounted on your camera, you can get slightly better results with shiny objects if you bounce the light from a white card fastened at an angle above the head of the flash.

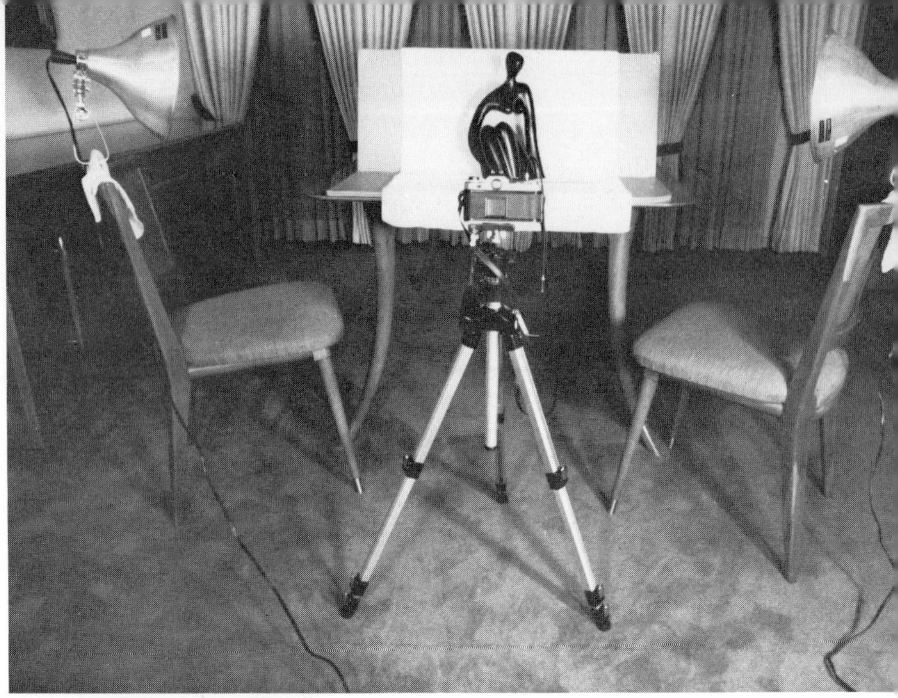

This is a typical arrangement for table-top photography. Two clamp lights are attached to the backs of kitchen chairs. The camera is on a tripod in front of the table. A board holds up the background cloth, which covers both board and table top.

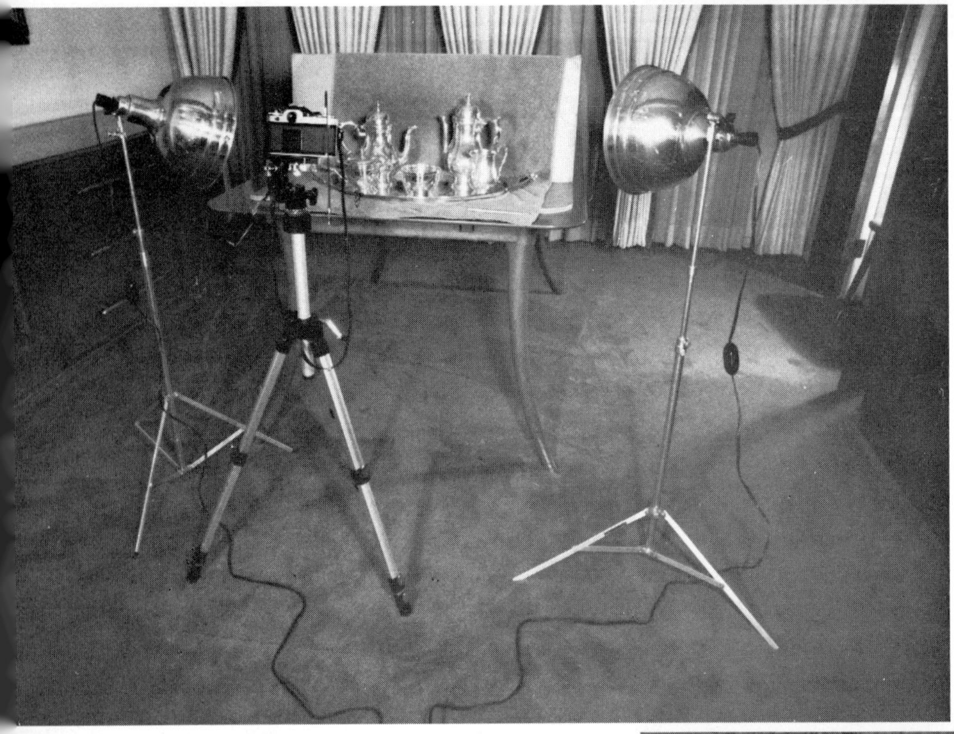

This arrangement is similar to the first, except that the lights are on stands, which permit greater flexibility in placement and height than clamp lights.

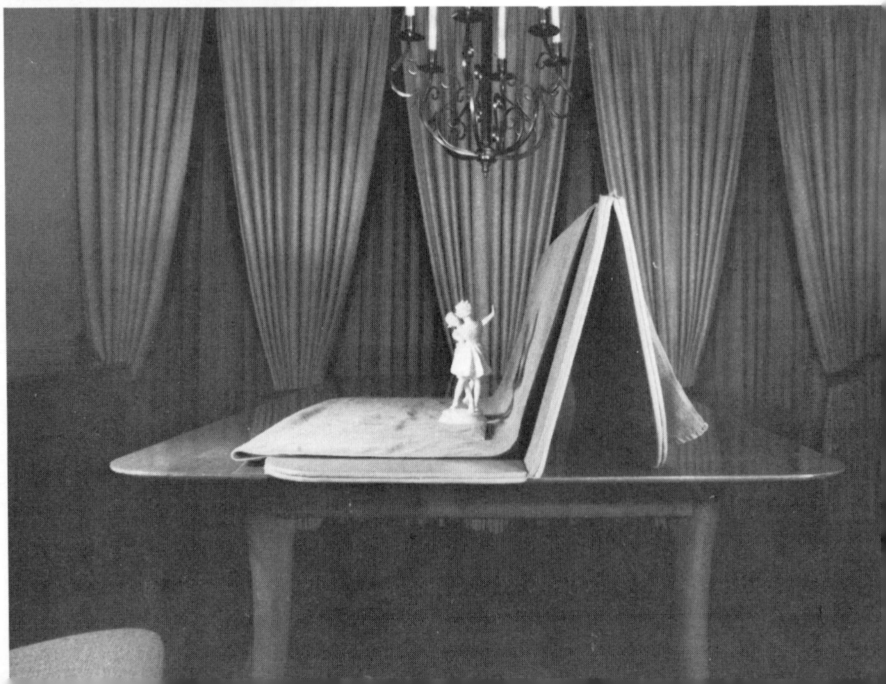

Dozens of readily available items can be pressed into service as background cloth holders. Here, a table pad is used.

Alternatively, use a diffuser in front of the flash. These and other special techniques for flash are described in Chapter 5.

If you feel that your floods are giving you too much glare, you can try diffusing the light using any of the diffusers on your reflectors or a sheet of tracing paper suspended 8 to 12 inches in front of your lights. These techniques, which scatter the direct beam of light from your floods, produce photos that may be aesthetically more pleasing, but we have found that just making minor adjustments in the position of the floods will usually eliminate serious problems. The few glare spots that remain do not diminish the value of an inventory photo.

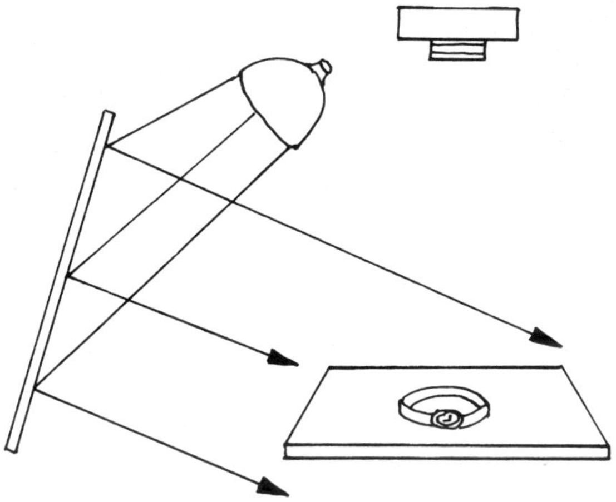

A simple way to diffuse light and reduce glare is shown in this diagram. Suspend a sheet of paper and bounce the light off it towards the subject.

Once your set-up is complete, begin bringing small objects to the table. There is no need to bring everything, just the valuable or potentially valuable items. Forget about electric can openers, pots and pans, tools, and so on. Those will appear in your overall or small-group shots. What you should be interested in now is getting detailed shots of silverware, crystal, fine china, and small collectibles—coins, porcelain figurines, small pieces of sculpture, valuable miniatures such as Chinese snuff bottles, and so on.

Remember to include your scale indicator (ruler) in all shots.

A SET-UP FOR FLAT SUBJECTS

You can use the background board arrangement to photograph documents and other flat subjects by leaning them against the backboard. On the other hand, if you have an extensive collection of documents, stamps, coins, medals and other flat items, then you might want to make a copy set-up. To do this, adjust the tripod head so that the camera is pointed at the floor. You can then lay the background cloth on the floor, set up two lights on either side at a 45° angle, and photograph that way, or put the tripod on the table and use the table as your copyboard. If your tripod has a removable head, you might be able to take it off and mount it underneath the center column. Then you can attach your camera so that it is suspended between the legs of the tripod. This is a good way to support the camera when you make ultra-close-ups of stamps and other tiny, flat subjects.

SUBJECT HANDLING

There are some tricks to arranging subjects for inventory photos that you should know. An inventory photo, like a scientific photo, must contain the maximum amount of information possible. For example, in photographing collections of plates, glassware, silver and so on, you must arrange the collection so that a person looking at the slide could project it and easily count every item.

China: Fine china should be stacked and the camera positioned so that you can count the edges of the plates. Arrange the stacks so

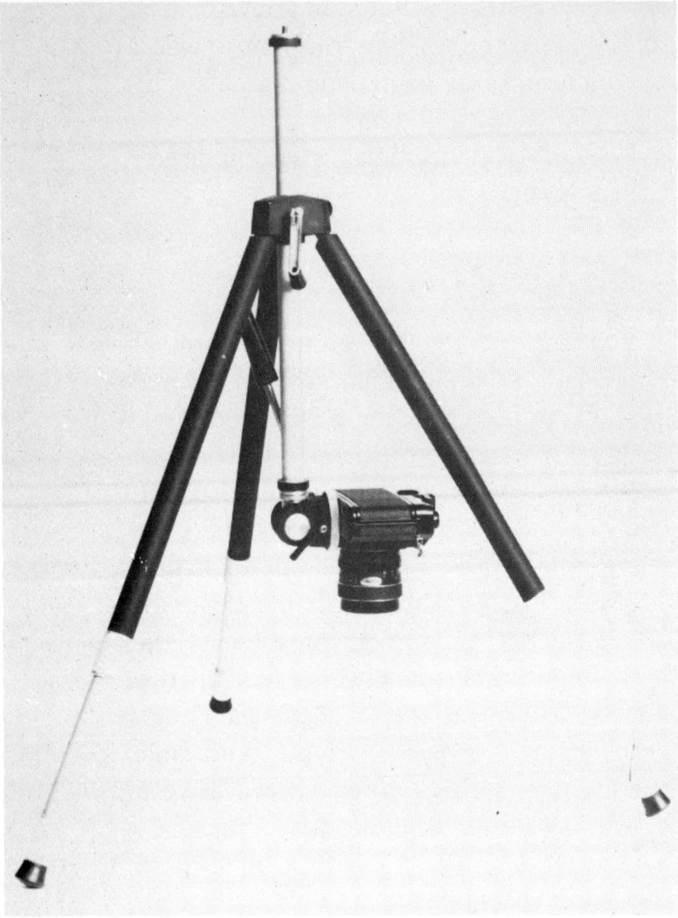

A tripod is needed to make a copy set-up for flat objects such as documents. If your tripod has a removable head, you can mount the camera underneath the center column, as shown in this photo. If not, adjust the tripod head so the camera points towards the floor. It's best to use a cable release when taking close-ups, as even a slight movement of the camera will cause blurring.

that no stack is hidden completely behind any other. Cups can be stacked as well and taken in the general shot or separately. Serving platters will have to be photographed in a separate shot.

The next step in photographing china is to take a close-up that will identify the pattern and the china mark. You can do this by standing up two plates on edge, side by side, one with the pattern facing the camera, the other with the reverse side facing the camera. Just lean the plates against the stacked china for this shot, or if you prefer, remove the other pieces and lean the plates against the background board. If you wish, you can also move in for an ultra-close-up of the china mark, but this is not really necessary. When you project the slide of the two plates, the china mark should be clearly visible.

Silverware: Make your first shot of silverware in the case or cloth rolls in which it is stored. Next, lay out the individual pieces on the background cloth in groups. By that we mean photograph all your knives together, forks together, and so on. Spoons and forks can be fanned out so that you can easily count them. Knives can be laid out side by side, as can serving pieces. Be sure to take a close-up shot of the mark on the back of a typical piece. On the average, it takes about five or six photos to fully document a silver dinner service. A typical sequence is shown in the accompanying photos.

Porcelain figurines: One-of-a-kind pieces should be photographed twice. The first shot will show the entire figure. For the second shot, lay the figurine on its side and photograph the mark on the bottom. If you have two or more identical pieces, you can lay one down so the mark shows and leave the other standing.

Remember to include at least an end of your ruler in each shot. Without that there is no way to tell how large the pieces are.

Jewelry: There are a number of ways to handle jewelry, depending on the uniqueness and value of the pieces. Less valuable items can be grouped together, along with your ruler, and recorded in one shot. Pieces of unusual value or unique design should be taken individually.

An easy way to photograph rings is to put them on your fingers, or on the fingers of an assistant. The hand is the ideal stand for rings

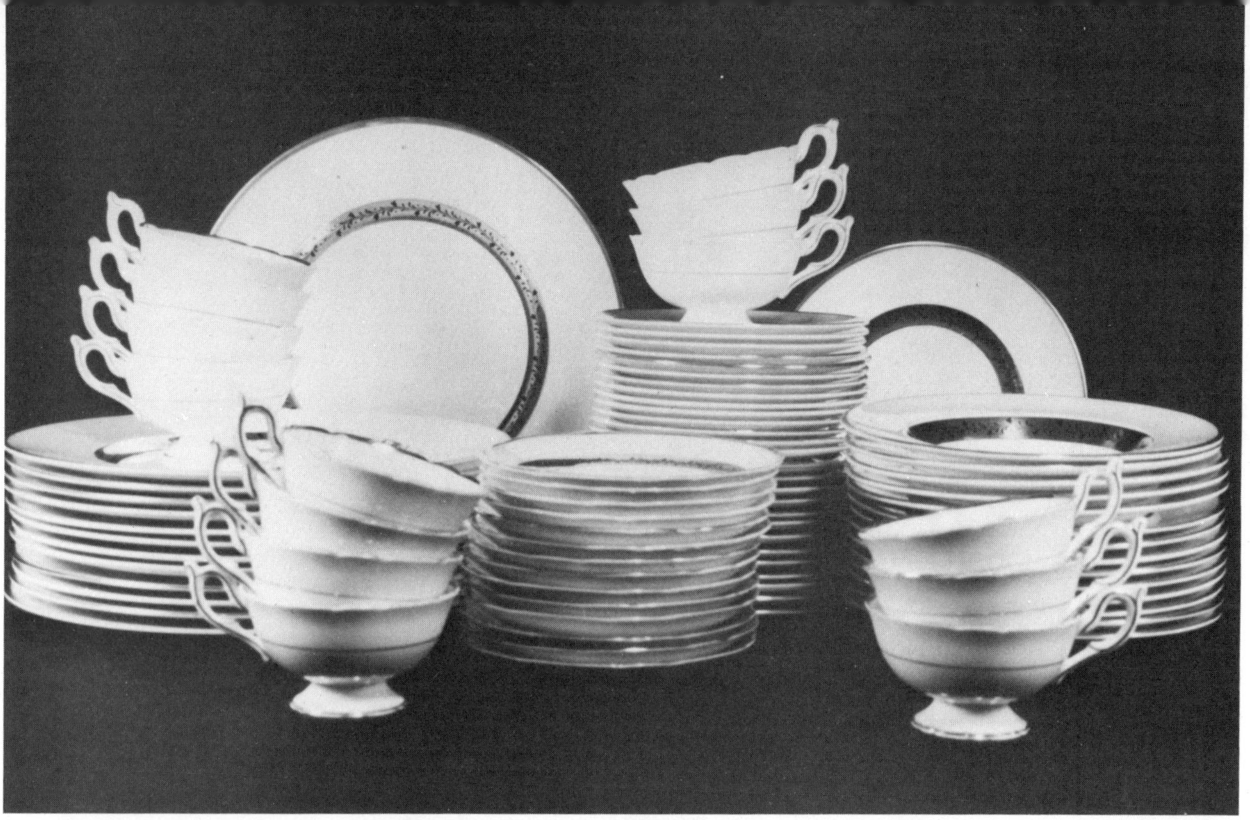

Two slides document this china dinner service. The first shot shows the entire set stacked so that every cup, saucer and plate can be easily counted, with two plates leaning against the background board so that the pattern can be identified. The second slide shows one of each. Note that one plate has been reversed to show the mark on the bottom and a similar plate faces forward to show the pattern.

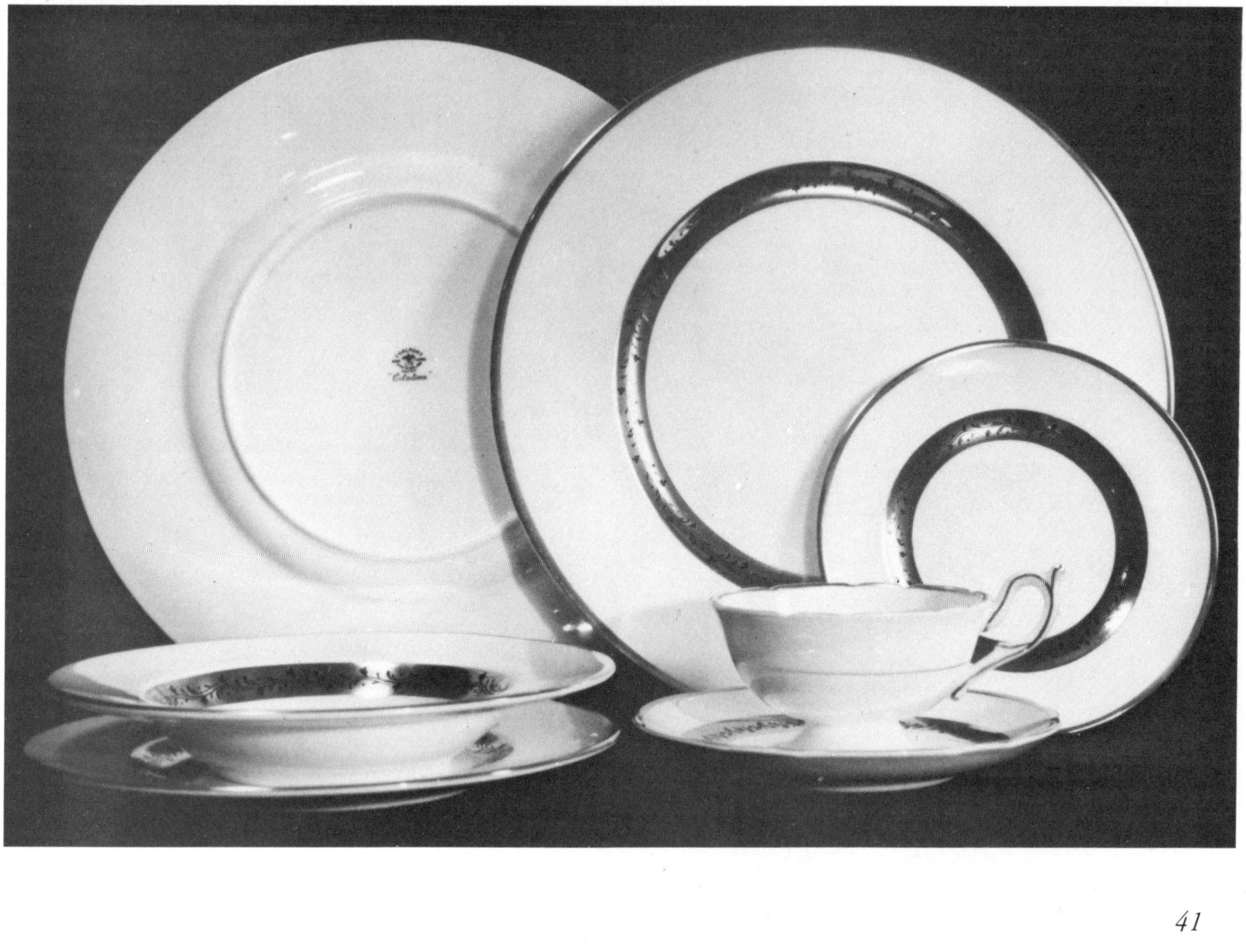

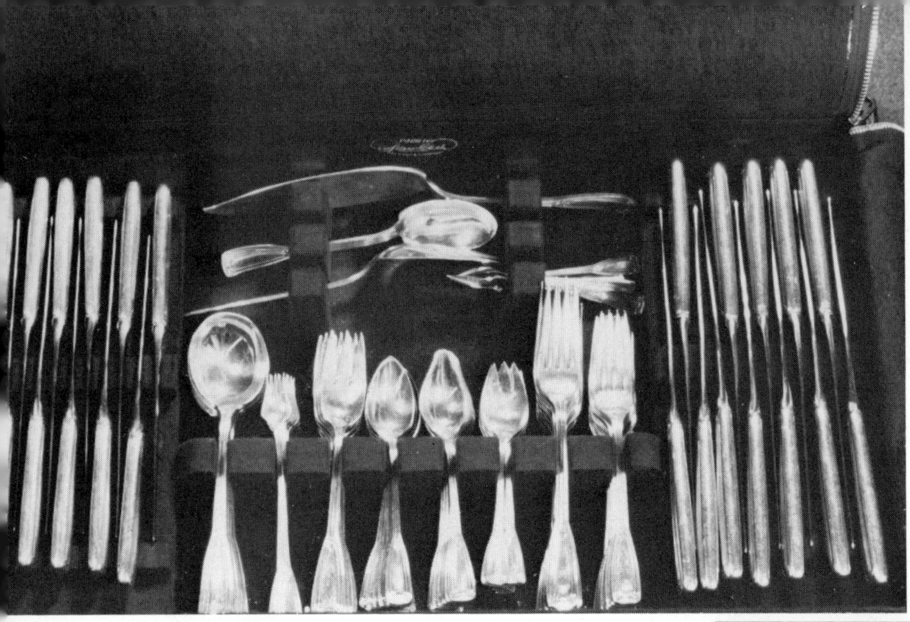

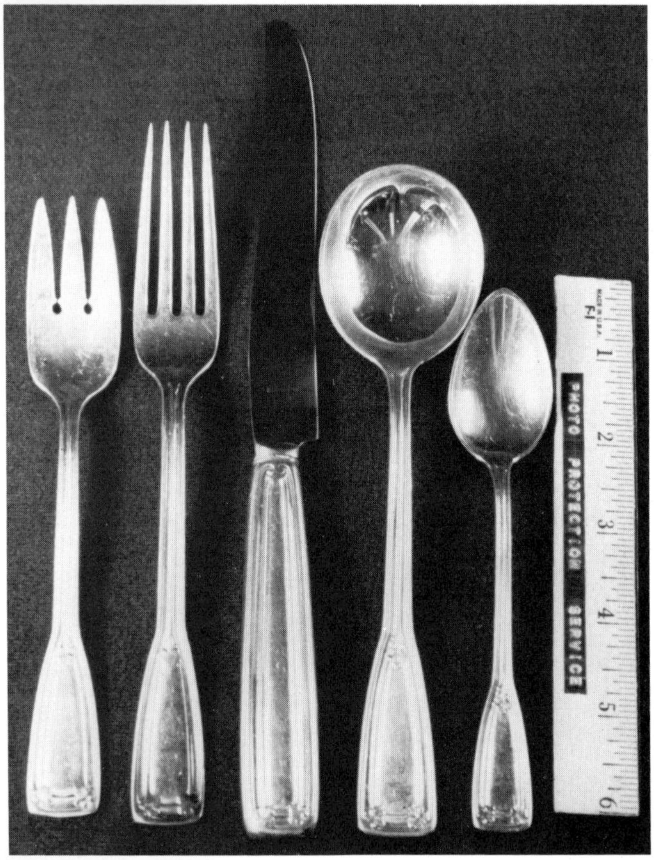

This sequence of slides shows how you would go about documenting a complete, five-piece setting of silver. First, the complete set is shown in its box. Then one of each piece is laid out along with the ruler and taken as a group. Next, the complete set of each piece is laid out so that every fork, knife or spoon can be counted; each group is then photographed.

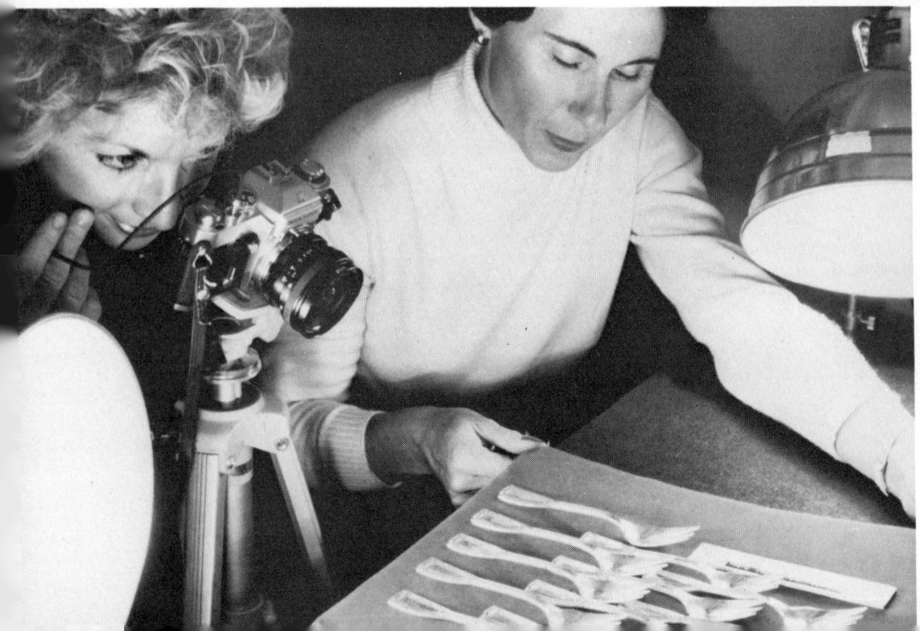

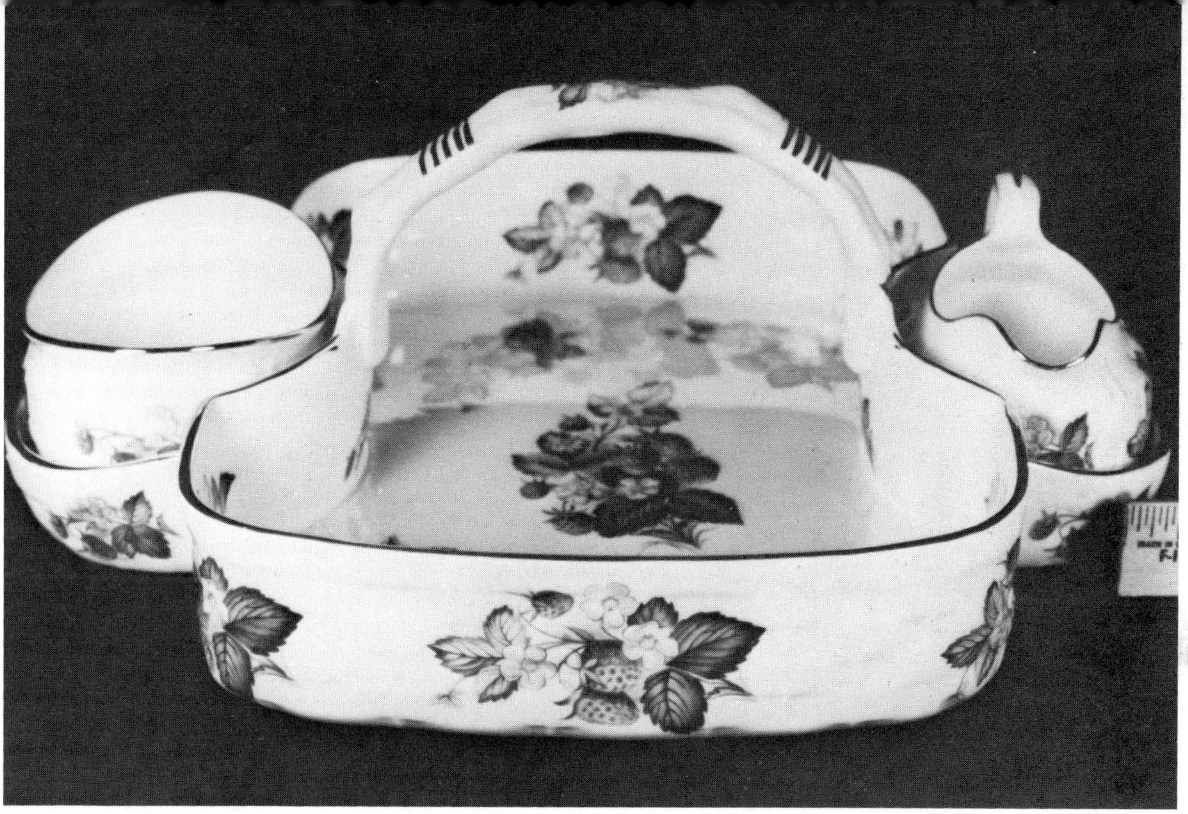

This china strawberry dish was photographed from a higher camera position than would be used for china plates so that a viewer can see the design inside the dish.

Group serving pieces according to pattern.

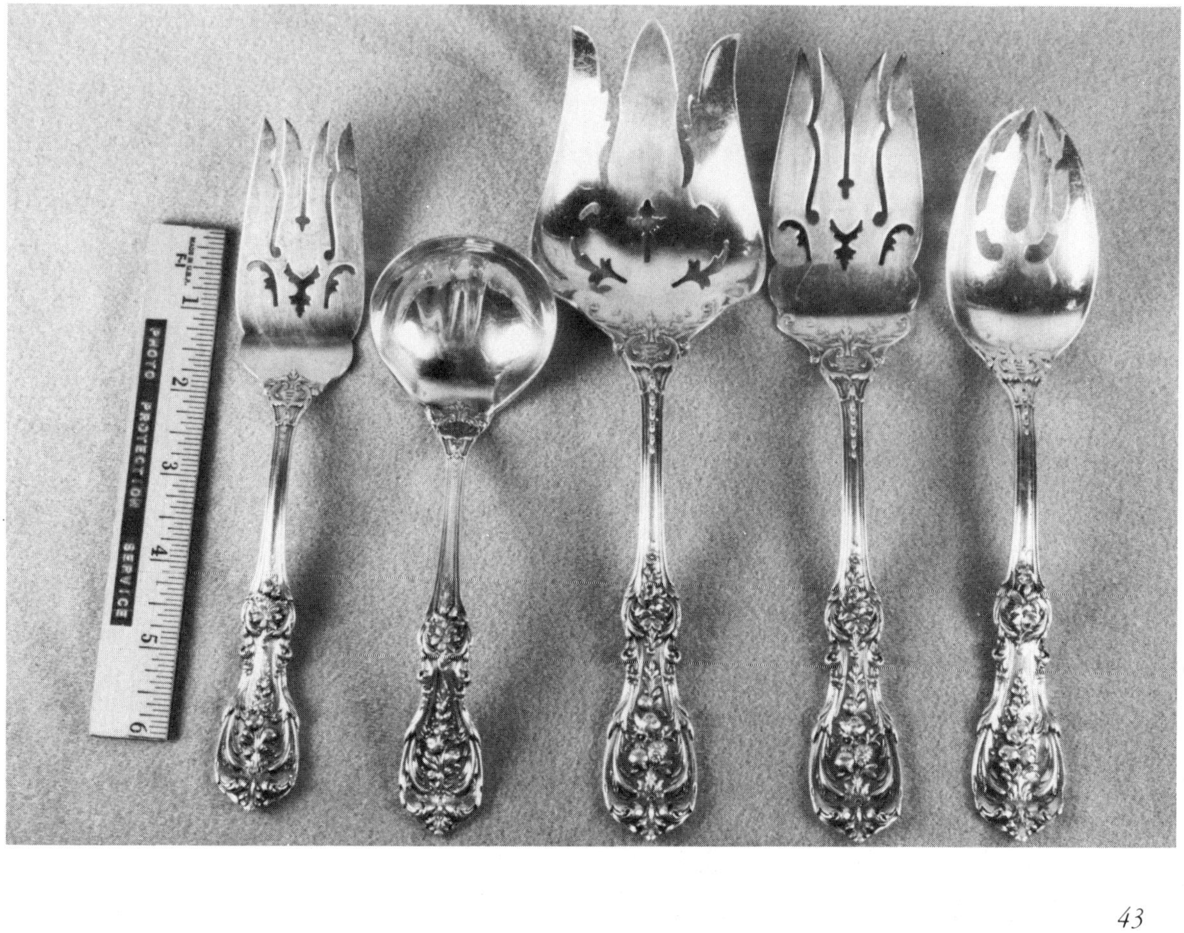

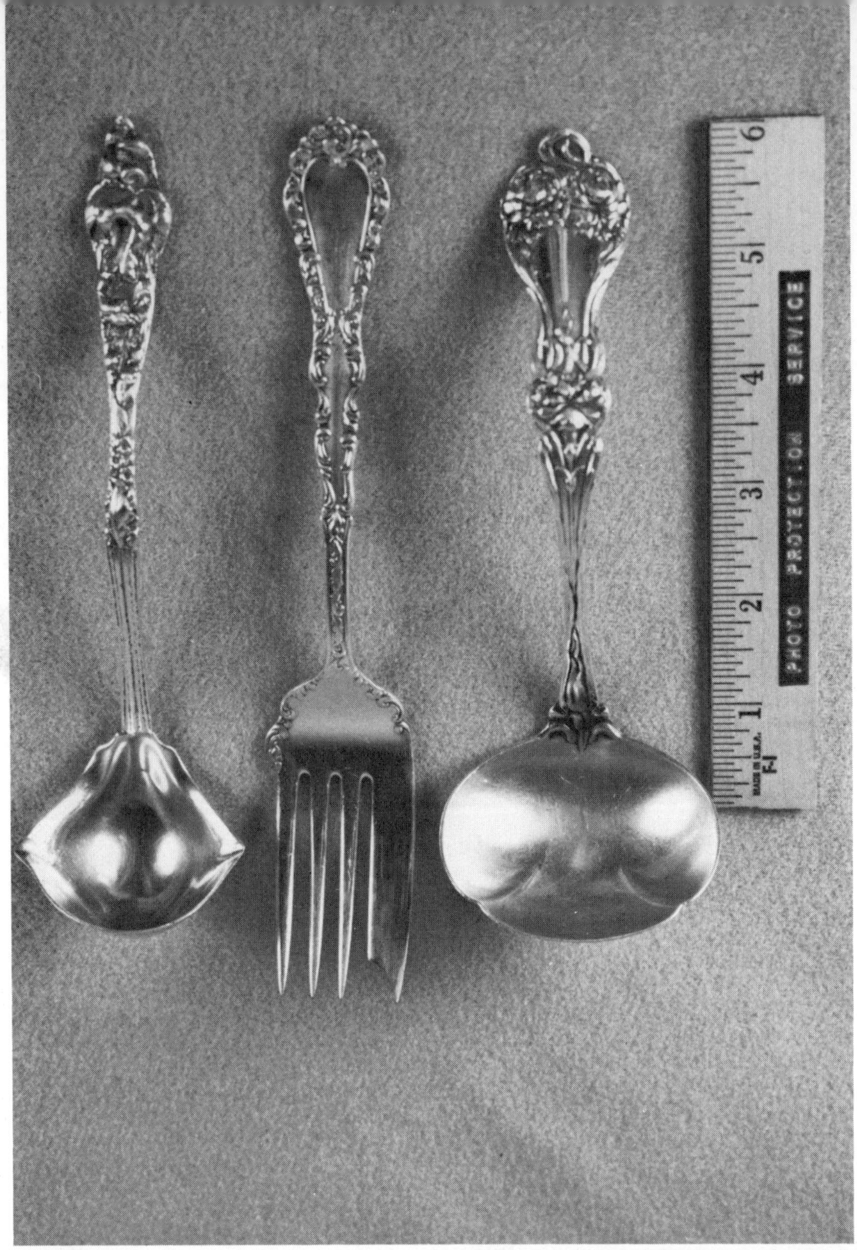

Sterling silver pieces such as these generally have a mark on the back, which you should photograph close-up. The mark on the back of one will do to identify the entire group as sterling.

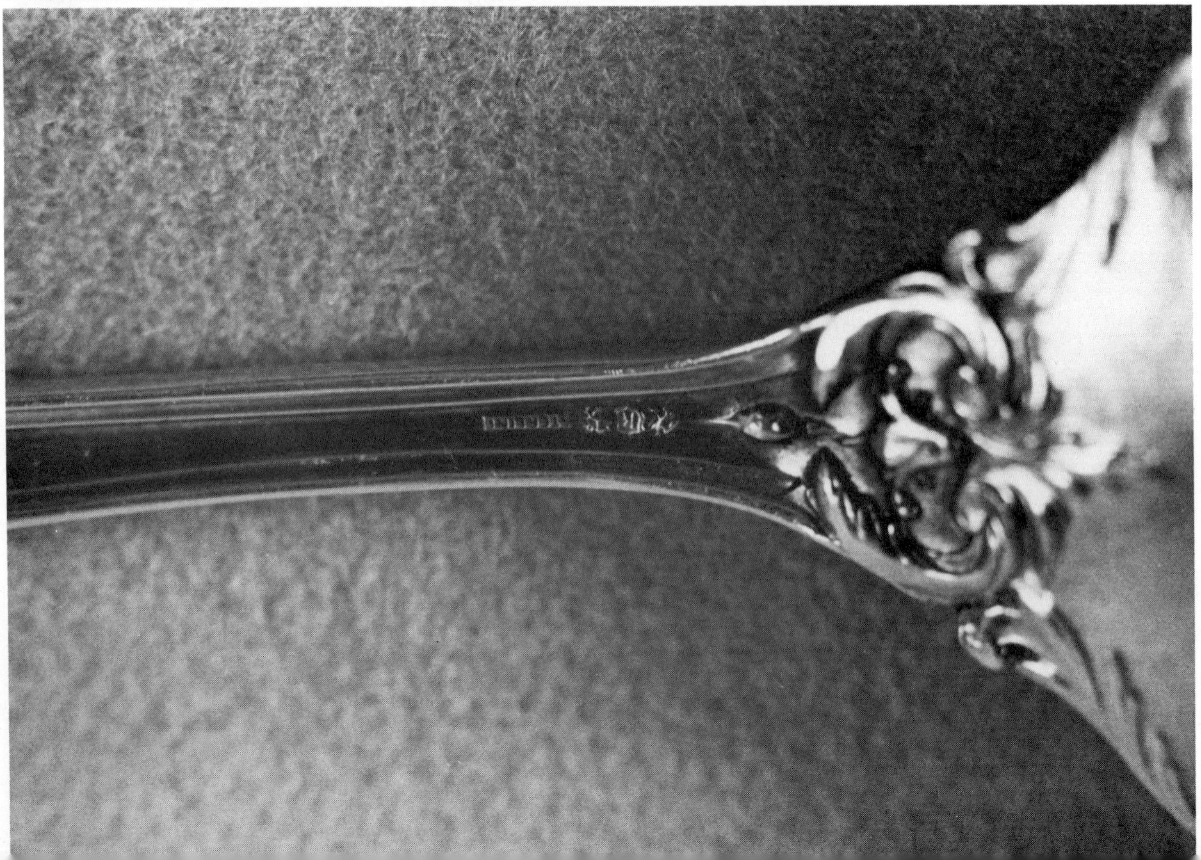

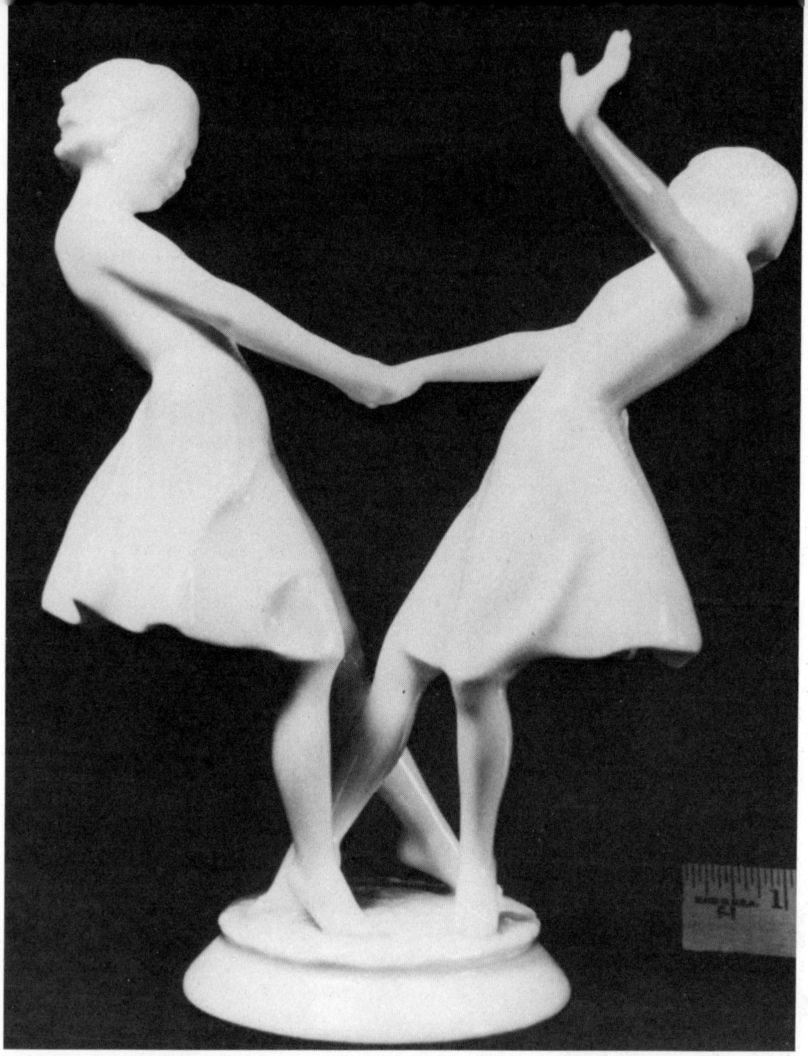

Two slides were taken to record this porcelain piece, the first to show the figures, the second to show the mark on the base.

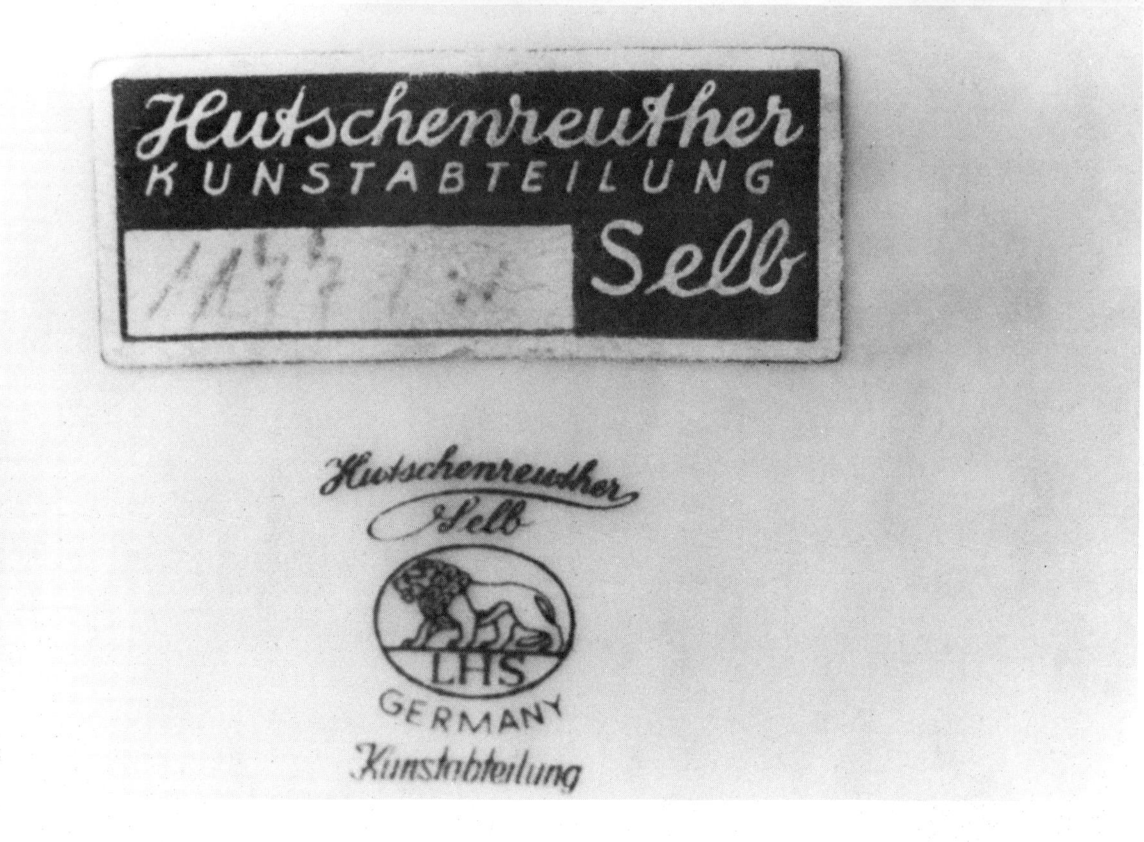

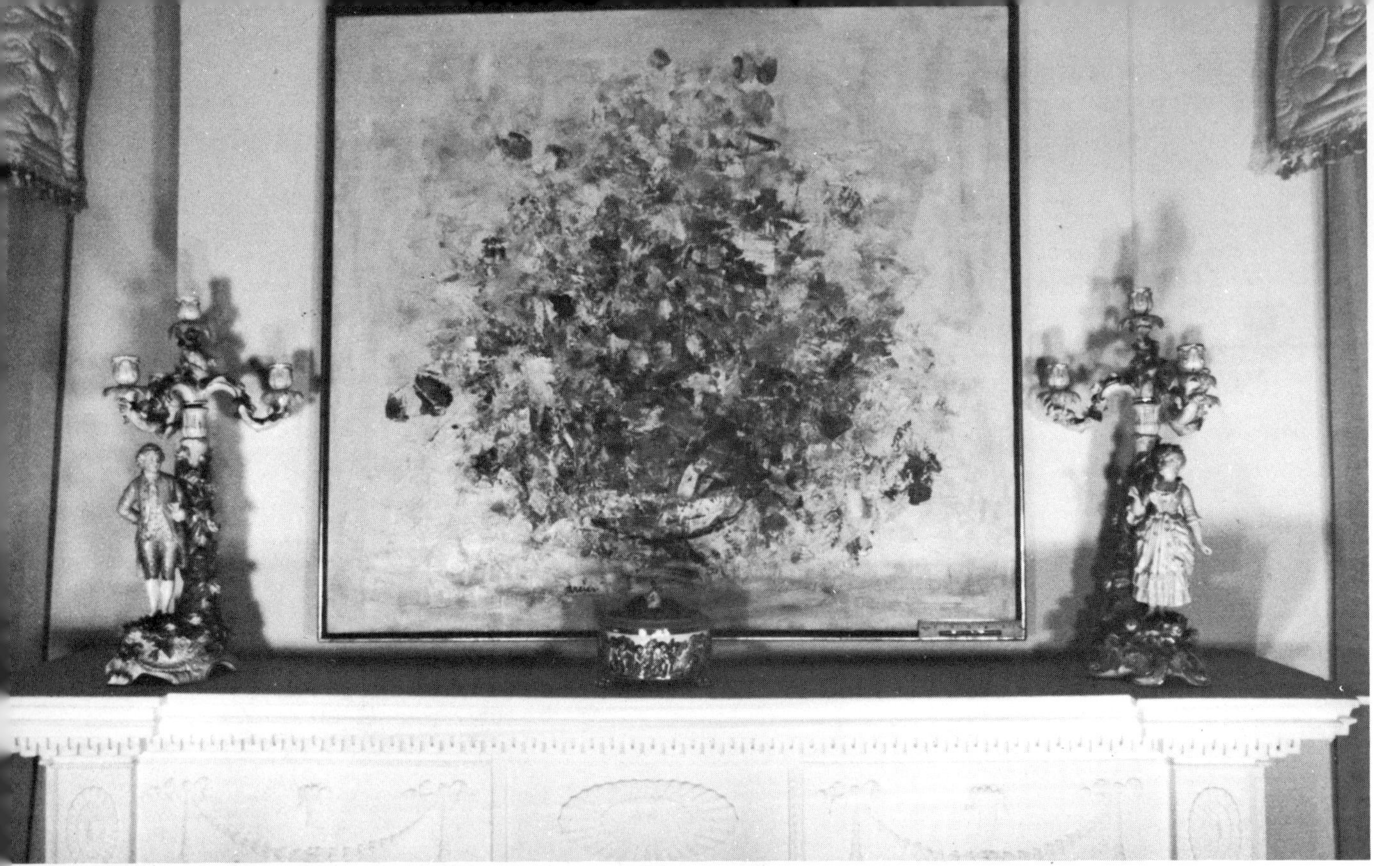

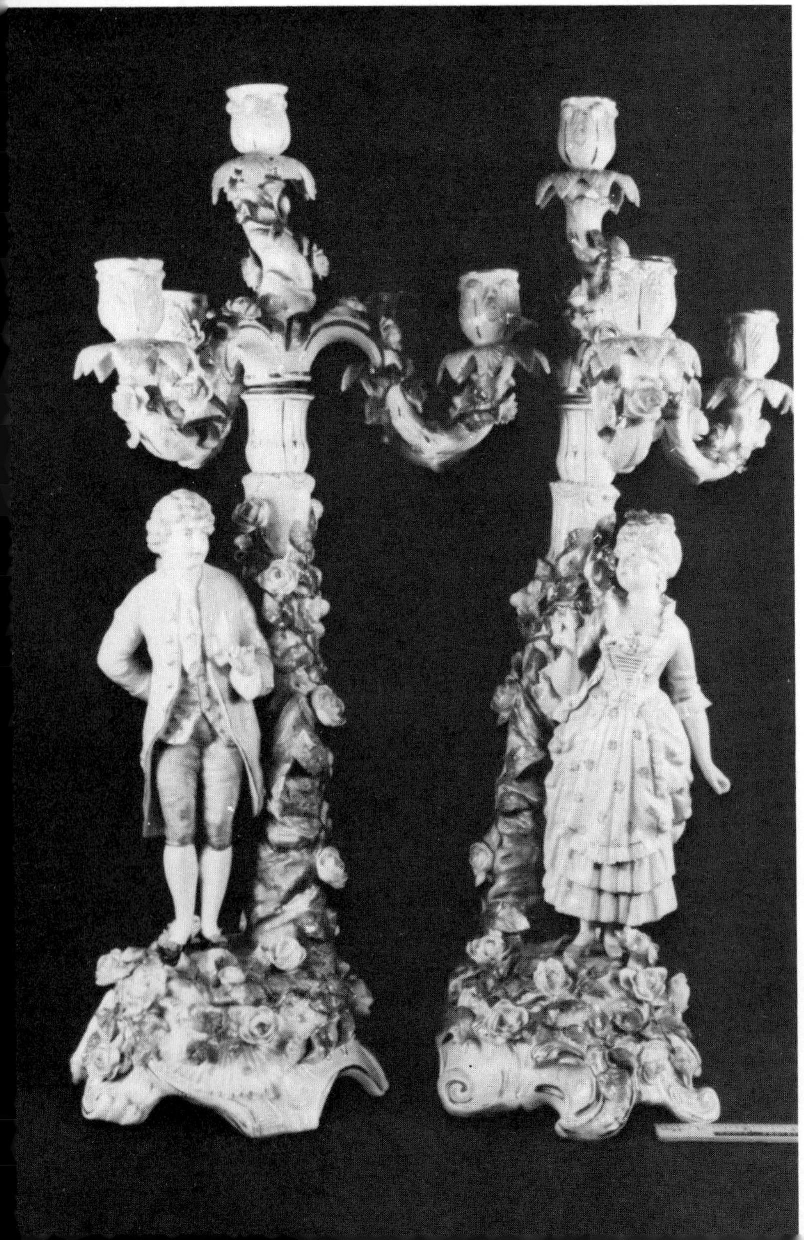

The small-group photo of these Dresden figures was not sufficient to document their intricate detail, so the pair was photographed again in the table-top set-up.

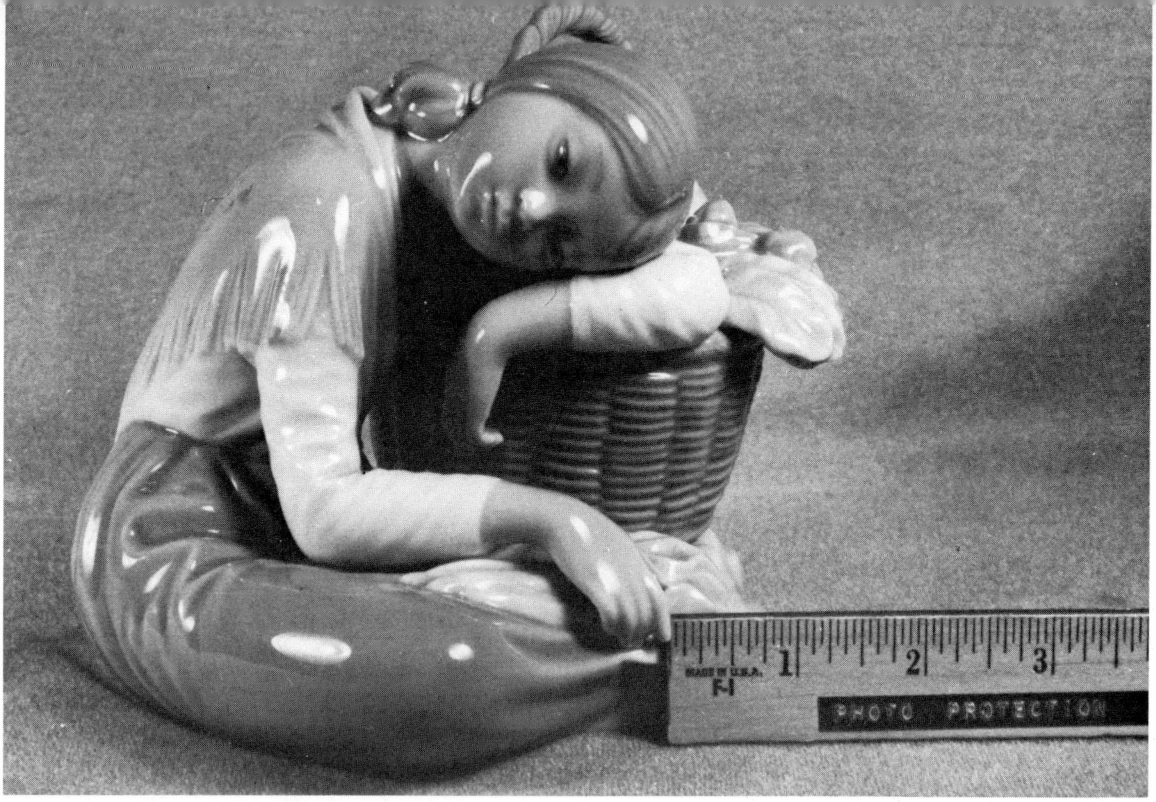

This is one of the pieces visible in the slide of the table on page 24.

and also functions as a size indicator. If you prefer, you can stand the rings up in the small, black cases in which jewelers often pack rings and cuff links.

If your jewelry has a maker's mark on the back, and it is important, you should take an ultra-close-up to show the mark. To do this, you may have to adjust your lights a bit. One trick is to move one light closer to your subject and lower it so that the light strikes the piece at an oblique angle, just skimming across the surface and illuminating the edges of indentations. It helps if you have an assistant to move the light while you observe the effect through the camera viewfinder.

Guns: A gun collection can usually be photographed as a group. Then you can move in for close-ups of unique pieces to get a clear record of etching, carved handles and stocks, and so on. Serial numbers can be recorded on the inventory sheet, but you may also want to photograph them. To get a clear photo of etching and serial numbers, use the side-lighting technique described for photographing maker's marks on jewelry.

Crystal: Handle crystal as you would china. Group all the glasses, cups, and so on. Large serving bowls can be photographed individually.

Tea and coffee services: Normally you can photograph these as a group. The only exception would be if you happen to have an antique service with etched scenes on each piece.

Stamps: The easiest way to keep a large collection of stamps straight is to place a small number beside each stamp or page of stamps as you photograph them. You can write the numbers on a small square of paper, or buy numbers from a stationery store. The numbers should be keyed to the inventory or catalog sheet of the collection. A small section of ruler can also be included with individual stamps of special interest to give the scale. By numbering each stamp or page, anyone can identify the stamps by referring to the inven-

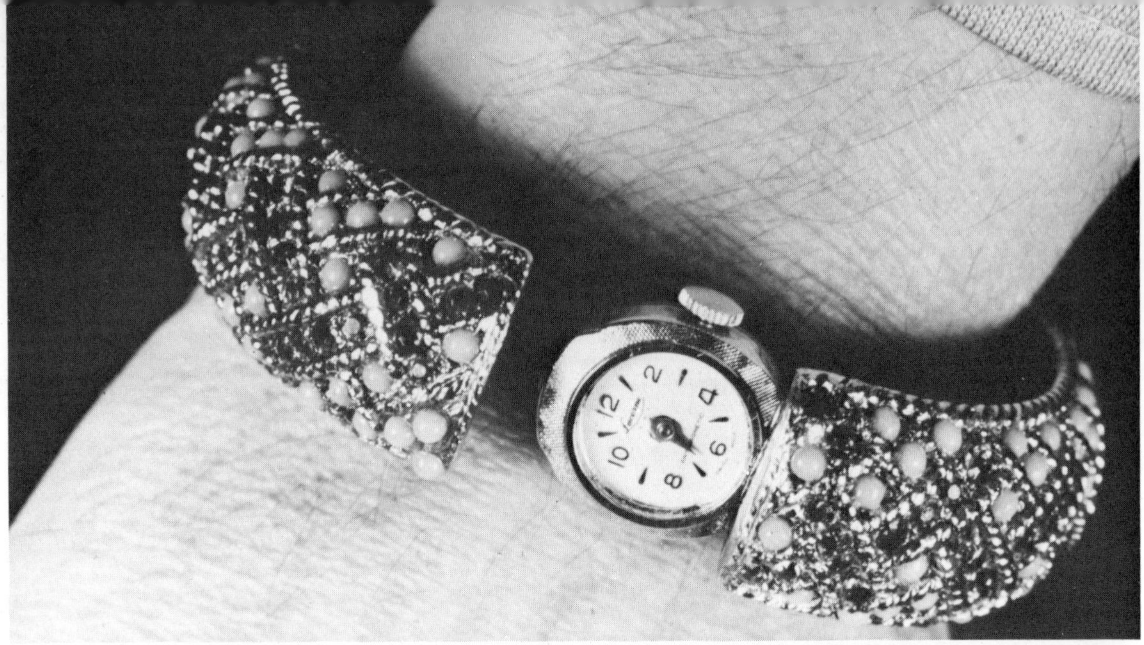

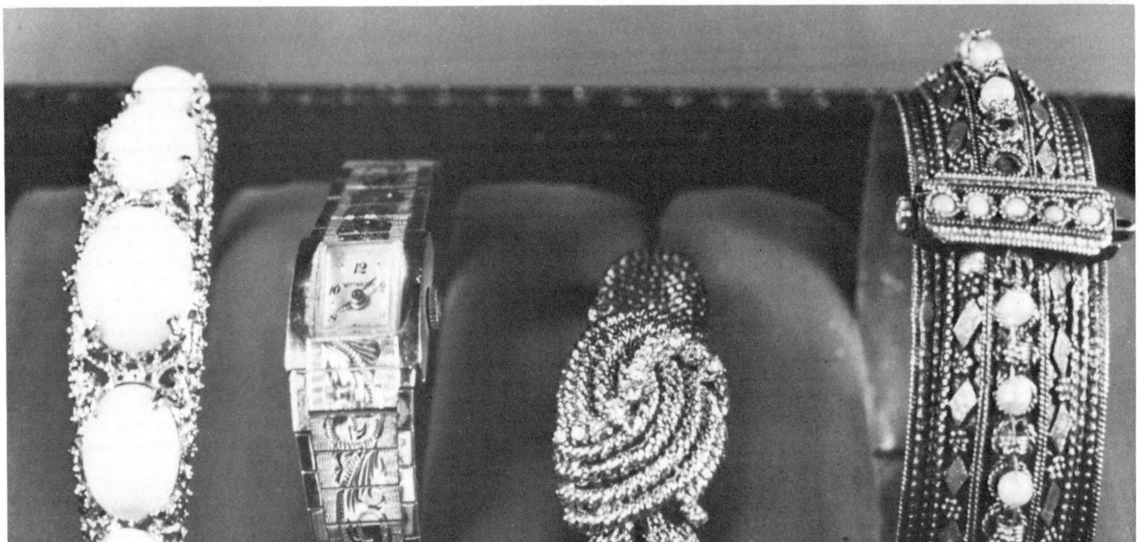

Here are three acceptable ways to photograph bracelets. An important piece can be displayed on your wrist. You can group less valuable pieces together in a bracelet box, and take a single photo that also serves to identify their usual storage place. Flexible bracelets can be laid out flat and photographed as a group or individually, depending on estimated value.

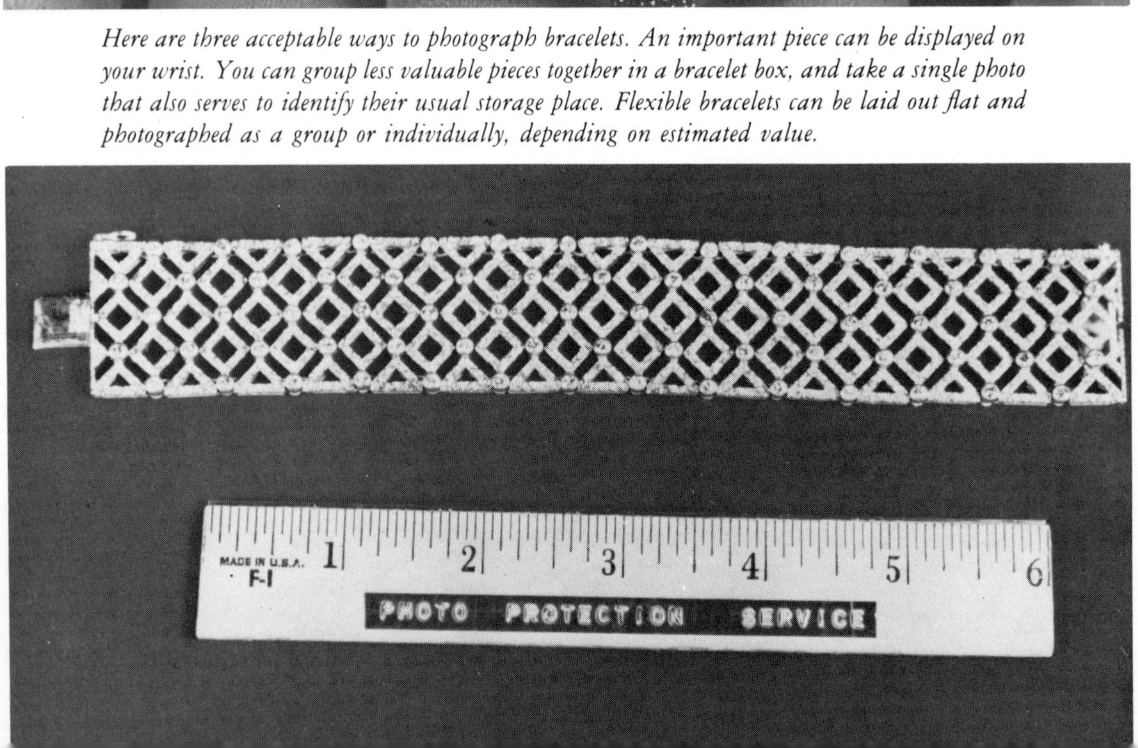

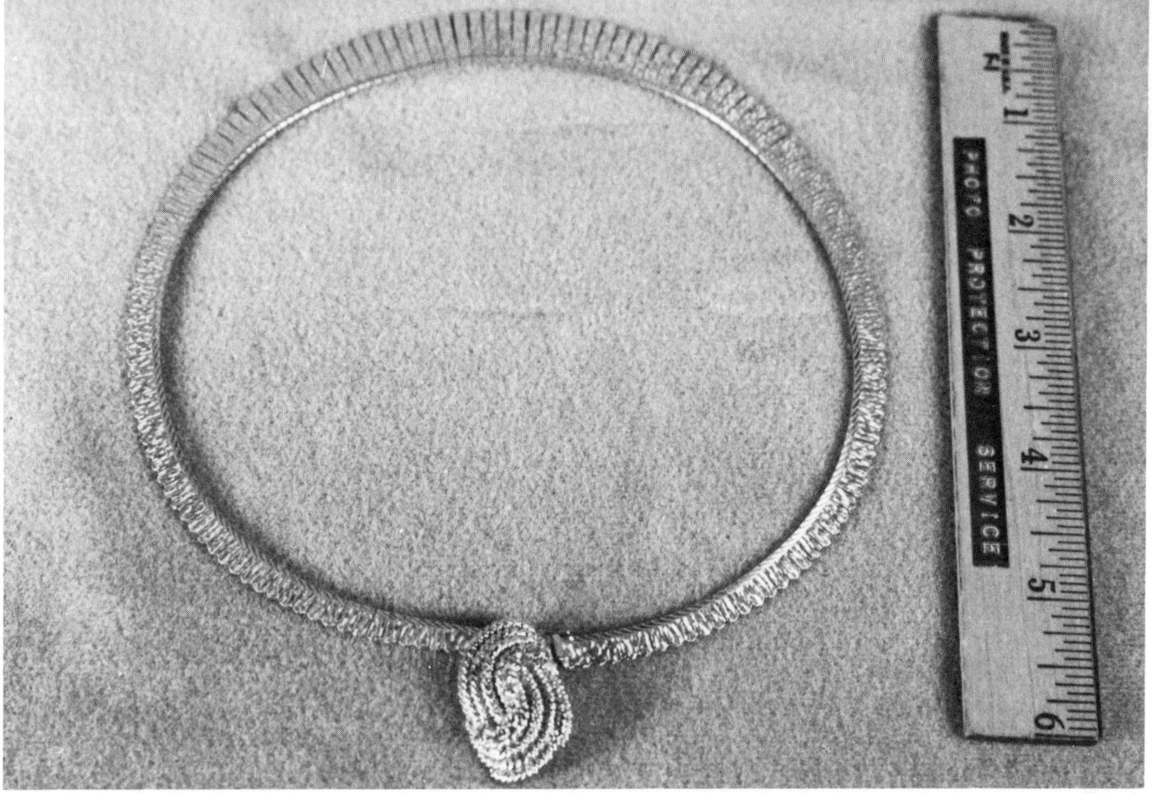

Here are two ways to handle necklaces.

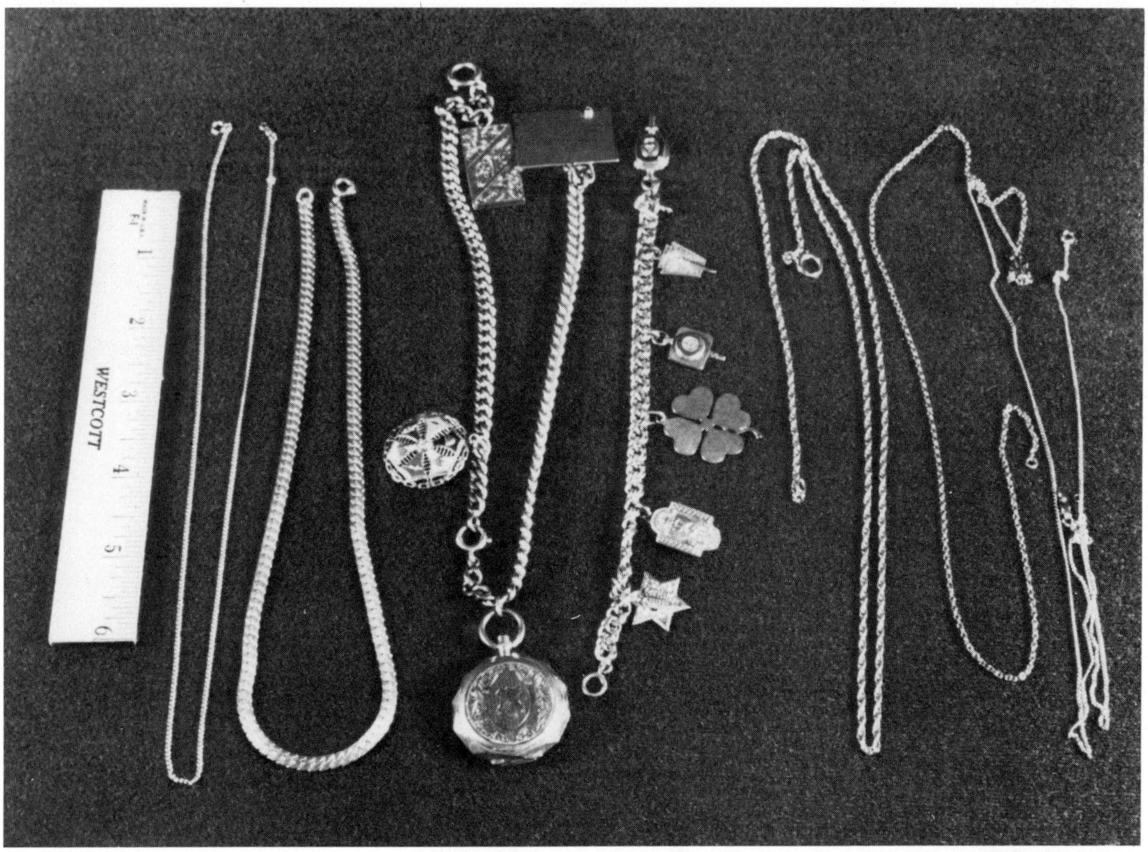

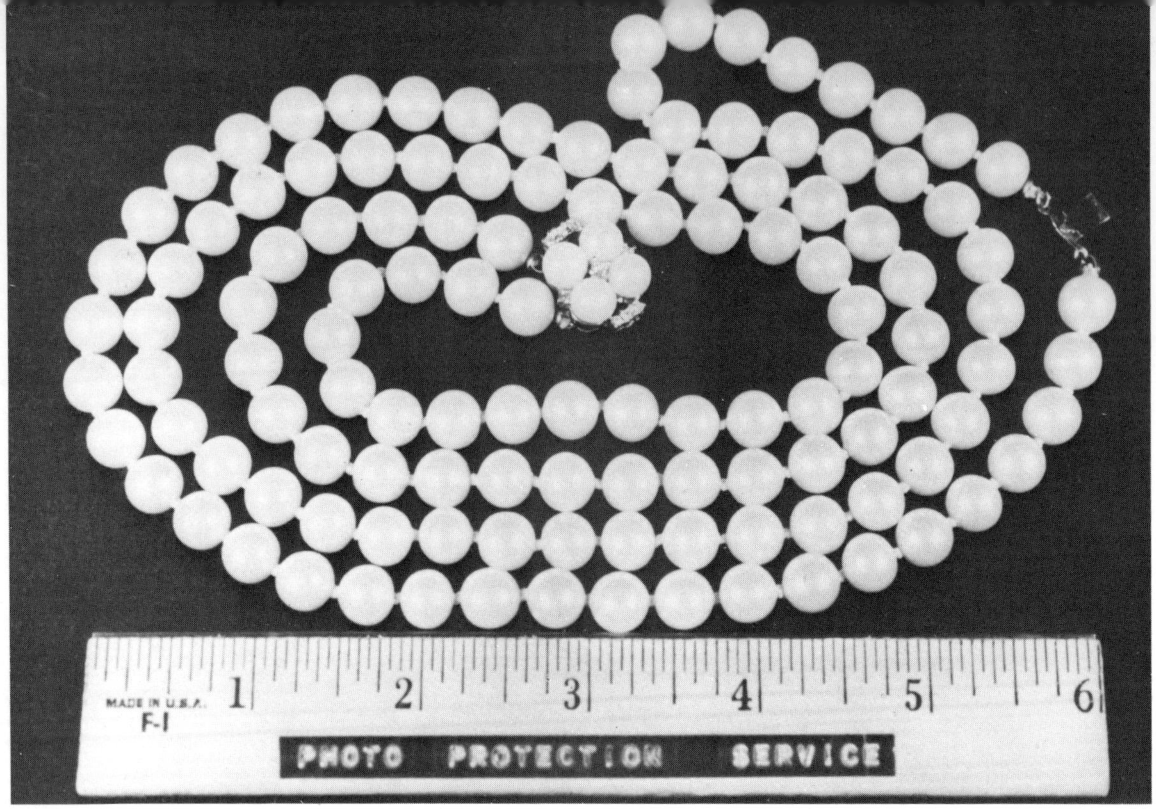

In this shot of the pearl necklace, note how the ruler has been placed to indicate the size of the pearls.

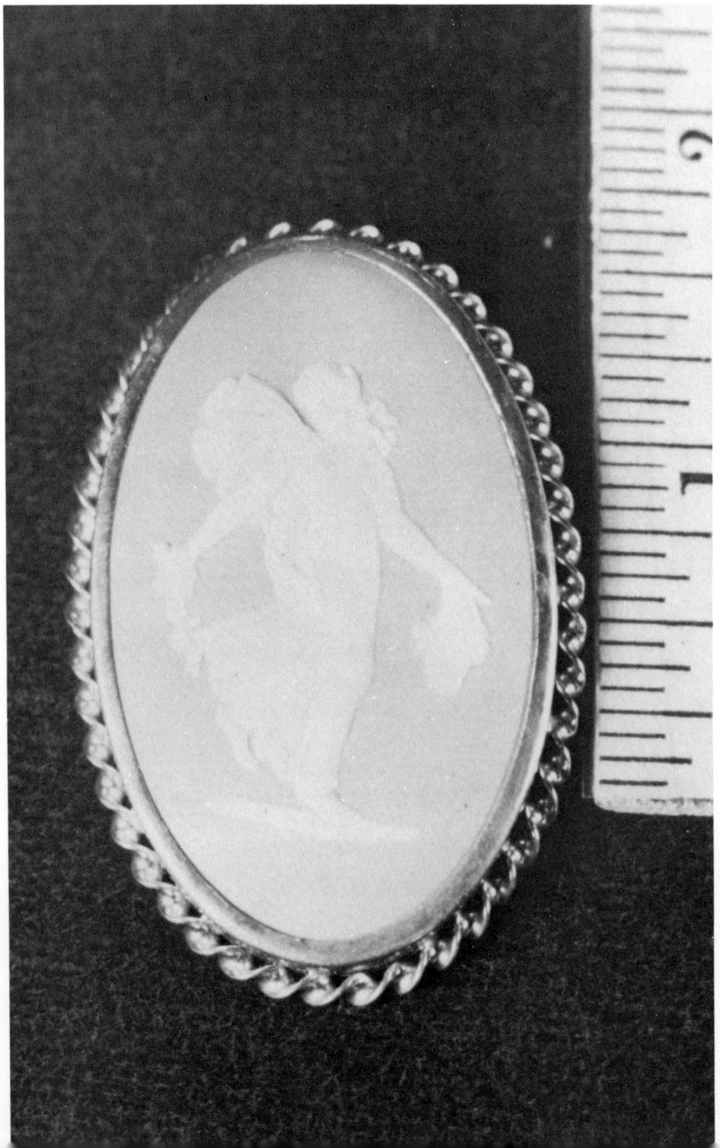

Pins can usually be documented in one group slide, but a special piece such as this Wedgwood cameo deserves individual treatment.

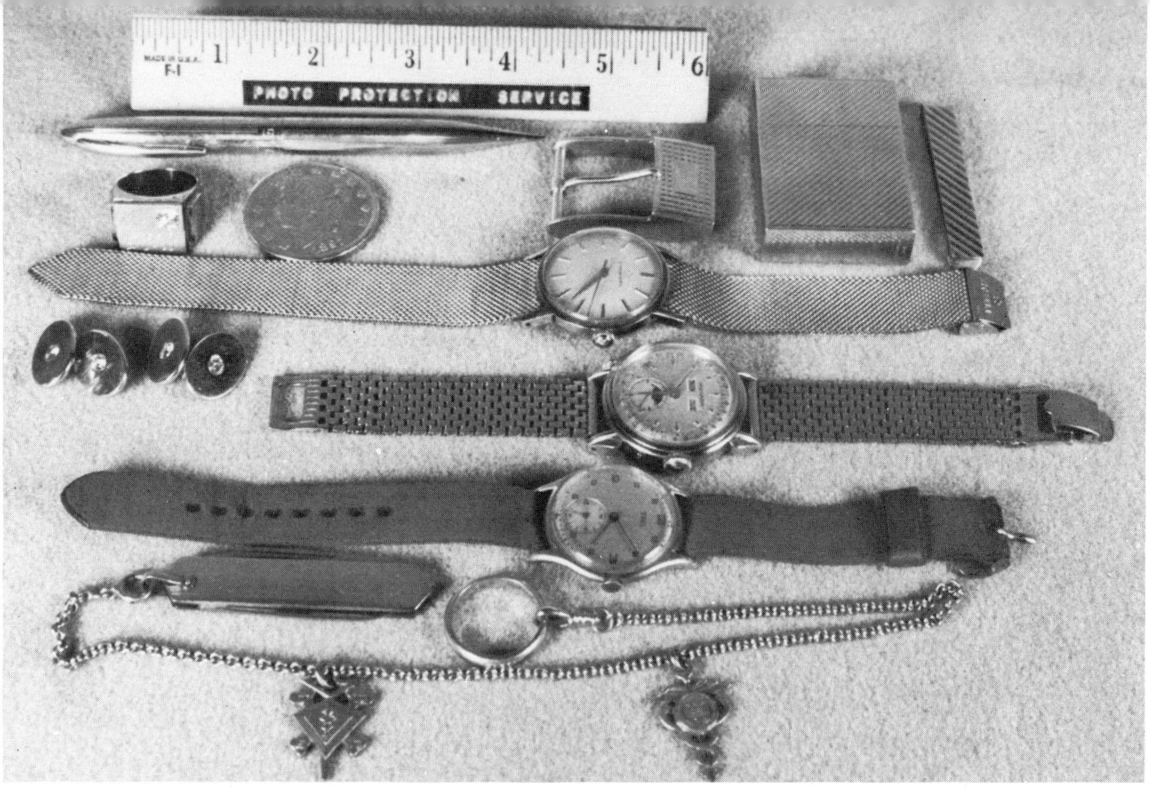

Men's jewelry can be valuable. Don't forget to take a group shot, and take close-ups of important pieces such as an heirloom pocket watch.

Crystal glasses should be grouped so that they can be counted easily.

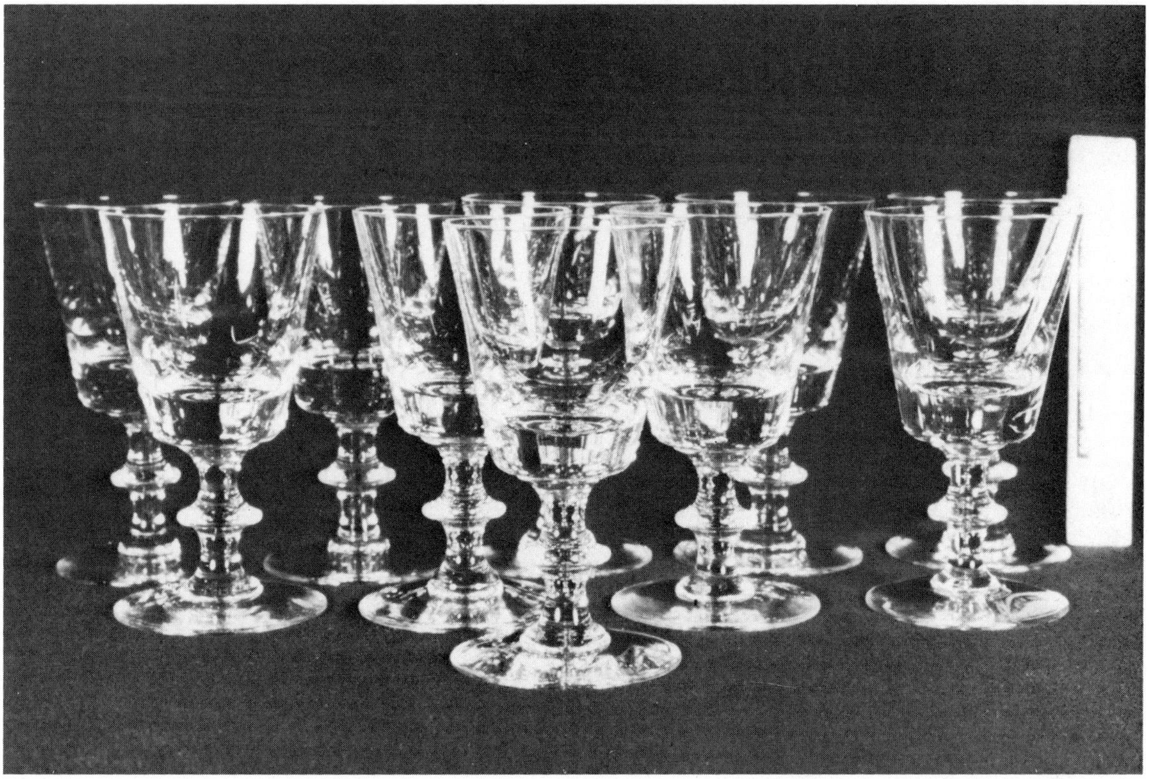

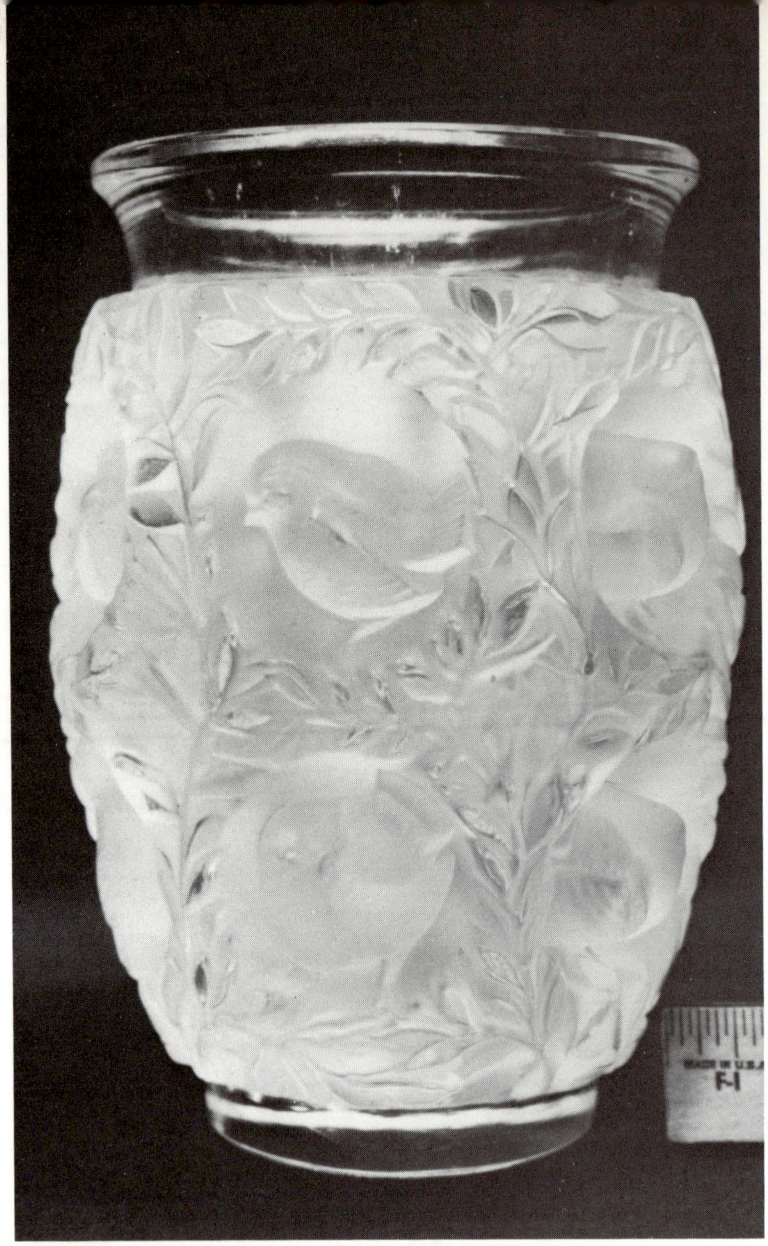

The photographer had to move the lights around, experimenting with a number of positions before one was found that would bring out the design of this Lalique vase.

One photo is usually sufficient to document a silver tea service.

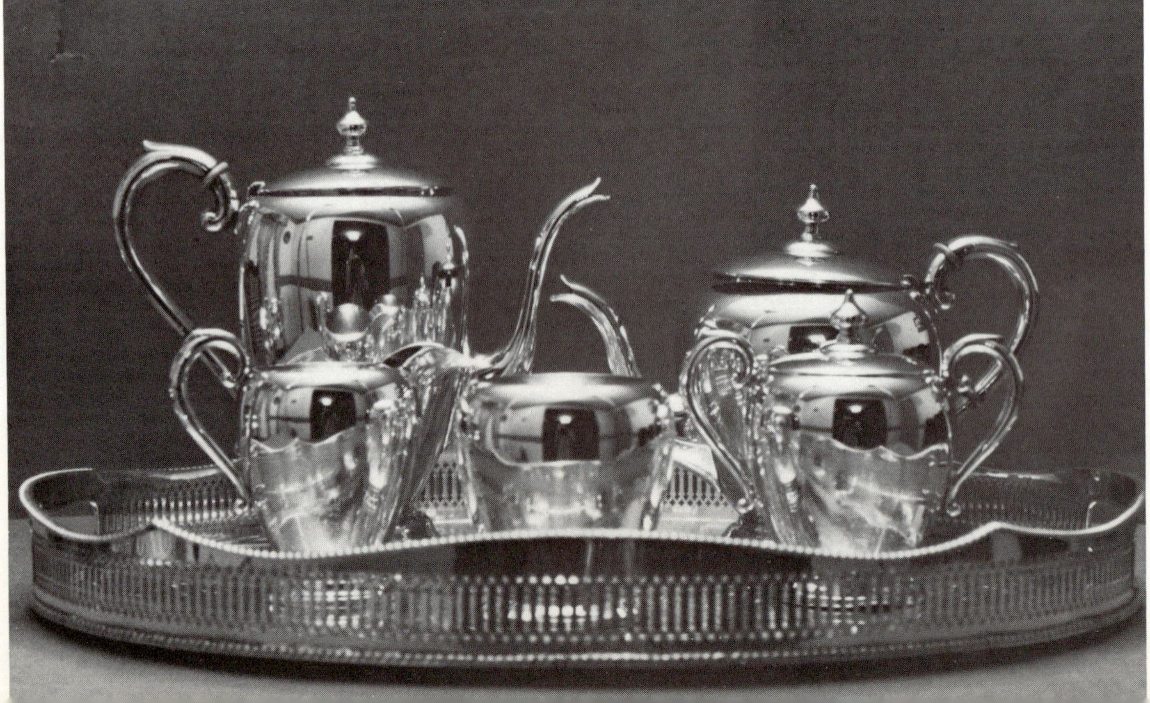

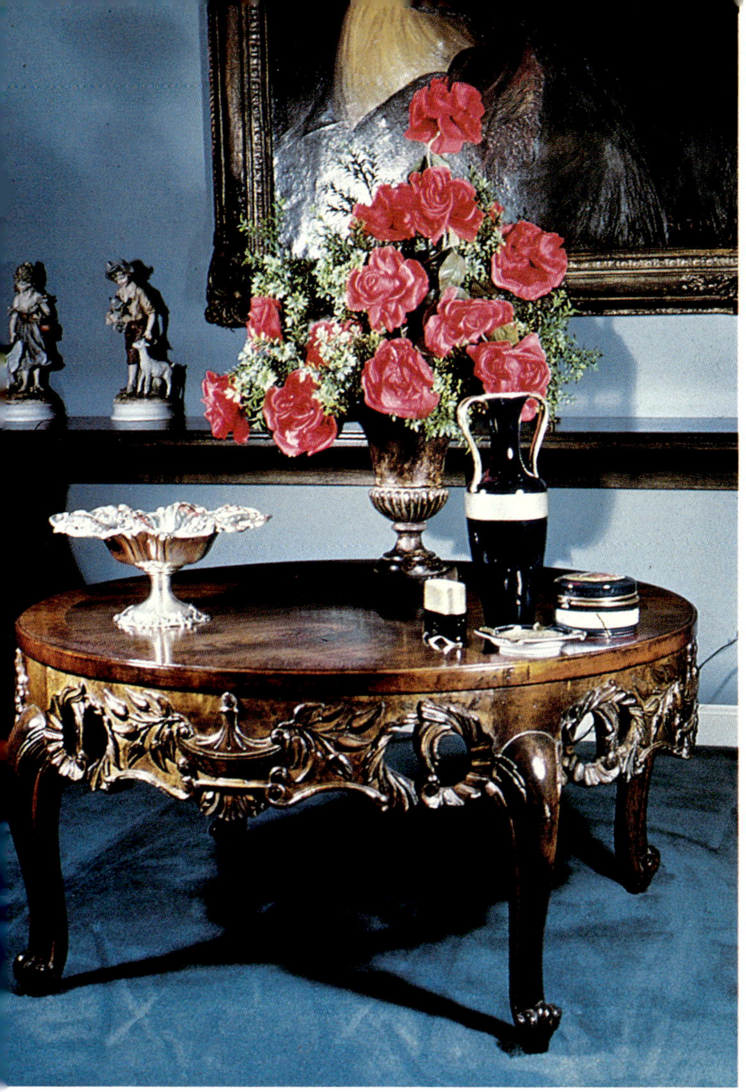

First, take an overall view of a room. Then, after photographing small groups of furniture and large objects on the wall, bring the small objects, such as the silver dish or the vases, to a table-top set-up where you can make close-up photographs.

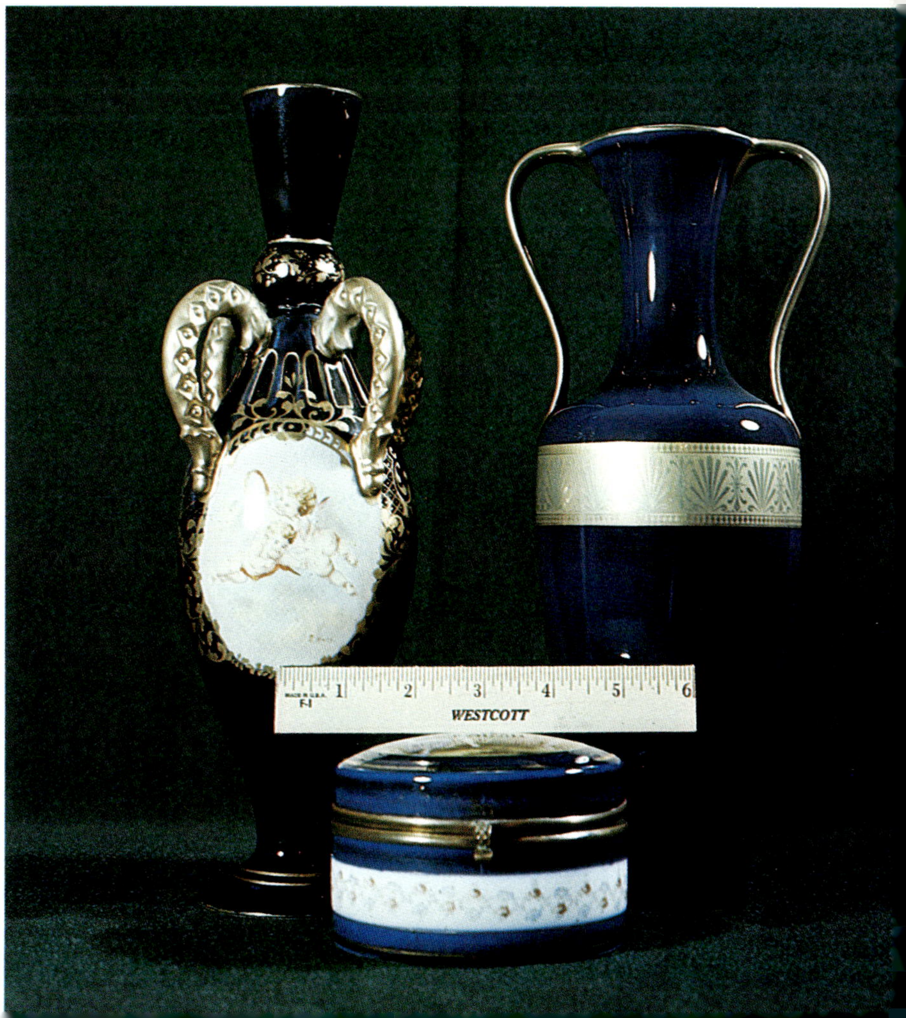

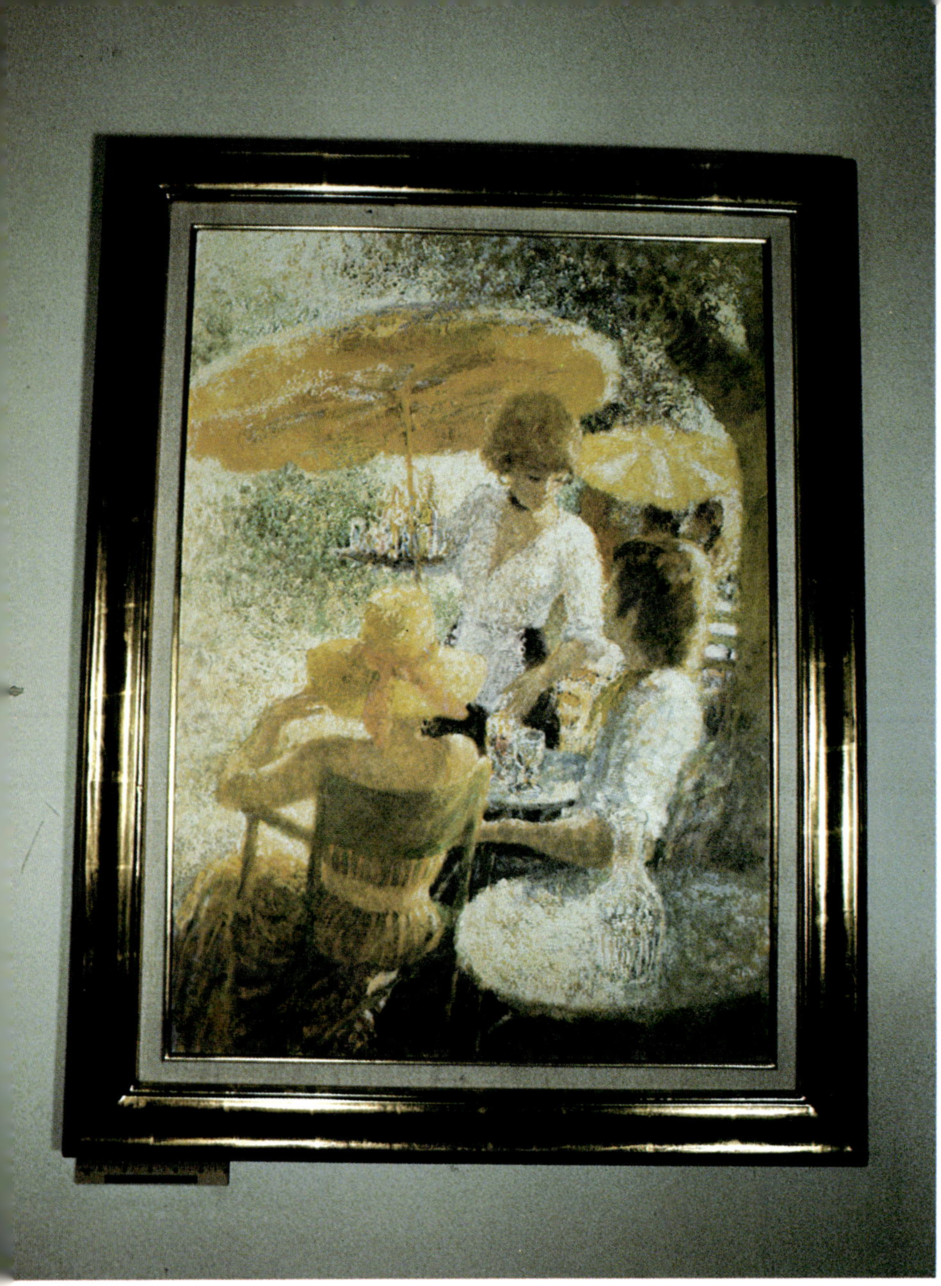

This is a close-up view of a painting for clear identification. Note the ruler taped to the wall beneath the lower right-hand corner of the picture frame.

In this case, the name of the painter was considered important, so a close-up of the signature was taken to supplement the shot of the painting alone.

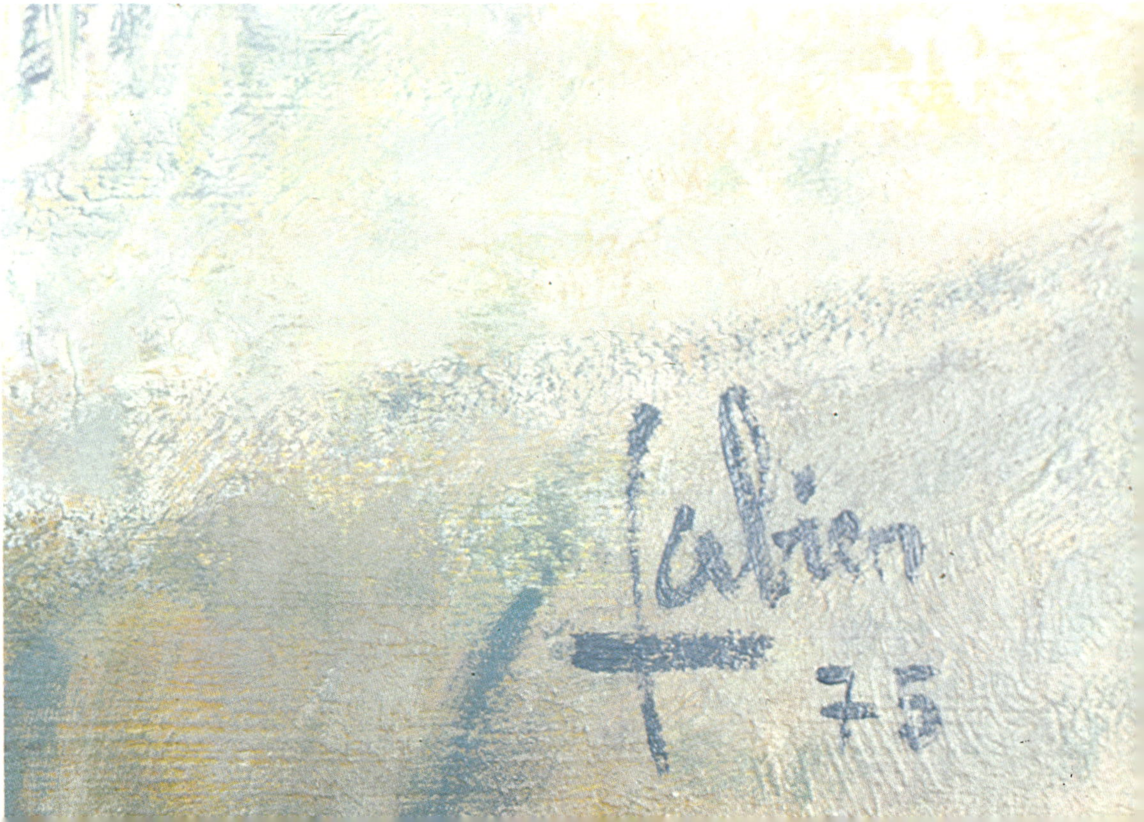

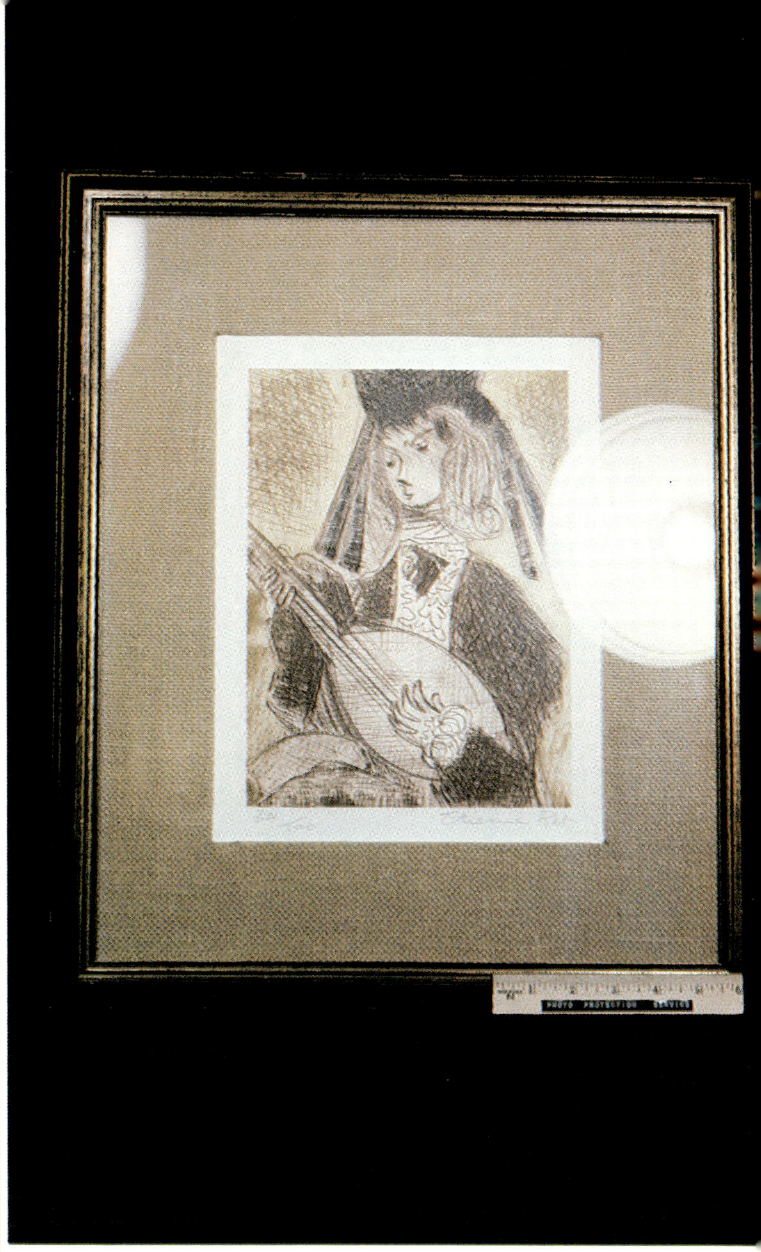

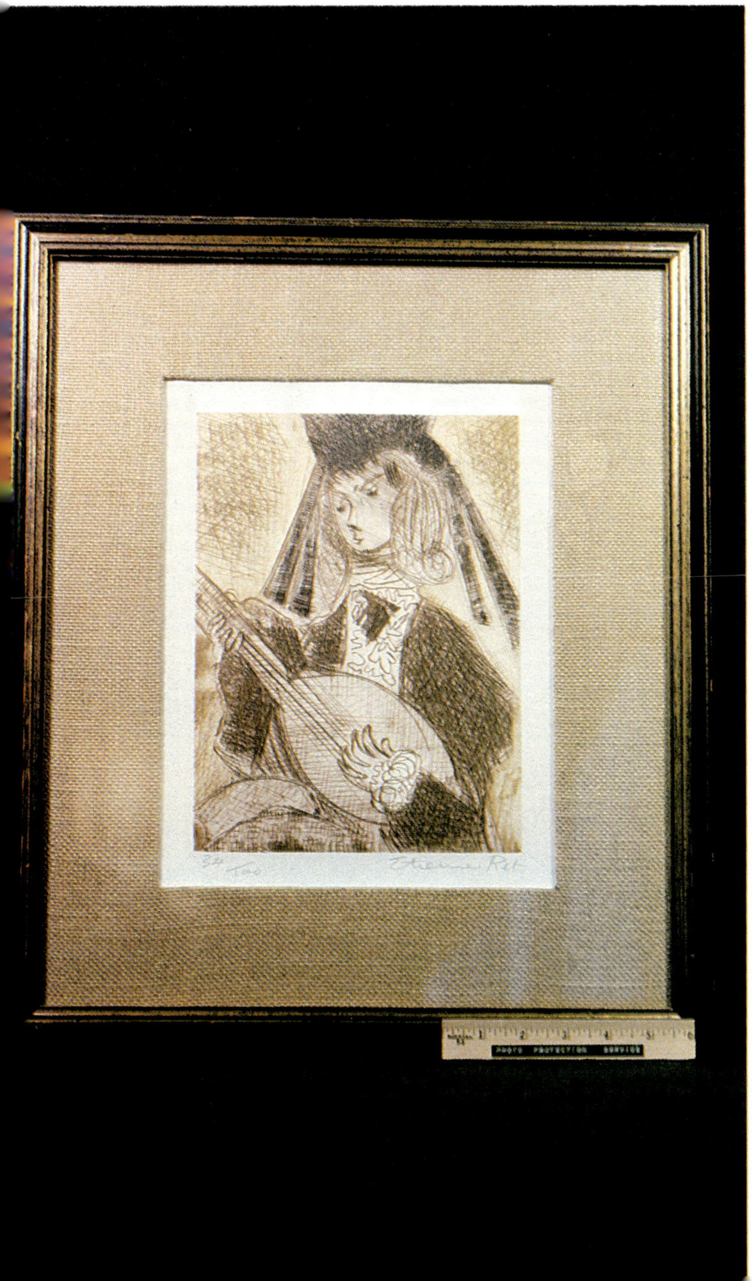

Watch out for reflections and glare from your lights when you photograph drawings and documents under glass. The situation can usually be corrected by making a minor adjustment in the position of your lights, as was done here. Note that some glare spots remain along the frame in the corrected version. This is within acceptable limits for inventory photographs.

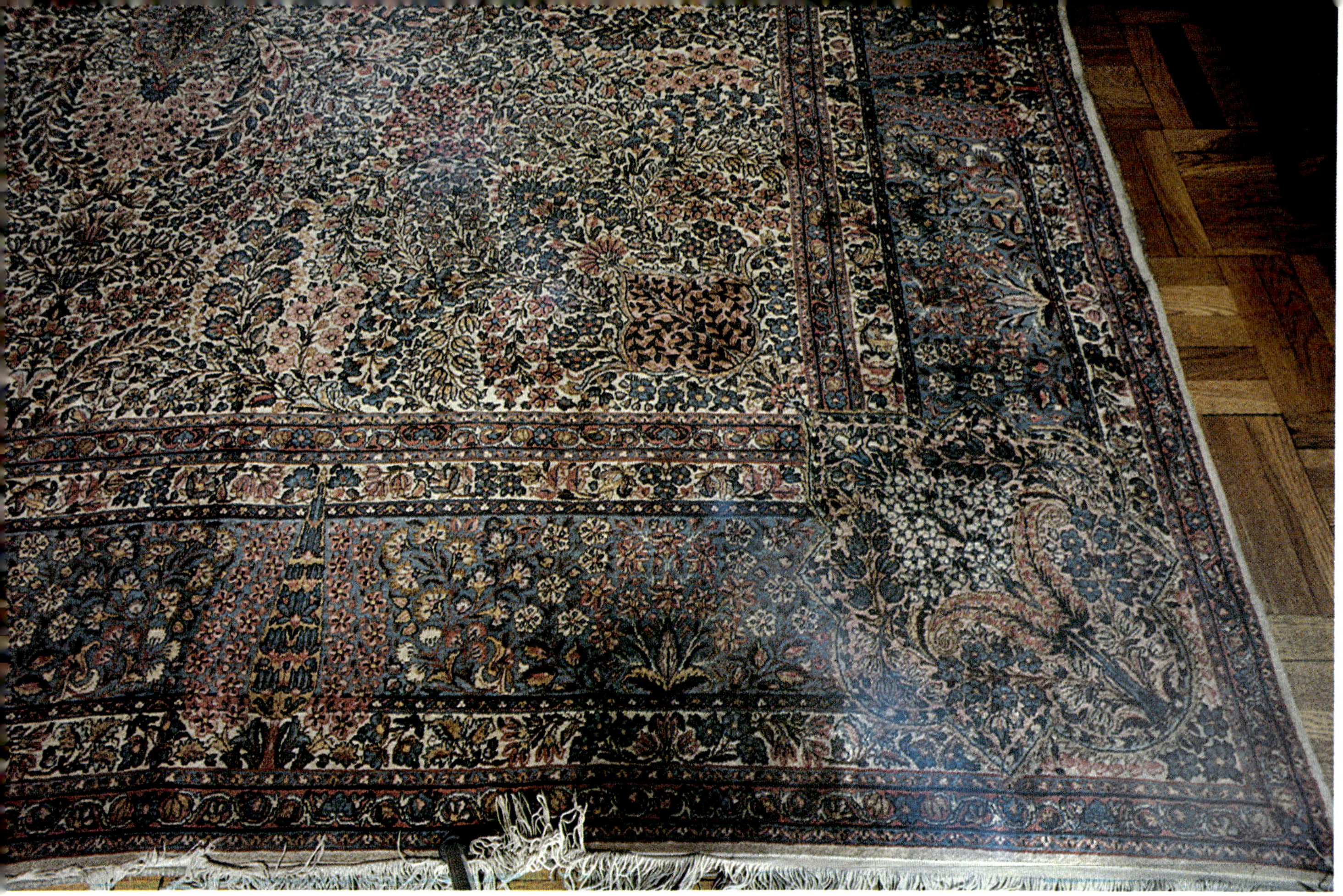

Take individual shots of large, valuable items such as this Persian rug.

A diffuser on the light and a polarizer on the lens help reduce glare and bring out the detail in this sculpture.

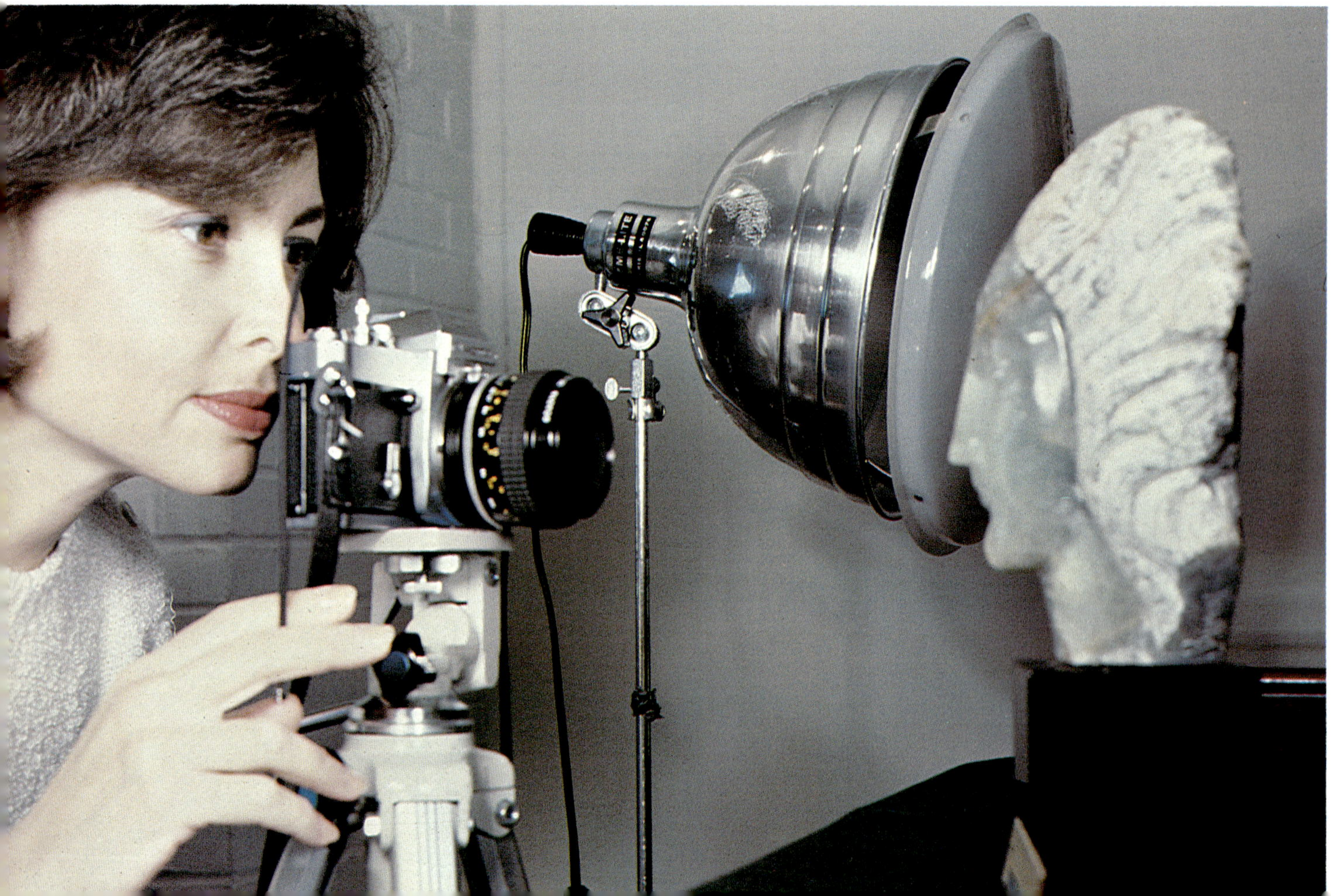

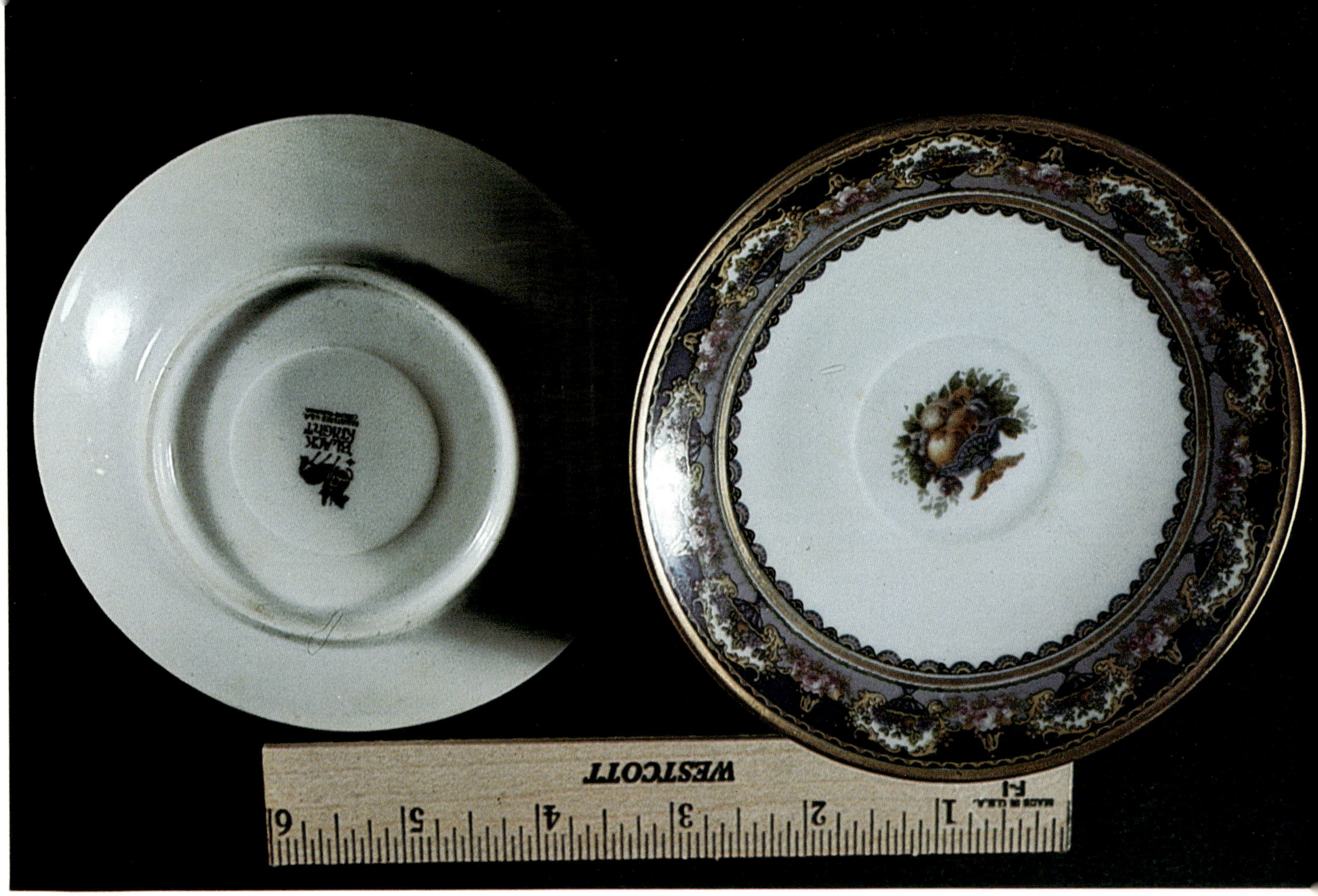

The ruler beneath these tiny three-inch plates provides a clear record of their unusual size. One plate is reversed to show the china mark.

Use a ruler to show the sizes of silver serving pieces.

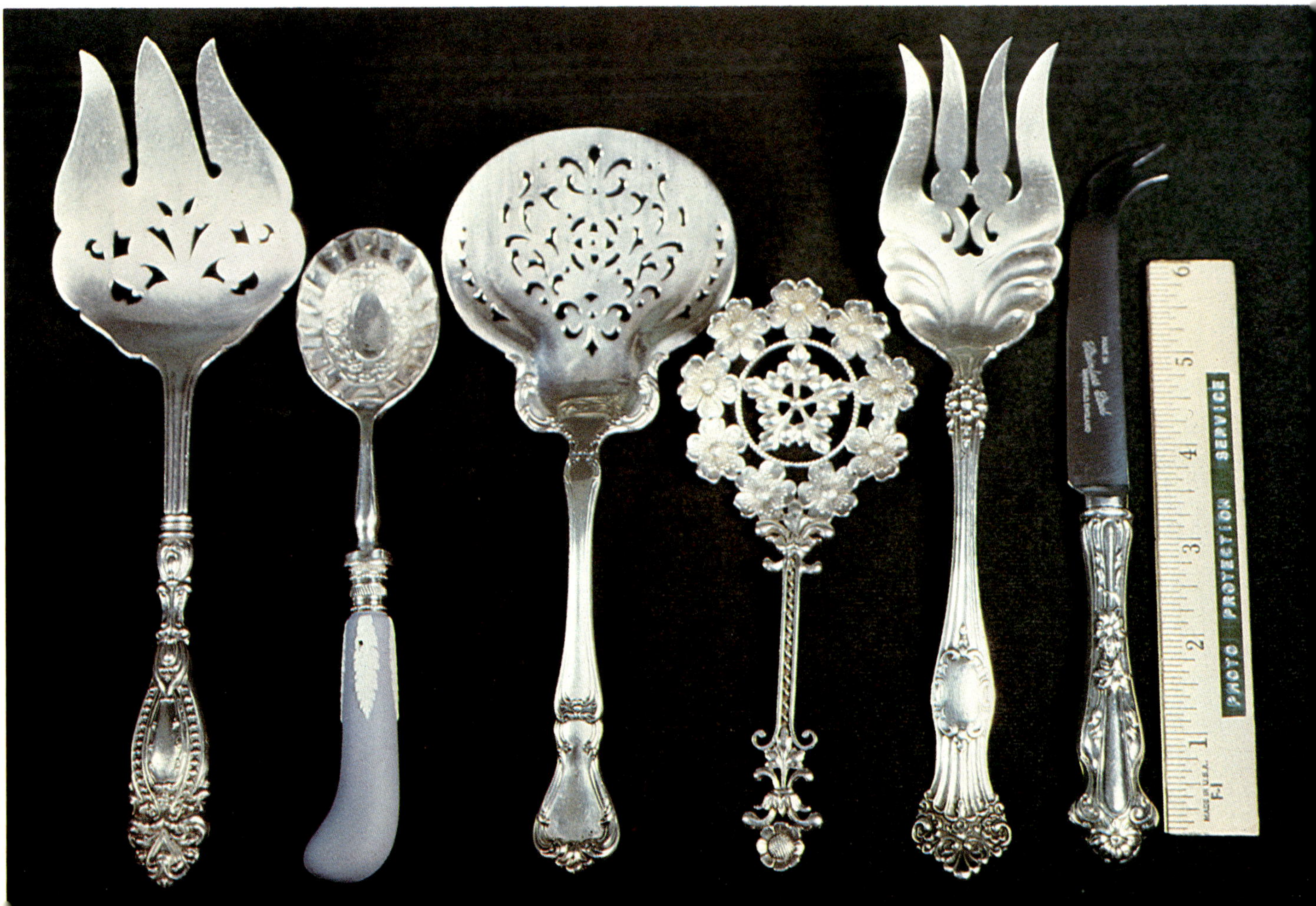

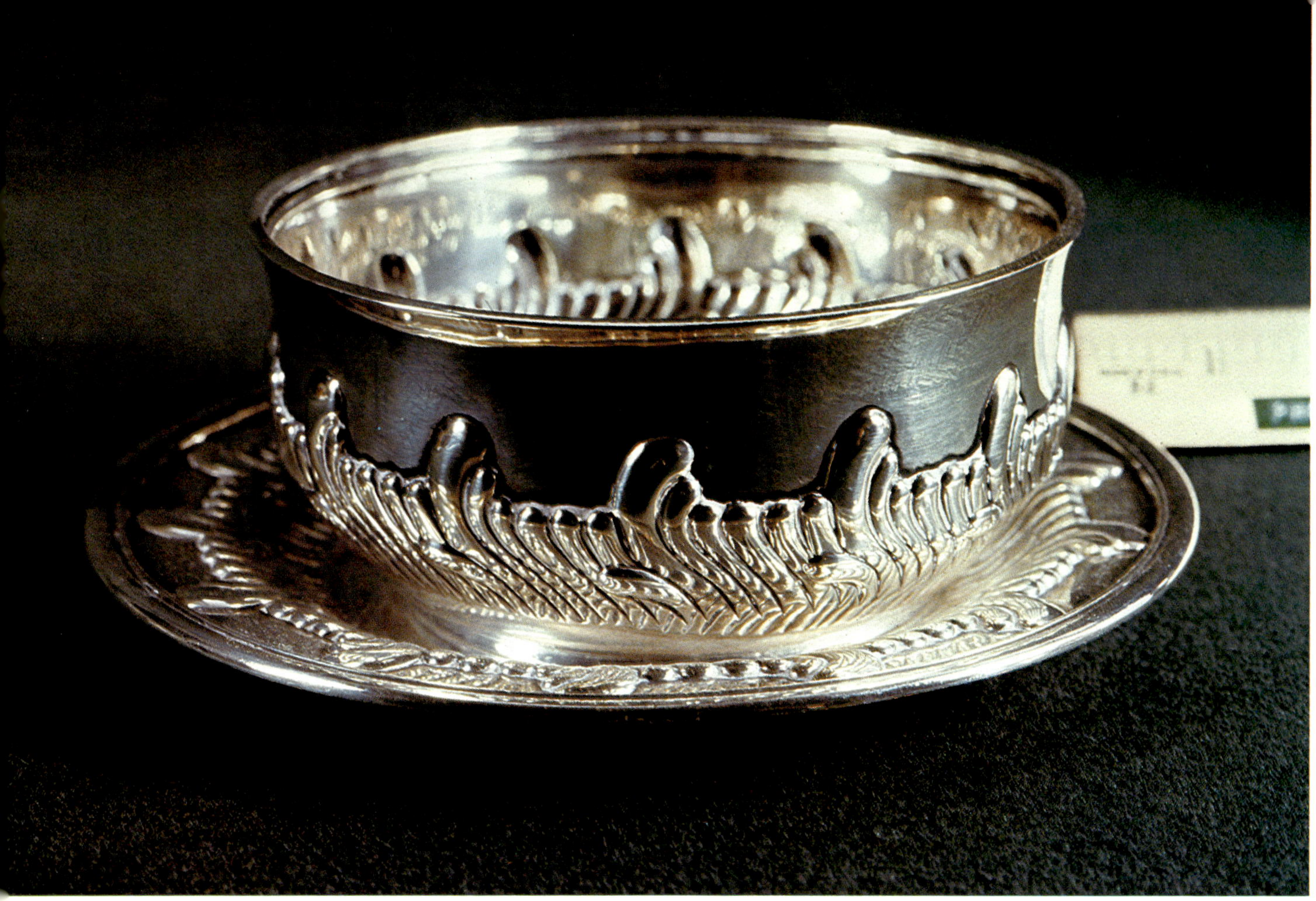

The photographer felt it was worthwhile making two slides of this silver bowl, the first from a camera position slightly above the bowl so that the outside and inside design could be seen, the second a close-up of the Tiffany mark.

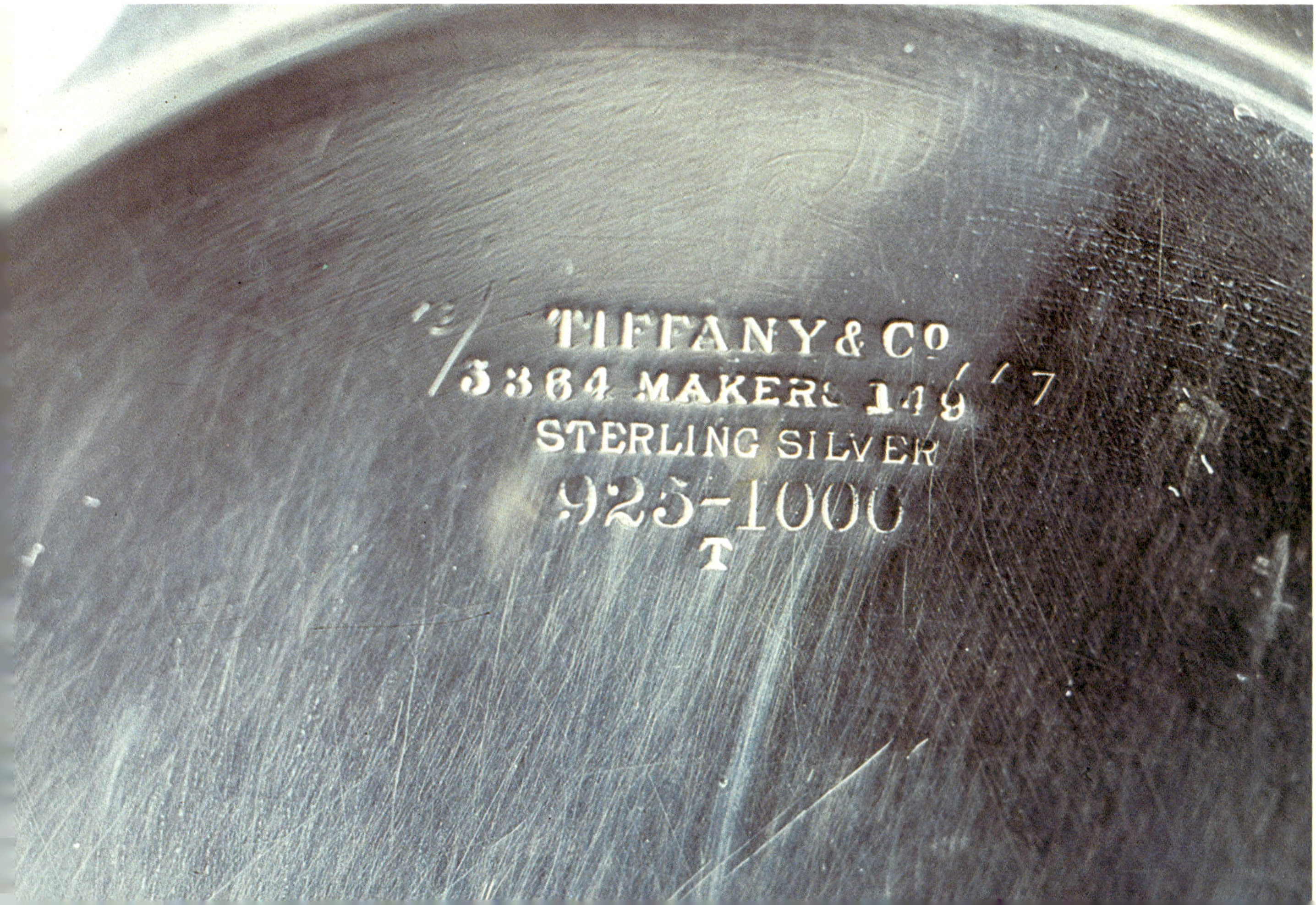

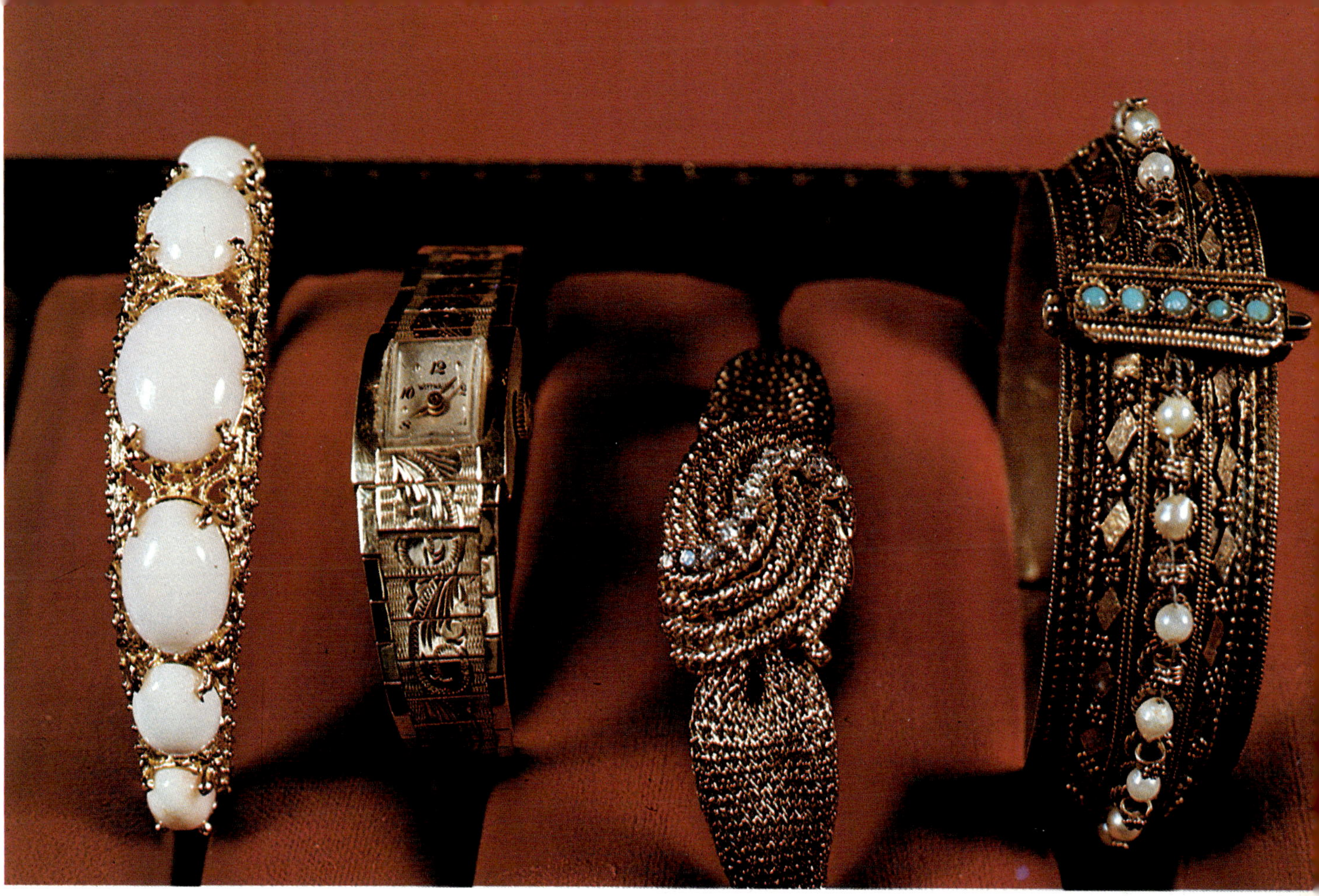

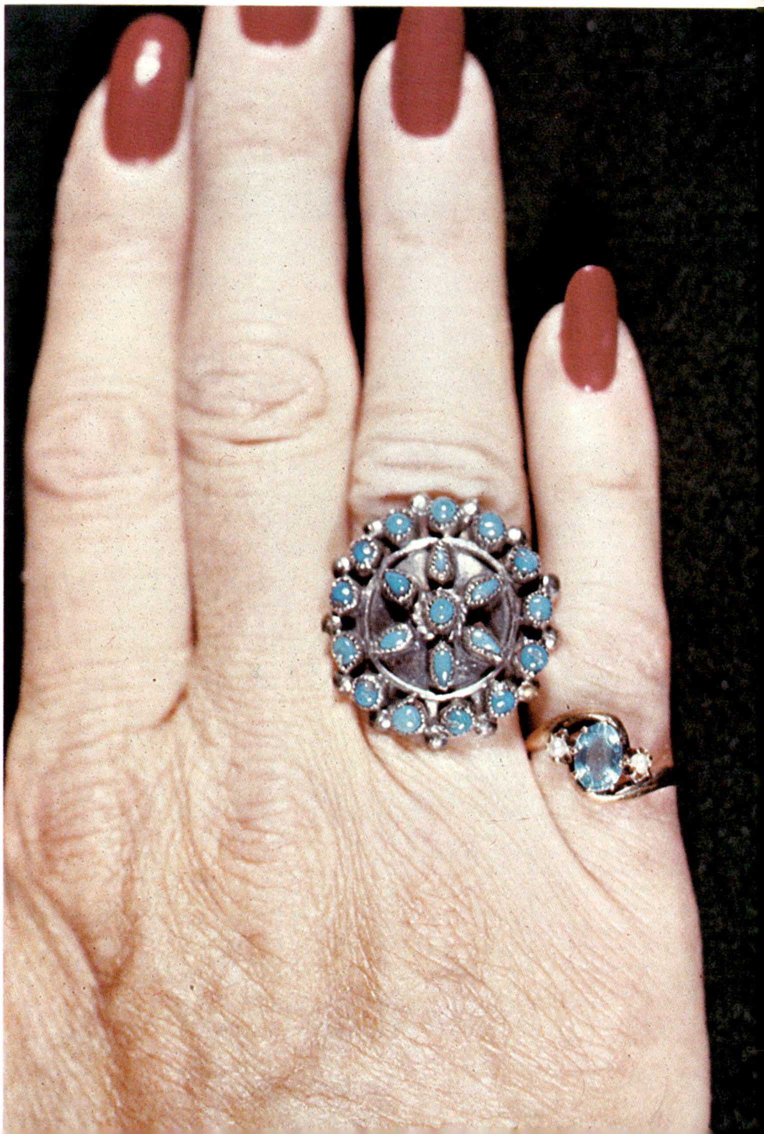

A jewelry box is an ideal holder for inventory purposes, but for valuable rings, your hand is an even better holder and has the added advantage of functioning as a scale indicator.

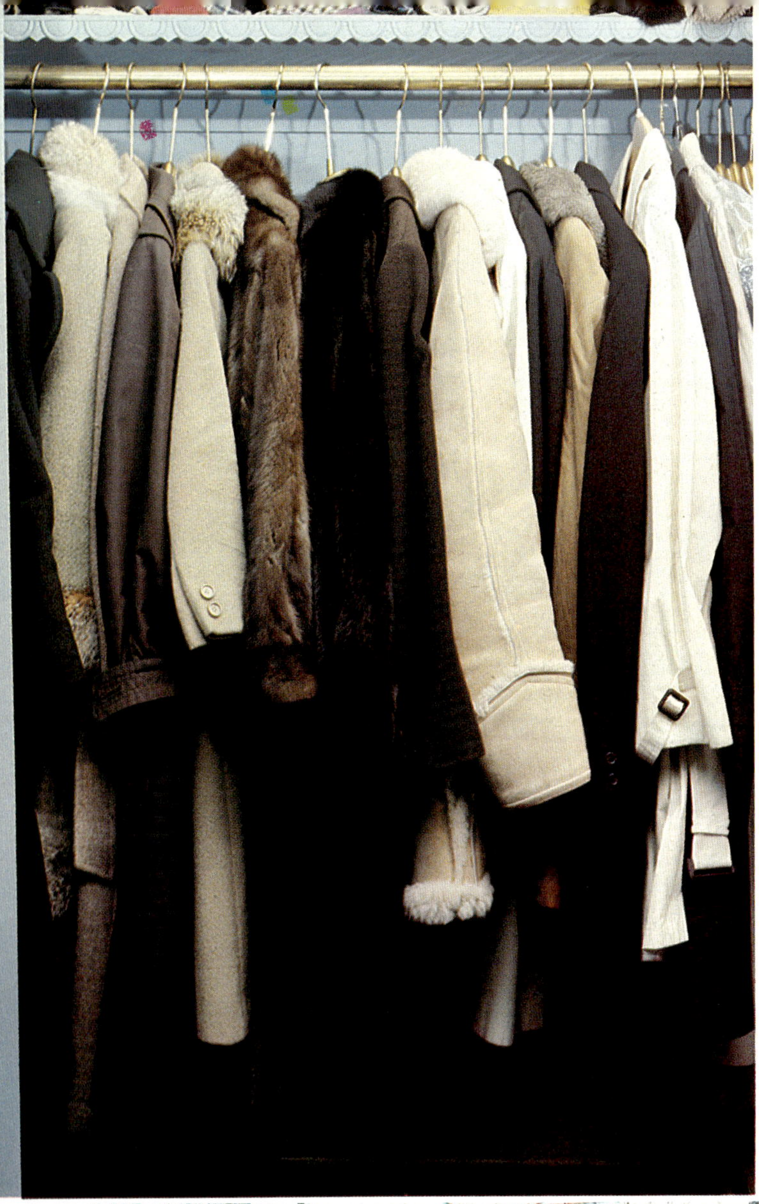

Be sure to take pictures of your closets.

Landscaping is costly to replace and should be documented. A few long shots will do the trick.

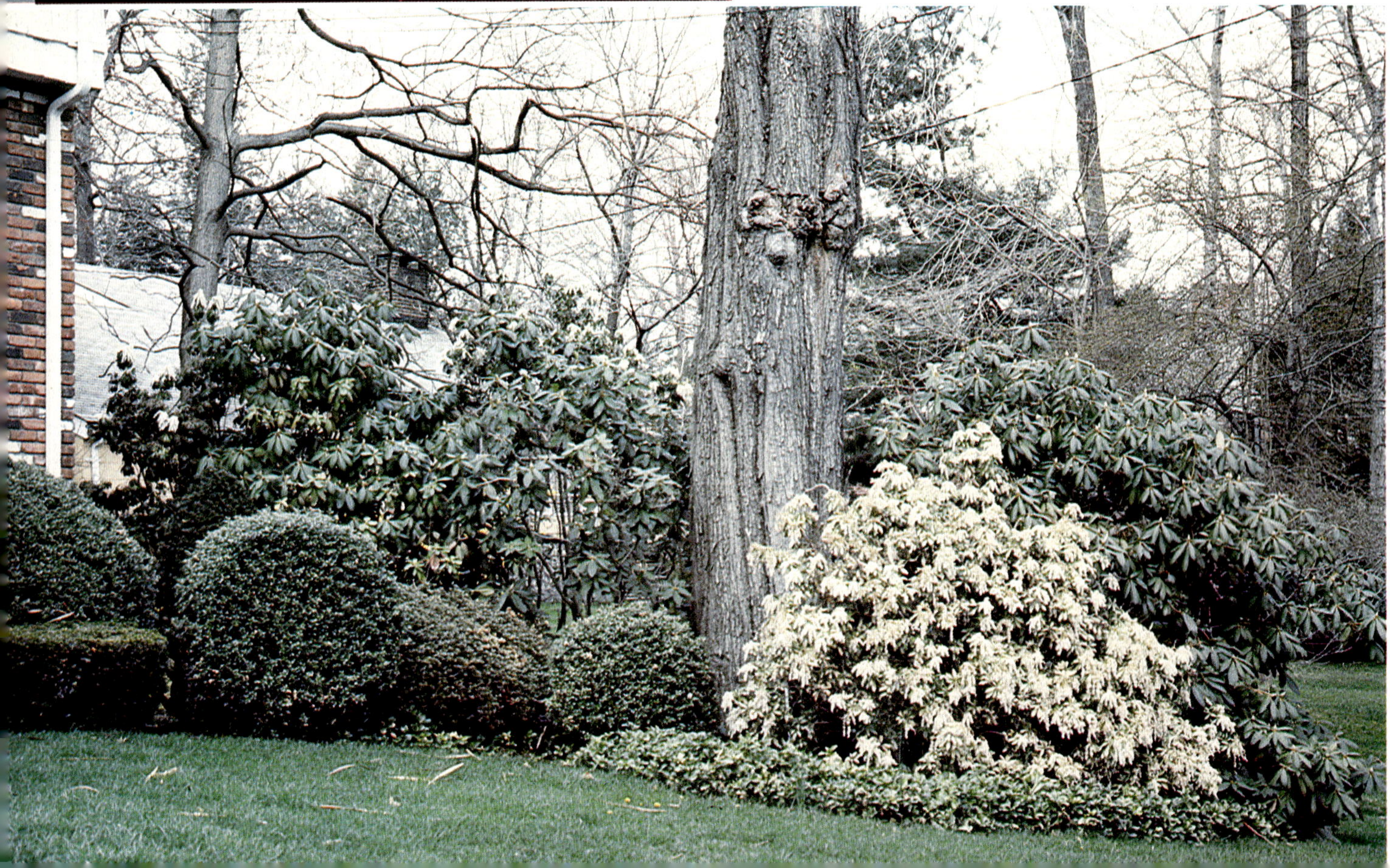

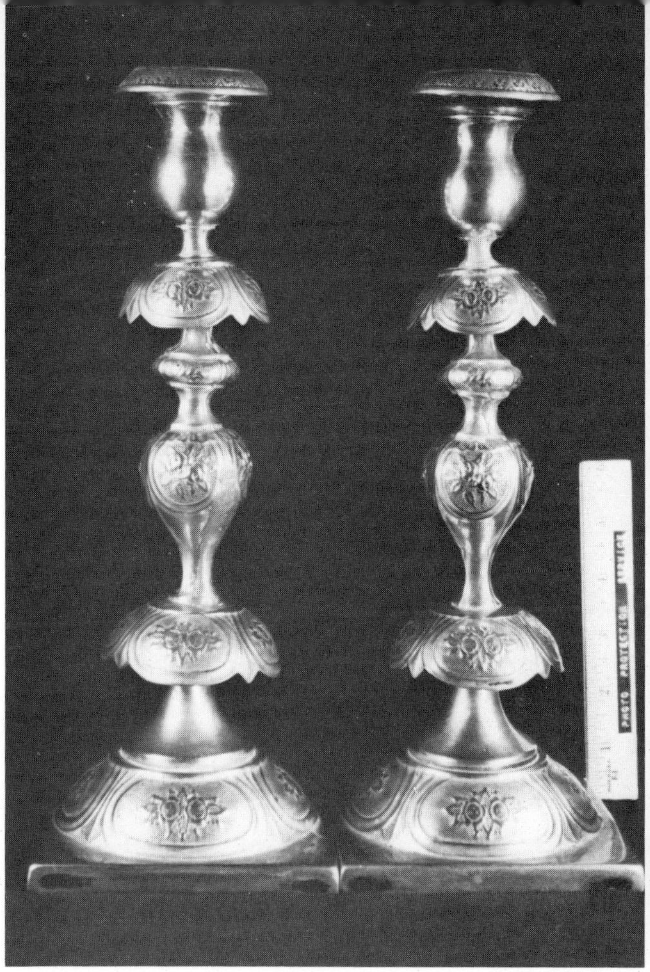

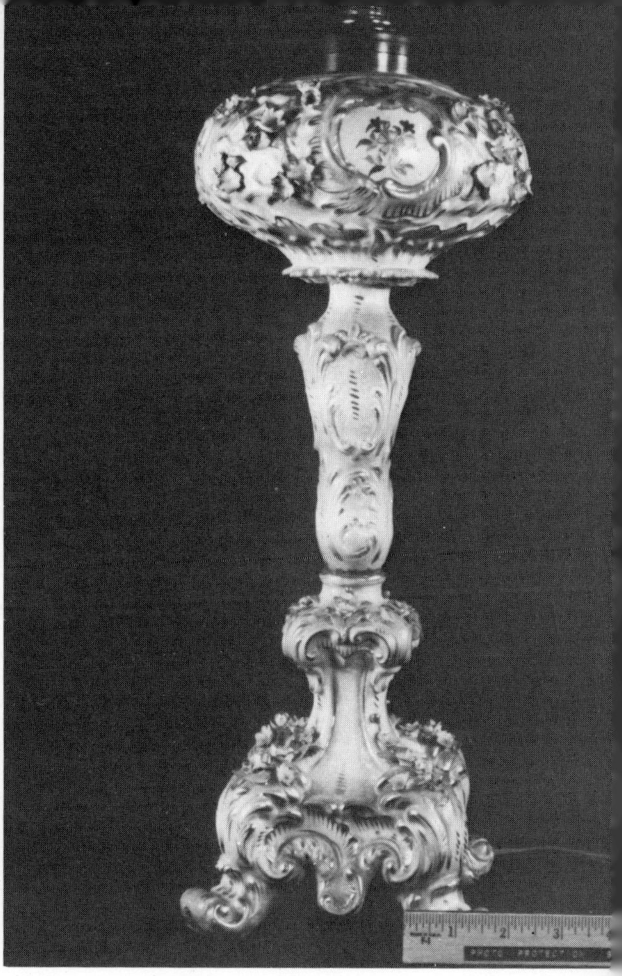

Bronze, brass and marble collectibles generally deserve individual treatment.

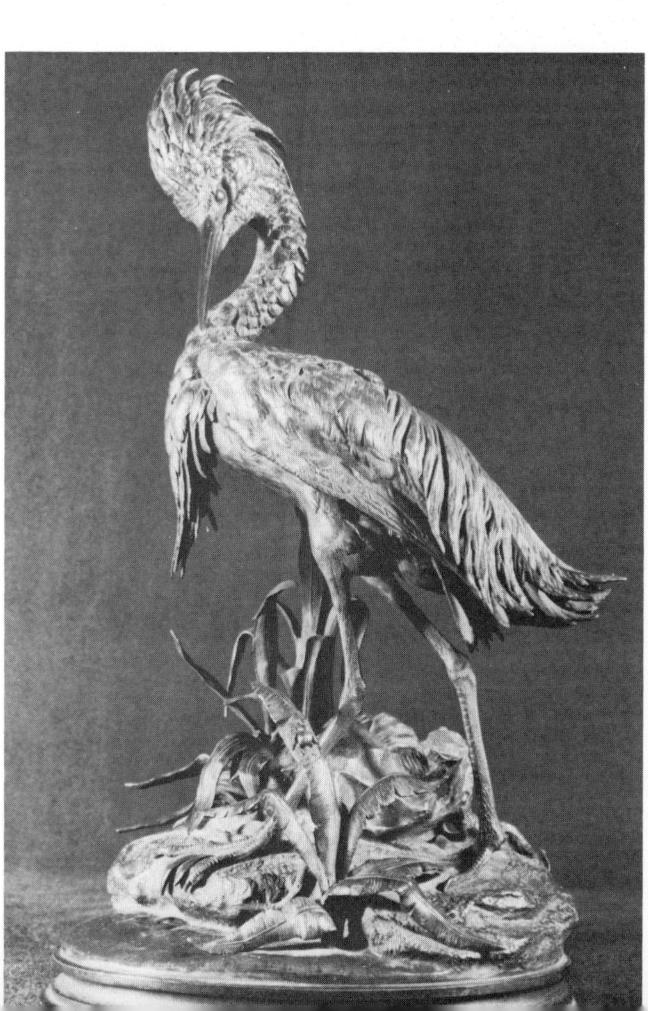

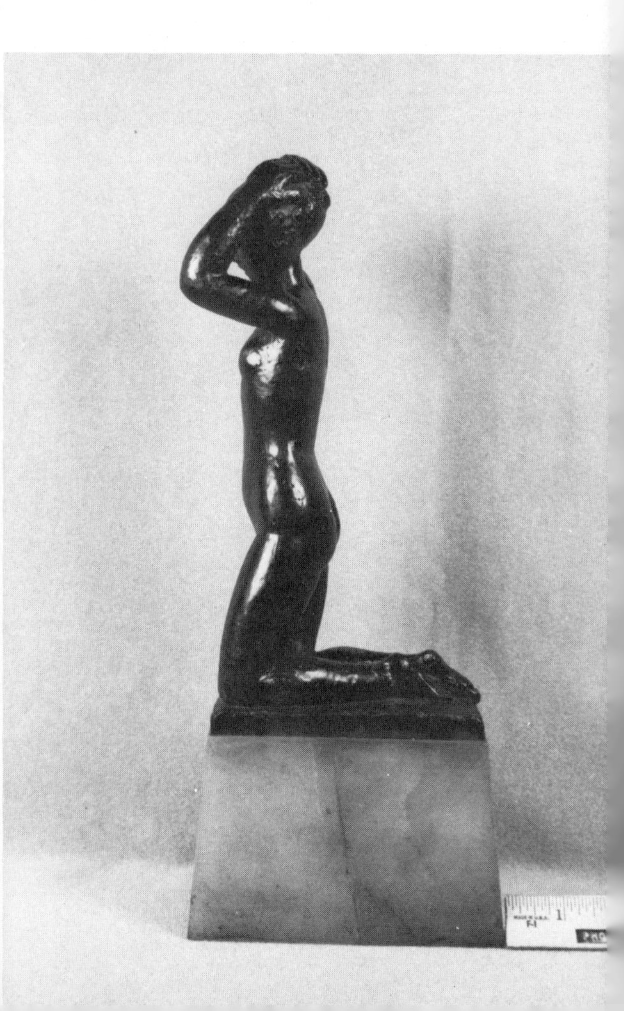

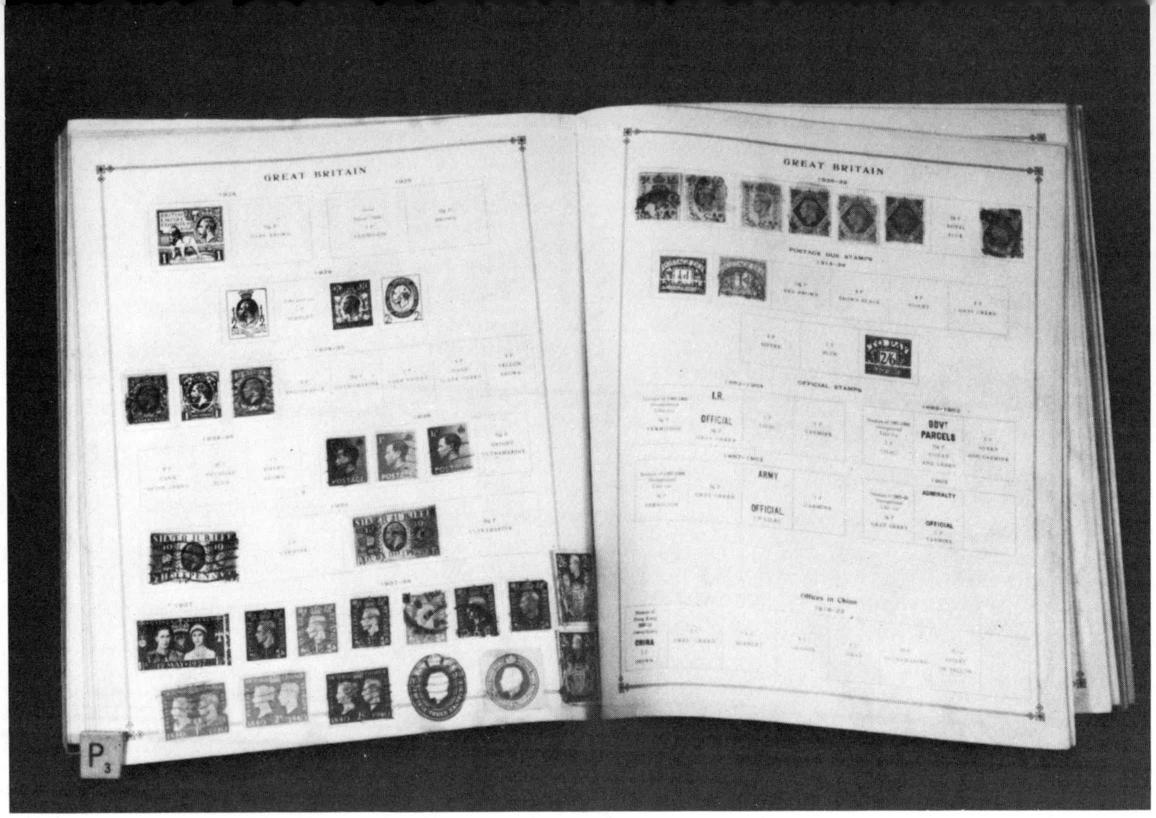

When photographing stamps, place a small number or letter next to each page or individual stamp. The photo can then be keyed to correspond to an inventory or catalog sheet. In this picture, a Scrabble® piece provides the key letter.

If coins are in plastic pouches, leave them there unless you are sure you know how to handle them correctly. This group photograph allows the enitre collection to be counted easily. The more valuable coins would be photographed individually using ultra-close-up techniques.

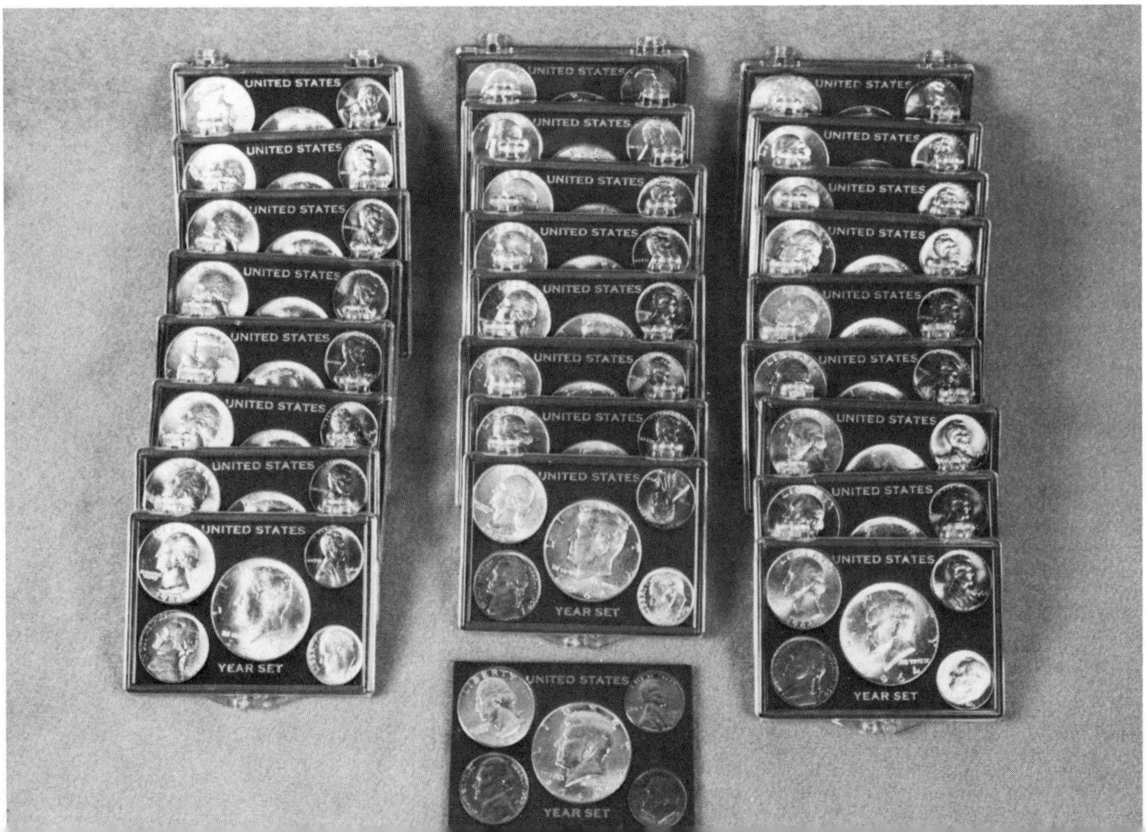

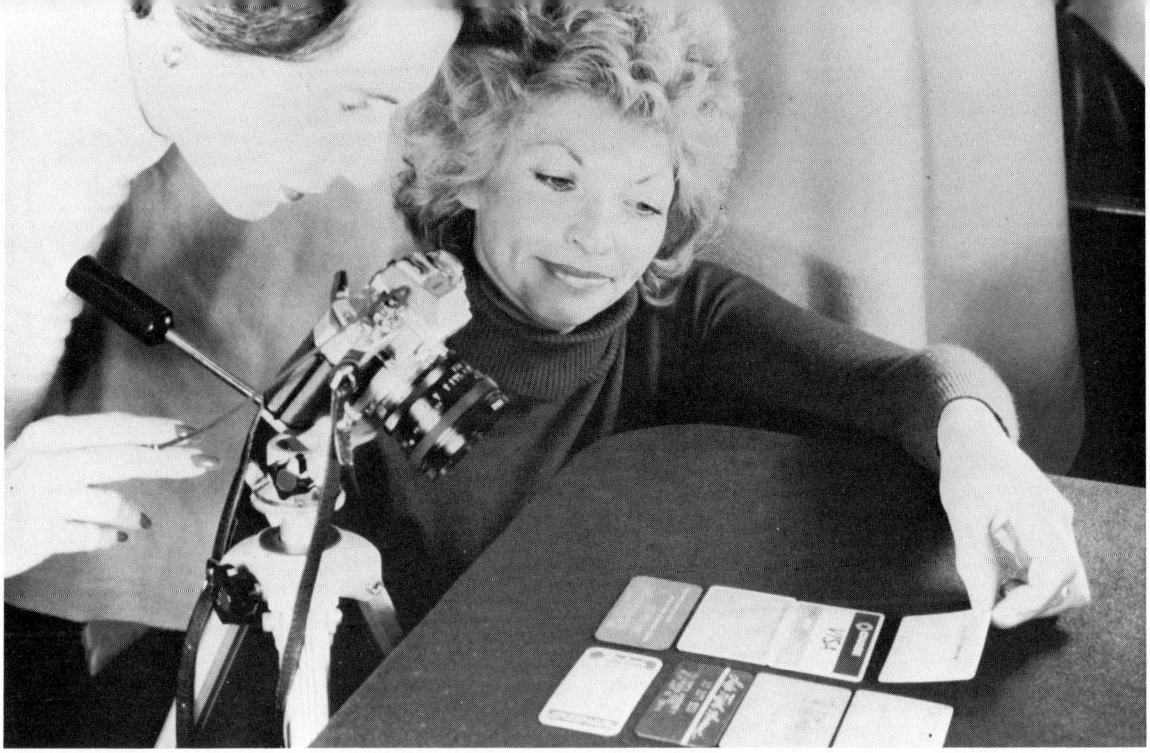

Replacing your credit cards if you don't have a record of the numbers can be a real headache. Avoid the problem by photographing your cards using the set-up shown here.

tory sheet. Without that, identification can become a tedious, difficult process.

If you are photographing stamps and are unfamiliar with handling them, remember not to put your fingers on the stamps. If the stamps are protected in plastic sleeves, leave them in the sleeves. Handle unprotected stamps only by the edges, using a pair of tweezers, or wear clean, white, lint-free gloves. If you are photographing someone else's collection, it is best to let the person actually responsible for the collection do the handling.

Coins: You should photograph both sides of a rare coin. To do this, identify each coin with a number to be included in the shot. Photograph the face of the coin (obverse), then the back (reverse), giving both the same number. That way you can pair up the two shots. Use a bit of ruler in the frame to indicate size.

Never touch the surface of a collectible coin with your fingers. Acids normally present in the fingertips can ruin the surface of a coin, and in the case of mint specimens could do incalculable damage that might result in a decline in value of hundreds, or even thousands, of dollars.

Today, many collectors keep their rare coins in see-through plastic pouches. Leave the coins in their protective pouches when you photograph them. Some collectors working with coins that are not protected by plastic wear clean, lint-free white goves whenever they handle them. You can buy these gloves in photo stores, where they are sold for film editing, and also from numismatic supply companies.

Credit cards: Group your credit cards together, laid out so that you can read the numbers, and photograph them. You now have a complete record of your cards.

PHOTOGRAPHING FLAT COPY

In standard copy work, photographers can spend a great deal of time making sure that the camera is parallel with the baseboard on which the copy rests. This meticulous alignment is not necessary for an inventory photo, the purpose of which is simply to document the existence and general characteristics of the subject. On the other hand, if the camera is not reasonably parallel with the baseboard, you will get a keystoning effect, in which rectangular pages look slightly trapezoidal, or lopsided. It pays to take a few extra seconds in aligning the camera so that things seem reasonably square when you look through the viewfinder.

Most documents lie flat and present little difficulty as subjects. But occasionally we run into items such as maps that have been rolled up. To photograph these, you have to unroll them and weight the edges. Pennies work well as weights. Don't use push pins. If a document is valuable enough to inventory, then you do not want to go sticking holes in it.

Documents and small paintings under glass can sometimes be tricky. Watch out for glare spots and reflections that obliterate the subject. By playing with the adjustment of your lights, you should be able to eliminate most of the problems. If necessary, you can shade the subject from the direct glare of lights by using a couple of sheets of tracing paper as a diffuser. But remember that a few glare spots in unimportant areas of your subject—such as along the edges or margins—will not affect the value of an inventory photo. You need be concerned only when glare obliterates important details, and these situations can usually be handled by making minor adjustments to the lights.

Once you have your camera set up for copy work, there is no need to make constant adjustments in the camera-to-subject distance, because there is no need to always fill the frame with your subject. As long as the documents fill at least one-third the area of your viewfinder, the photo will contain plenty of detail.

If you have a large number of documents to photograph, try grouping them by size category. Three categories—large, medium, and small—will do it for most collections. That way you need move the camera only three times. Once the camera is set up and you have found the right focus and exposure, you can run through a pile of similar-sized documents in minutes.

Close-Up Techniques

This section deals with some of the technical problems that are unique to close-up photography and contains tips that make it easier to work with some of the specialized equipment involved.

THE BASICS

As a general rule, you should work at the smallest possible apertures—*f*/11 or *f*/16—with your camera mounted on a tripod. If you have an SLR with through-the-lens metering and use 250-watt ECA bulbs or No. 1 photofloods, then close-ups and ultra-close-ups will simply be an extension of normal photography. The biggest difference is that for fine focus it is easier to move the camera toward or away from the subject, or move the subject itself back and forth, to get it sharply imaged. Using the focusing ring on the lens mount is generally a waste of time. Another point to remember is that if your eye is away from the finder eyepiece and you have an automatic camera, light coming in through the eyepiece can cause the camera to underexpose slightly. Some cameras have a built-in eyepiece blind that you can snap into place for these situations, but if your camera does not come with this bit of exotica, don't worry about it. Just lay a small square of cardboard over the eyepiece before you make your shot or keep your hand close to the eyepiece so that it shadows the finder. Since exposures are normally long in ultra-close-up work, use a cable release or the camera's built-in self-timer to trip the shutter and don't touch the camera while the exposure is being made: your body has vibrations that will transmit themselves to the camera and cause blur.

HOW TO USE AUXILIARY CLOSE-UP LENSES

An auxiliary close-up lens attaches to the filter mount of your regular camera lens and changes it into a close-up lens. You should attach it with the convex side out, so that it faces your subject. If you have the screw-on or bayonet type, there is only one way that you can put it on, so you don't have to think about it. If you are using series size close-up lens, you have to pay attention, because the series size is simply a metal-bound disk of glass that you drop into a retaining ring, which in turn screws into an adapter ring that goes on the lens. The series size lens has a small arrow engraved on the rim. You should position the lens so that the small arrow points away from the camera and toward your subject.

When you use a close-up lens with an SLR camera, focus as you normally would, by looking into the finder and moving the camera toward or away from your subject until you get it in sharp focus. You can fine-focus, and get a slightly larger or smaller image, by turning the focusing ring on the lens. You will find that the close-up lens restricts your focusing range to close-ups only, so you don't have much leeway.

If you are using a rangefinder camera, or a camera that depends on scale-focusing, or a fixed-focusing camera, then you will have to measure the distance between the close-up lens and your subject in order to get sharp focus. Since the right lens-to-subject distance changes, depending on the distance to which you have your lens set, you have to pay attention to the numbers involved. The chart on page 58 gives the correct lens-to-subject distances for close-up lenses from +1 through +10 at various footage settings. In addition, the chart gives you the area in inches seen by the lens, which will help you in positioning your subject.

The complexity of the chart, and the fact that you can't see what the lens sees with rangefinder and other non-SLR cameras, makes it obvious why an SLR is the first choice for close-up work. These other cameras are limited-function tools that do certain jobs, such as photographing people or scenery, admirably well. But things get uncomfortably complex when you try to use them to do work for which they were not designed. On the other hand, with an SLR, which lets you focus and compose while looking through the lens, close-up work is a snap.

Auxiliary close-up lenses require no exposure compensation, so you can expose as you would for a normal scene.

EXTENSION TUBES

In theory, extension tubes, which fit between the lens and the camera, should give

CLOSE-UP LENSES WITH STILL CAMERAS

Close-up Lens (diopters)	Footage Setting on Camera	Inches from Subject to Close-Up Lens	Area Seen by Lens (inches)*: 45mm Lens 24×36mm Negative	50mm Lens 24×36mm Negative	50mm Lens 28×40mm Negative	75mm Lens 2¼×2¼ in. Negative	100mm Lens 2¼×3¼ in. Negative
	Inf.	38¾	20½ ×31	18⅝×28	21⅞×31¼	30×30	22⅛×32
	50	37		17¾×26⅝	20½×29¼	28×28	21×30¼
	25	34¾		16⅝×25	19¼×27½	26⅛×26⅛	19⅝×28⅜
	"FIXED"	33¾		16×24	18¾×26¾	25½×25½	19×27½
	15	32⅜		15⅜×23	17⅞×25½	24½×24½	18¾×27⅛
+1	10	29⅝	15½×23	14×21	16⅛×23⅛	22×22	16⅜×23⅝
	8	27⅞		13⅛×19¾	15⅛×21⅝	20½×20½	15¼×22⅛
	6	25½		11⅞×17⅞	13¾×19⅝	18⅝×18⅝	13¾×19⅞
	5	23¾	12½×18	11×16⅝	12¾×18¼	17⅛×17⅛	12¾×18⅜
	4	21⅝		10×15	11½×16½	15⅜×15⅜	11⅜×16⅜
	3½	20⅜	10¼×15½	9¼×14	10¾×15⅜	14⅜×14⅜	10½×15¼
	Inf.	19½	10½×14⅞	9⅜×14	10⅞×15½	14¾×14¾	11⅛×16⅛
	50	19⅛		9⅛×13⅝	10½×15⅛	14⅜×14⅜	10¾×15⅝
	"FIXED"	18½		8⅞×13¼	10¼×14⅝	13⅞×13⅞	10⅜×15
	15	18		8⅜×12⅞	10×14¼	13½×13½	10⅛×14⅝
+2	10	17¾		8½×12¾	9⅞×14	13⅛×13⅛	9⅞×14⅜
	8	16⅞	8½×12¼	8×12	9¼×13¼	12½×12½	9⅜×14
	6	16⅜		7¾×11½	8⅞×12¾	12×12	8⅞×12⅞
	5	15½		7¼×10⅞	8⅜×12	11¼×11¼	8⅜×12
	4	14⅞	7⅜×10½	6⅞×10⅜	8×11½	10¾×10¾	7⅞×11⅜
	3½	14		6½×9⅝	7½×10¾	10×10	7¼×10½
		13⅜	6¼×9⅛	6⅛×9¼	7⅛×10⅛	8⅞×8⅞	6⅞×10
	Inf.	13	6⅛×9¼	6¼×9⅜	7¼×10⅜	9⅞×9⅞	7½×10¾
	50	12⅞		6⅛×9¼	7⅛×10¼	9⅝×9⅝	7¼×10½
	25	12½		5⅞×8⅞	6⅞×9⅞	9⅜×9⅜	7⅛×10¼
	"FIXED"	12⅜		5⅞×8⅞	6⅞×9¾	9¼×9¼	7×10
	15	12¼		5¾×8¾	6¾×9⅝	9⅛×9⅛	6⅞×9⅞
+3	10	11⅞	6×8⅞	5⅝×8⅜	6½×9¼	8¾×8¾	6½×9½
	8	11½		5⅜×8⅛	6¼×8⅞	8⅜×8⅜	6⅜×9⅛
	6	11⅛		5⅛×7⅞	6×8⅝	8×8	6×8⅝
	5	10¾	5½×8	4⅞×7½	5¾×8¼	7¾×7¾	5¾×8¼
	4	10⅜		4¾×7⅛	5½×7⅞	7⅜×7⅜	5⅜×7¾
	3½	10	5⅛×7½	4½×6⅞	5¼×7½	7×7	5¼×7½
	Inf.	9⅞	5¼×7½	4⅝×7	5½×7¾	7⅜×7⅜	5⅝×8⅛
+4	"FIXED"	9½		4½×6⅝	5⅛×7½	7×7	5⅜×7¾
	3½	8	4×6	3⅝×5⅜	4⅛×6	5½×5½	4⅛×6
	Inf.	7⅞	4×6	3¾×5⅝	4¼×6¾	5⅞×5⅞	4½×6½
+5	"FIXED"	7⅝		3½×5⅜	4⅛×6	5⅝×5⅝	4¼×6⅛
	3½	6½	3¼×4⅝	3×4⅜	3½×4⅞	4½×4½	3⅜×4¾
	Inf.	6½	3¼×4⅞	3×4⅝	3⅝×5⅛	4⅞×4⅞	3¾×5⅜
+6	"FIXED"	6⅜		3×4⅜	3⅜×4⅞	4¾×4¾	3⅝×5¼
	3½	5⅝	2¾×4⅛	2½×3¾	3×4¼	3⅞×3⅞	2⅞×4¼
+8	Inf.	5⅛	2½×3¾	2¼×3⅜	–	–	–
	4	4⅝	2¼×3¼	2×3	–	–	–
+10	Inf.	4¼	2⅛×3⅛	1⅞×2¾	–	–	–
	4	4	1⅞×2⅝	1⅝×2½	–	–	–

*Data is approximate. The area seen by lens depends in part on the separation between supplementary and camera lenses. All focal lengths given are considered average. Information courtesy of Tiffen Manufacturing Corp.

you slightly better image quality than auxiliary close-up lenses, because you are not adding any lens elements to the optical system. But in practice, the difference is probably not worth the added bother of taking the lens off the camera, putting the tube or tubes on, and then putting on the lens. And if you do not have a through-the-lens metering system, then the work of figuring out exposure factors may be enough in itself to tip the scales in favor of the close-up lens. To calculate close-up exposure when you use a hand-held light meter, you need to know the reproduction ratio, which is the ratio of the size of the image on the film to the size of the original subject. For example, if your subject is two inches high and the actual size of the image on the transparency is one inch, then the reproduction ratio is 1:2, or one-half life-size on the film.

To find the reproduction ratio when you use extension tubes, set the focus on the lens to infinity. Then divide the tube length by the focal length of the lens. (The length in millimeters of extension tubes is generally engraved on the tubes and lens focal lengths are customarily given in millimeters.) For example, if you use a 25mm extension with a 50mm lens, the reproduction ratio is 1:2. When the tube is the same length as the focal length of the lens, the ratio is 1:1 or life-size.

The chart on this page shows the additional exposure required when you use a hand-held light meter, flash meter, or guide-number calculations for manual electronic flash.

Just to make things more difficult, some films become slower when exposures are longer than one second. This effect is known as *reciprocity failure,* and you will have to add on any time required to compensate for this as well. The instruction sheets packed with most films give reciprocity correction recommendations. Our advice is to keep your exposures shorter than one second and avoid the problem entirely.

EXPOSURE INCREASES FOR CLOSE-UPS WITH EXTENSION TUBES

Reproduction Ratio	Increase in *f*/stops
1:12	1/4
1:8	1/3
1:5	1/2
1:4	2/3
1:2.5	1
1:2	1 1/3
1:1.5	1 1/2
1:1.3	1 2/3
1:1	2

GETTING MAXIMUM DETAIL

Aesthetically, it may look nicer if you fill the frame with your subject, getting as large an image as possible. But the larger the image, the smaller the zone of sharp focus, and with small, three-dimensional subjects, you can often get sharper detail when you use less magnification, which will increase your zone of sharp focus. Any subject that fills one-third or more of your viewfinder will have plenty of detail when you project it, and often you can get away with an even smaller image on the film. So don't bother messing around with complex techniques in order to get maximum image size. The results won't be worth the hassle.

SOME GOOD ADVICE

Keep your working methods as simple as possible. You do not need to use sophisticated equipment and techniques just to take inventory photos of small subjects. As we have pointed out earlier, the normal lens on a modern 110 or 35mm SLR is capable of handling most of the close-ups you will need to take, and if you put a +3 or +4 auxiliary close-up lens on your normal lens, you should be able to handle the rest of your inventory.

When you try to modify other types of cameras to do the work of an SLR, you run into complex technical problems. Rather than getting involved with these difficulties, you are probably better off keeping within the limits of the camera and just ignoring the ultra-close-ups altogether. If you feel you must have them, then borrow or rent an SLR and do the job the easy way.

5 Special Techniques

This chapter is written for those of you who encounter special problems while making your photo inventory, either as a result of using non-recommended equipment, such as pocket and instant cameras or portable electronic flash, or as a result of trying to photograph unique subjects that do not lend themselves to standard lighting procedures.

If you glance through the various headings in this chapter, you will see that it is really a grab bag of tips and techniques, some of which may apply to your situation and many of which will not. Unless you have a general interest in the subject of photography, we suggest you skip those sections that don't relate directly to your equipment or subject matter and get on with the material that really counts.

NON-ADJUSTABLE CAMERAS

If you use an inexpensive, non-adjustable camera—one that won't let you change focus or exposure—then you have to modify your inventory procedure so that you stay within the limits of the camera. It does not matter whether your camera uses 110 (pocket), 126 (Instamatic) or instant (Polaroid or PR-10) film. The limits are roughly the same.

First, these cameras work best in bright daylight. As soon as you bring them indoors, you must use either very high-speed film or flash, or both, to get an acceptable picture.

The high cost of flashcubes, barflash and flipflash makes flash photography with these cameras relatively expensive. You will have to work out the economics for yourself, but as you do, keep in mind that your photo dealer probably has an inexpensive electronic flash designed specifically for your camera, and these flash units, with batteries, cost about the same as ten flipflash arrays.

Regardless of the flash you use with simple cameras, you get good exposure only with subjects that are seven to ten feet from your camera. Anything closer will be too light and anything further away will be too dark. (The outside limits are four to 12 feet.) This means that you will not be able to make any tight close-ups, and you will not be able to get good overall views of rooms when you use flash.

One way around these problems with pocket- and Instamatic-type cameras is to load your camera with Kodacolor 400 film and photograph during the daytime. For indoor shots, open up all your window shades and drapes to let as much light in as possible and turn on all your room lights. If you've got a lot of windows, this just might work.

To make your individual shots of small items, wait for a sunny day and set up a table

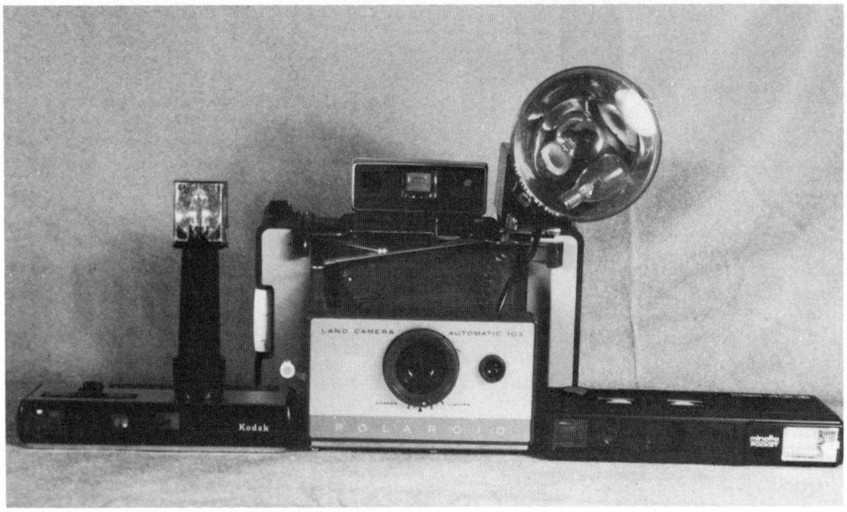

Good inventory pictures can be made using non-adjustable cameras such as those shown here, but the procedure requires some modification.

outside. Put a background board and background cloth on the table as described in Chapter 4 and bring your medium and small objects to the table to be photographed. If the table is in direct sunlight and you stay at least five feet away, you should get reasonably clear shots.

If you find that your Kodacolor 400 shots don't come out any lighter than similar shots taken under the same conditions on the much slower Kodacolor II film, then you may be using a camera that has a lever or button that you push when you load the camera with 400 film. If your shots are too dark and you have kept this lever set for 400, then next time don't push it. Keep the camera set for ASA 100 film instead. That way, when you load up with 400 film, you will get the benefit of the higher speed.

You will not be able to get good close-ups with very simple cameras. Your best bet is to group all your small items together and take them in a single shot. The group shot will contain enough detail for rough visual identification, and you can supplement it later in the "remarks" column of your inventory sheet. Forget about taking individual shots of tiny items that won't show up well anyway. It's just a waste of film.

Of course you can use close-up lenses with simple, fixed-focus cameras, but a set of these lenses costs nearly as much as the camera itself. Also, they have to be used with measuring tape and special attention to subject placement, as explained in Chapter 4, and if you use flash, you will have to cut down the light by putting a diffuser over it as explained below. When you've done all that, you still haven't got much because the lenses on these simple cameras are not very good to begin with.

HANDLING ELECTRONIC FLASH

There are two general types of problem that crop up with electronic flash. The first, characterized by consistently poor exposures or partially blank images, is caused by mishandling the equipment. The second, characterized by uneven light distribution—too light in front, too dark in the rear—or by image-obliterating glare spots with shiny subjects, is the result of limitations inherent in the equipment design. Both types of problem can be corrected, the first completely, the second partially through the use of a few lighting tricks.

Equipment handling problems: If your flash

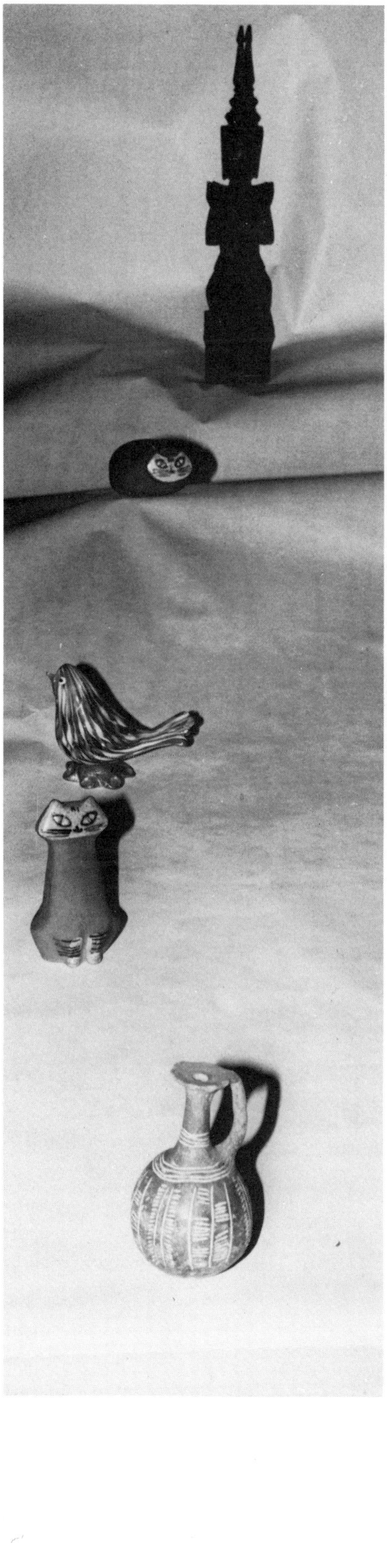

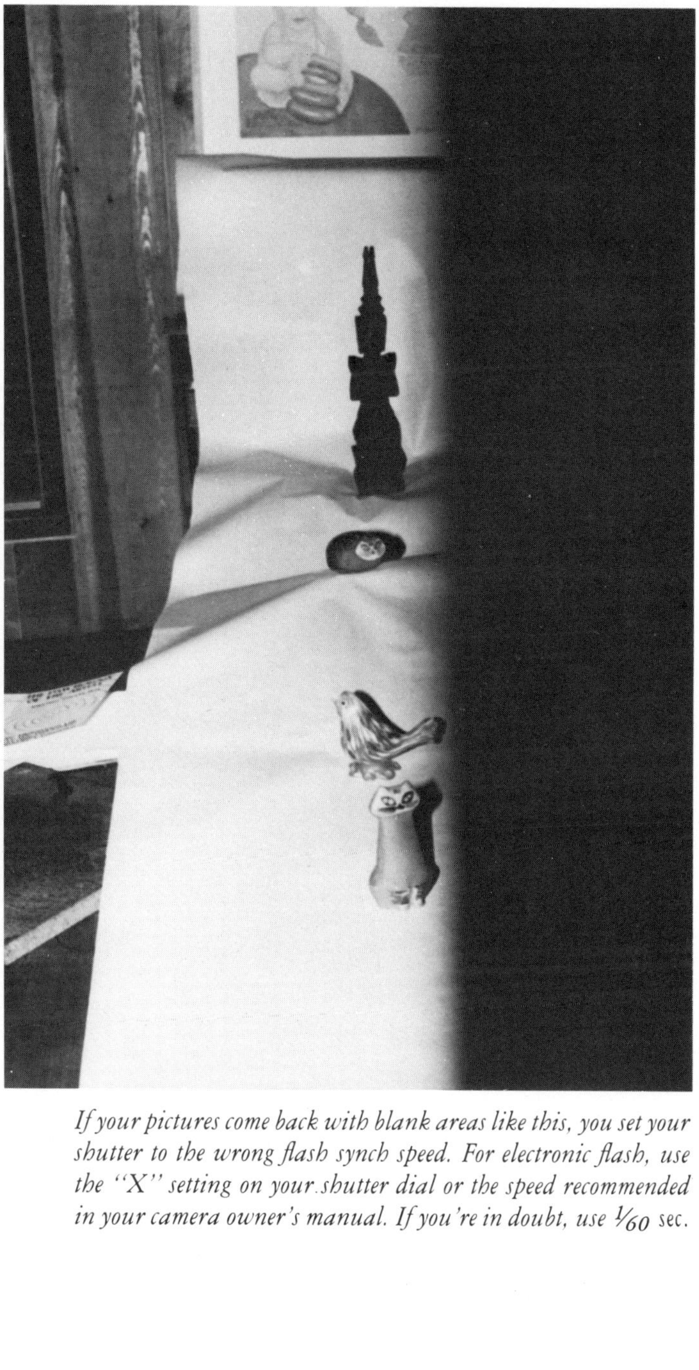

If your pictures come back with blank areas like this, you set your shutter to the wrong flash synch speed. For electronic flash, use the "X" setting on your shutter dial or the speed recommended in your camera owner's manual. If you're in doubt, use 1/60 sec.

Notice how the background becomes darker and the figures receive progressively less light, until the last figure is nothing but a dark shape without detail. This effect is called light fall-off and is a common problem when you use on-camera electronic flash: if objects in the foreground are properly exposed, objects in the background will be underexposed.

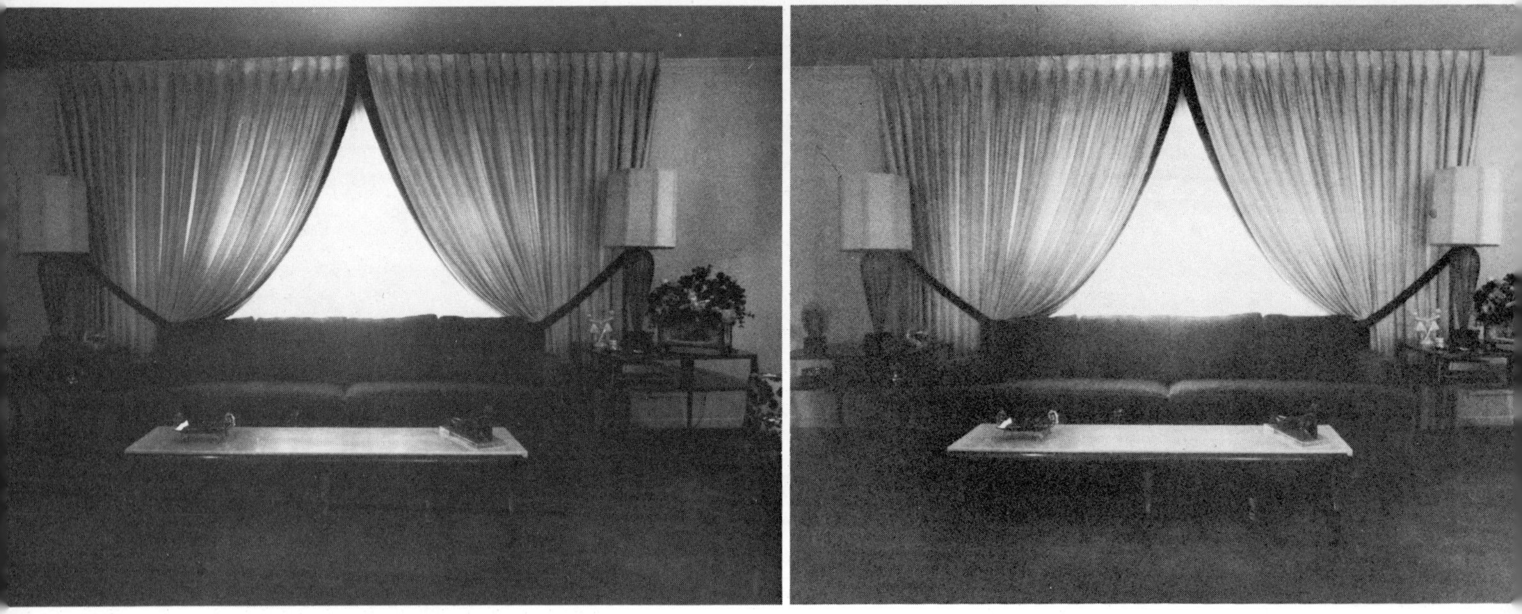

The photo on the left is over-exposed; the one on the right is under-exposed. Be sure your exposure is correct to get properly exposed pictures.

photos are consistently under- or over-exposed, then you are not calculating exposure correctly, in the case of manual units, or you are not programming correctly with an auto flash. To calculate exposure with a manual flash, use the guide numbers that are printed on a plate attached to the flash. When you divide the guide number by your flash-to-subject distance, you get the correct *f*/stop to use. The guide number (G.N.) depends on the film speed, so be sure you have the right one in mind. For example, your unit might have a G.N. of 80 for ASA 400 film. If your subject—a medium-sized painting, say—is 10 feet from the flash, then the correct *f*/stop to use is *f*/8 ($80 \div 10 = 8$). If the number doesn't come out to a full stop, then use the nearest half- or full-stop setting.

There are a handful of inexpensive units that provide only one G.N., usually a number for ASA 100 film, and the instructions that come with them leave you in the dark about figuring guide numbers for slower or faster films. In this situation, you can calculate new guide numbers for faster films by multiplying the ASA 100 G.N. by 1.4 for each doubling of the film speed. For example, if the flash has an ASA 100 G.N. of 40, then its ASA 200 G.N. is 56 and for ASA 400 film the G.N. is 80. Working in the other direction, the G.N. for ASA 25 film would be 20.

Automatic flash units, as well as dedicated units designed to work with special circuits in certain cameras, can be misprogrammed. Pay attention to the *f*/stop selection guides on the calculator dial, to the sensitivity setting on the light cell if your flash has a variable control on the front, and last but not least, to the *f*/stop you set on the lens. Autoflash units, particularly the more expensive ones, offer a large number of power options, so check your instruction book if you have any uncertainty about the way you are using it. If you have lost your instruction book, you can usually get a duplicate by writing to the manufacturer's customer service department.

On some camera lenses, it is all too easy to turn the *f/*stop selection ring accidentally when you change focus. Short of getting a different lens for your camera, the only way you can control this is to pay attention to the way your hand grips the lens. Learn to use more finger action and less palm when you focus.

Partially blank frames are the result of using too high a shutter speed. Use the "X" setting on your shutter speed dial, if it has one, or 1/60 sec. if you are in doubt about the top flash synchronization speed for your camera. If you are using a flash that connects to your camera via a p.c. (push-connector) cord, make sure you put it into the "X" synch terminal on the camera.

If you are calculating your exposures correctly and are still getting runs of underexposed shots, you may be using weak batteries, or it could be that you are not giving your flash unit time to fully charge up between flashes. If you wait until the ready light on the flash comes on before you make your exposure, you should get consistent exposures.

Overcoming equipment limitations: The biggest limitation with electronic flash mounted on the camera is light fall-off. Objects at different distances from the camera receive different amounts of light, which produces uneven exposure of room views and furniture groupings. The most expensive solution is to use several flash units. You place them just as you would continuous lights and synchronize them to the camera with remote triggers that fire these slave flash units in response to the burst of light from a flash unit attached to your camera.

If you are a one-flash photographer, a more practical technique is to bounce your flash from a white ceiling. To do this, you need a flash with a tilting head, or you need to

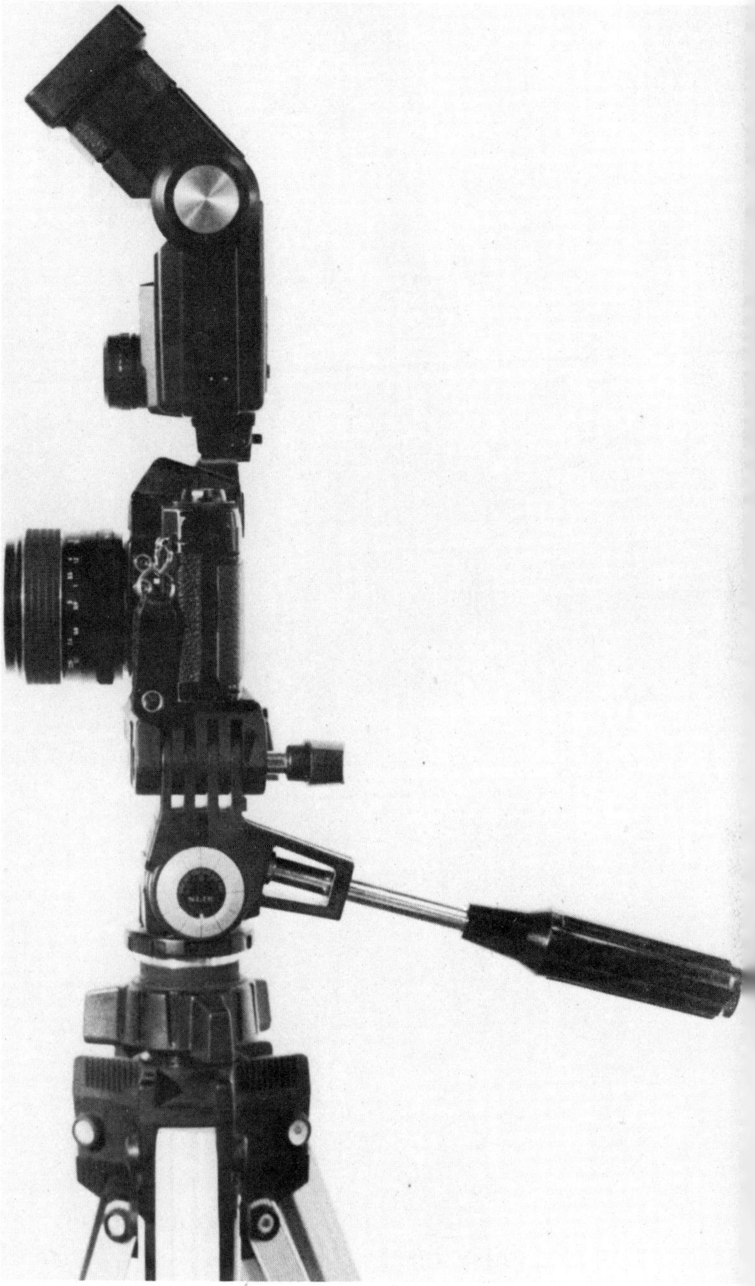

This flash is tilted to bounce light from the ceiling. If you use a small automatic flash, you may find this technique will not work for you with the flash on "Auto" because it does not have enough power. With a flash on manual, you must open up the lens at least two f/*stops from the indicated exposure for a normal flash shot.*

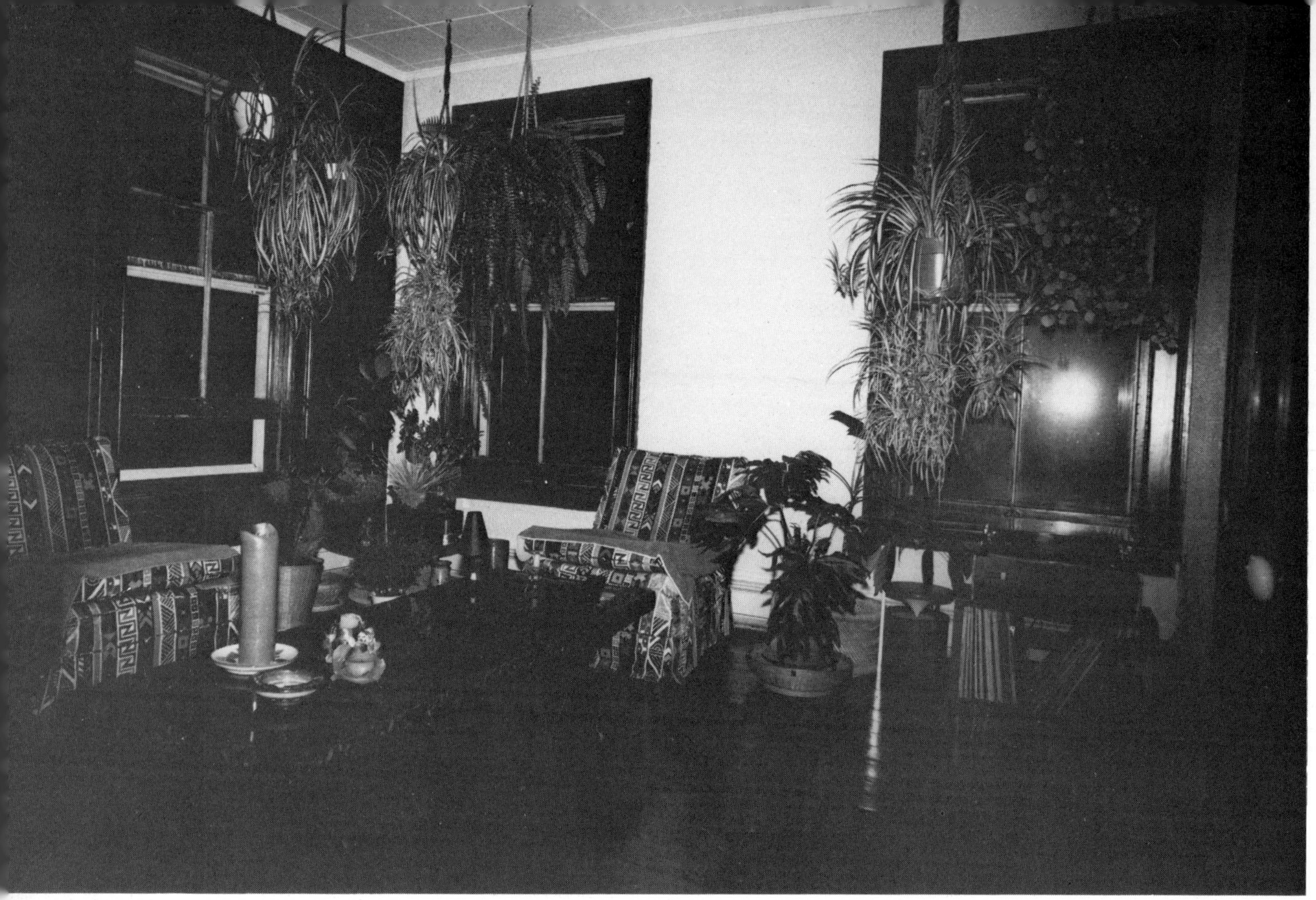

When you use flash with a wide-angle lens, you get darkening at the corners of the image area. In a large room, you will also run into problems of light fall-off and inadequate lighting of dark subjects. This photo has all of these problems. To correct them, use the painting-with-light technique.

To set your camera up for light painting, place it on a tripod, shelf or other solid support. Set the shutter to "B" and use a locking cable release. Next, turn off the room lights and open the shutter. In most cases, you will have to wait until it's dark outside before this technique will work.

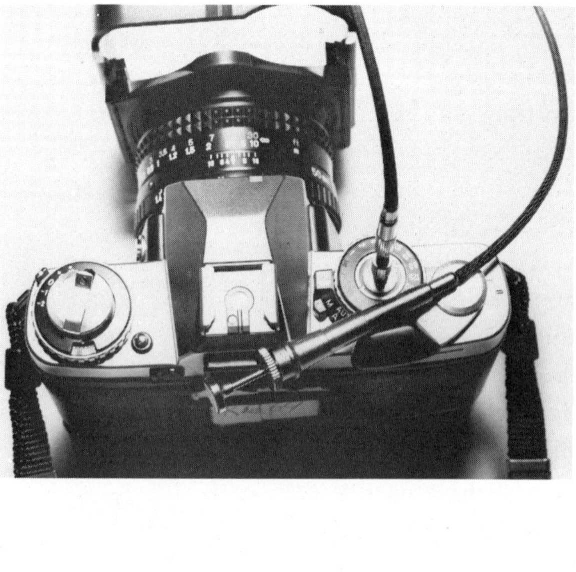

mount your flash on a bracket with a tilting flash mount. If you are using automatic flash, make sure the sensor is pointed at your subject. If you use a flash that does not have a tilting head, then use the unit on manual, calculate the *f/*stop using the flash guide number, and then open up two extra stops to compensate for the light absorbed by the ceiling. Then make three exposures, one at the corrected *f/*stop, one at a stop smaller and one at a stop wider. That way, you should come out with at least one usable slide.

An alternative to bounce flash in large rooms is the painting-with-light technique.

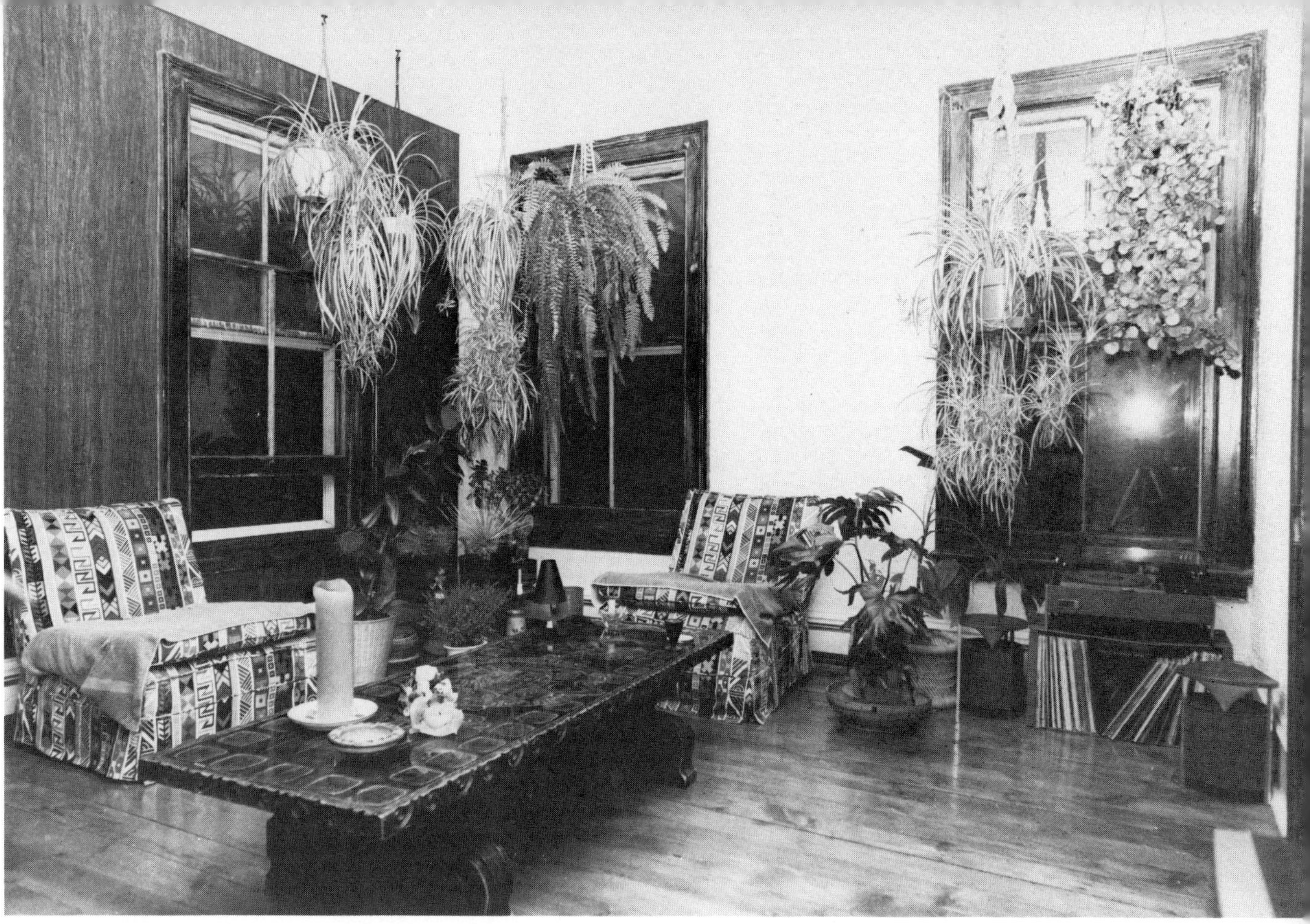

This room was "painted" with three successive bursts of light from a stationary position while the shutter was held open on "B." The flash, kept on the "Auto" setting, was hand-held and the test button on the flash used as a trigger. Three flashes, one aimed to the right, one to the center, and one to the left, were sufficient to paint this room. To be sure of proper exposure, try several shots with a varying number of flashes aimed in slightly different directions.

This is best done at night. You start by putting the camera on a tripod, composing and focusing. Then calculate the right *f/*stop to use for a subject that is about 10 feet from the flash. To do this set your flash on manual and divide the guide number for the film speed you are using by 10 to get the right *f/*stop.

Next, set your camera shutter to "B." You will need a locking cable release to keep the shutter open, or an assistant who will hold down the shutter button. Turn off all the lights in the room and then open the camera shutter.

Now walk around the room with your flash and flash the various objects in the room, keeping the flash about 10 feet from the objects you light. Be sure not to get between the flash and the camera. If you do, you'll get your own silhouette in the photo. Try to aim the bursts of light so that they will overlap slightly at the edges. To trigger the flash, use the test button of the flash. If your unit does not have a test button, you can use a paper clip to short out the p.c. terminal connector.

The painting-with-light technique can also be used with small objects set up on a table and with very large subjects, such as a building. The only change you need to make for small subjects is to select an *f/*stop that will let you make your flashes from one or two feet away and for very large subjects to select an *f/*stop that will let you work about 20 to 30 feet away.

After you have painted your subject with successive flashes, return to the camera, and close the shutter. This is a surprisingly effective technique that is employed with great success by commercial photographers.

Glare from the surface of shiny subjects, such as silverware or paintings under glass, can be an annoying problem when you use on-camera flash. The easiest way to overcome the problem is to direct your flash at a reflector that bounces the light onto your subject. A low white ceiling makes an excellent reflector, as does any large piece of white paper or cardboard.

Some automatic flash systems offer accessory reflector holders and umbrella reflectors. Both types reduce glare and produce a softer, more pleasing light for photographing objects about the size of a human head and smaller.

You can purchase inexpensive reflectors and diffusers designed for use with just about any flash. One example is the Air-Brella, which looks something like a plastic balloon that attaches by straps to your flash head. Another is the Air-Diffuser, a balloon made of translucent material that produces a soft, scattered light.

A sheet of tracing paper suspended about 8 to 12 inches in front of your flash also does an effective job of softening the light. You can make a holder for the tracing paper out of a few strips of cardboard and some masking tape.

All of the above methods for reducing glare can be used with both on- and off-camera flash, but your chances for success are much greater if you use the flash off the camera and synch it with a p.c. extension cord.

CLOSE-UPS WITH FLASHCUBE, FLIPFLASH AND BARFLASH

If you have a camera that will focus close up, such as a Polaroid Sonar SX-70, and you want to use barflash, or one of the new 110 miniature SLR cameras and you want to use flip- or cube-flash—depending on what your camera accepts—then you can reduce the power of the flash for close-ups by putting one or more layers of Scotch Magic Transparent Tape over the flash, or by draping a thin handkerchief or piece of nylon over the flash.

If you have an instant picture camera, you can preview the results immediately and add or remove layers of tape or handkerchief until you get properly exposed close-ups. If you use conventional color print or slide film, then you should experiment. Take several shots using different thicknesses of tape or handkerchief and keep a record that includes the camera-to-subject distance and layers of material used for each shot. When you get your prints back from the lab, match them up with your record to find the thickness that works.

INSTANT CAMERA EXPOSURE CONTROL

It is sometimes desirable to get more or less exposure than is possible using the lighten-darken control on instant picture cameras. Most of these cameras have a light sensor that is independent of the lens. To trick this sensor into giving more exposure, put one or more layers of tissue paper, nylon stocking, handkerchief or translucent tape over the sensor eye. It seldom takes more than two or three trial exposures to determine the right amount of material to use.

This series of photos show the effect of reflectors and diffusers on an electronic flash. In this photo, the characteristic beam pattern of an portable electronic flash is shown.

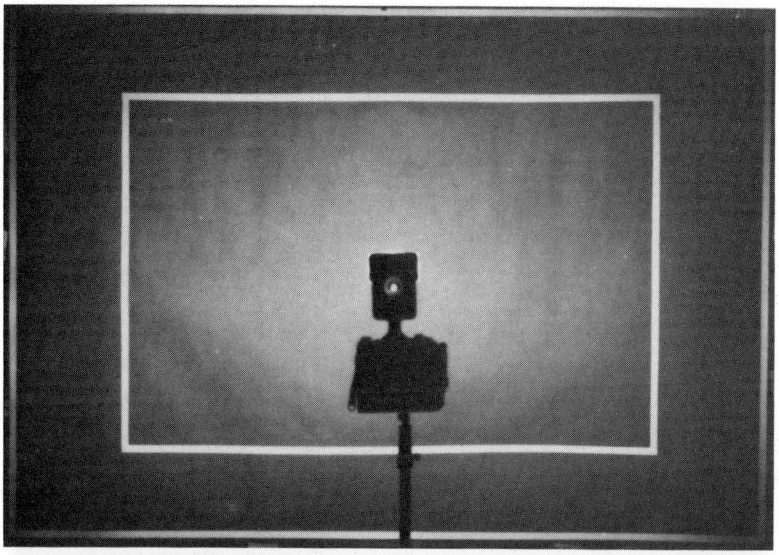

In this photo, the simple Air-Diffuser has been strapped to the flash. Glare is reduced and the light is softer.

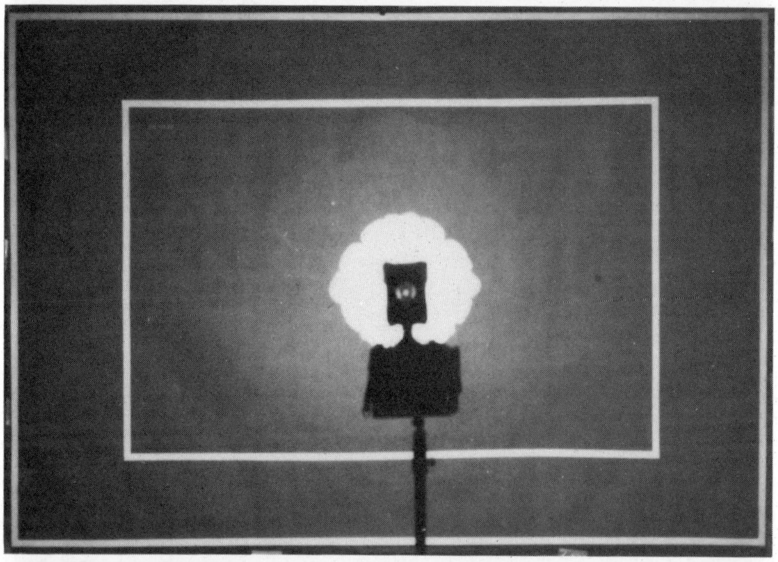

This photo shows the use of the Air-Brella to reduce glare and soften the light even further.

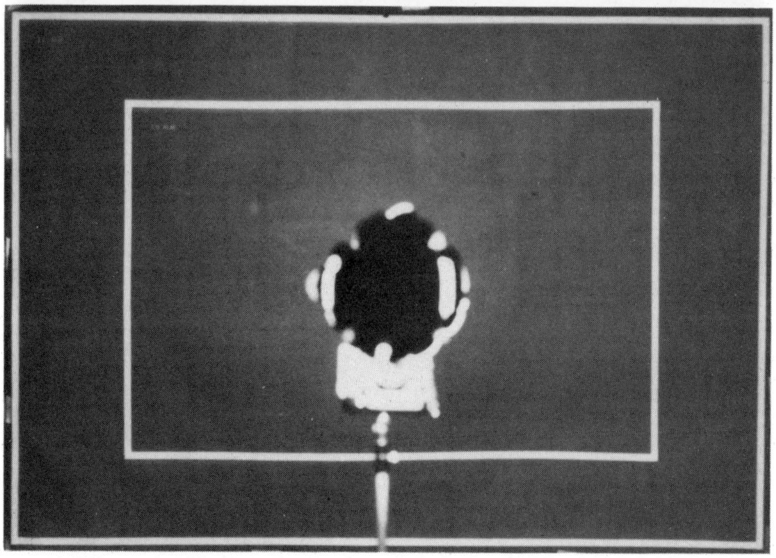

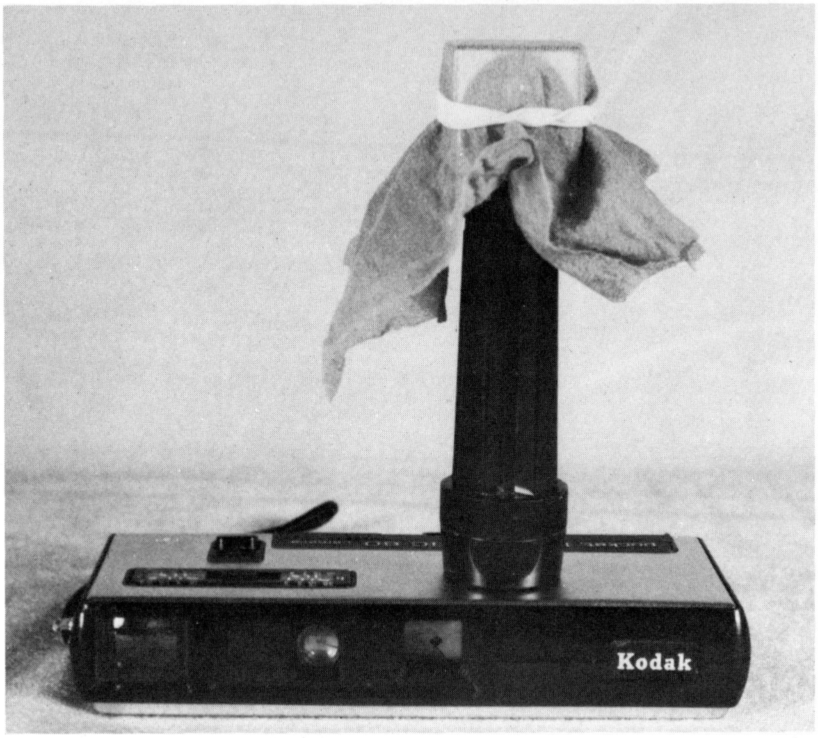

You can reduce the power of flashcubes, flipflash and flashbars by draping a thin piece of cloth or nylon over them.

DOCUMENTATION OF WORK IN PROGRESS

Occasionally you may want to keep a photographic record of work in progress with dated photos that show construction and other projects in various stages of completion. A photo record of this type can be a useful source of reference if disputes arise concerning schedules or the quality of materials and workmanship that went into the job.

When you use photos to document work in progress, proper dating is critical. One way is to write the date in large numbers on a sheet of typing paper, photograph it, then take your record shots. But the easiest way is to use a data back on an SLR camera.

A data back contains a small light that projects a date or code number into the corner of each photo. Dials on the back allow you to reset the numbers at will. Canon, Minolta, Nikon, Olympus and Pentax all have some cameras in their lines that will accept data backs.

To use one of these backs effectively, compose so that a dark area of your subject falls in the corner where the data is printed. The projected data is white, and if it falls into a very light portion of the subject, such as dry concrete in sunlight, it is going to be difficult, or impossible, to read.

Data-back cameras are a useful tool for doctors, dentists, and any craftsperson who does custom work on another's property, because they can be used to routinely document the condition of the person, place or thing before starting work. If you have a dated photo, there is a good chance that a disagreement can be settled quickly without recourse to a lawyer. One quick and easy settlement can more than pay for the cost of the camera and film used for routine photo protection.

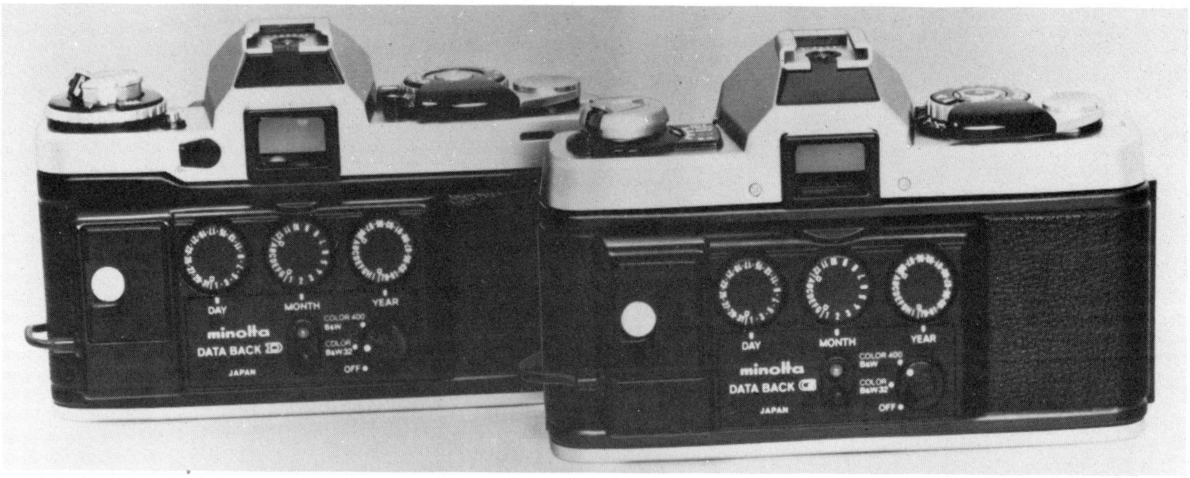

Data backs such as these from Minolta (above) print a date or code number on the film. In the photo (below), the date appears in the lower right-hand corner of the print. Try to compose your shots so the number falls into a dark area of the picture.

Photo courtesy of Minolta Co.

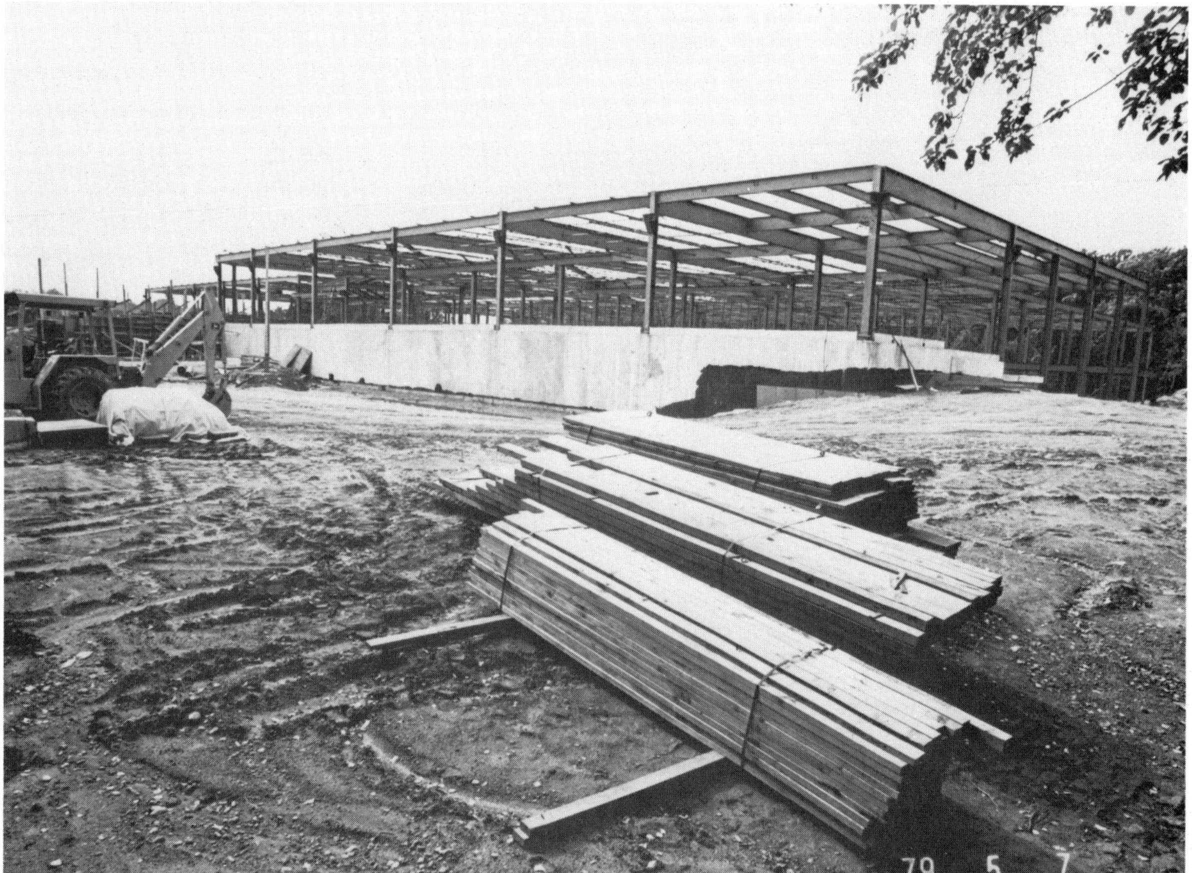

6 Finishing the Job

Once you have finished photographing your rooms and possessions, you are about three-quarters of the way through the inventory process. The rest of the job consists of filing and paperwork—not nearly as much fun as camera handling, but just as important.

PROCESSING

Get your exposed film processed immediately by a reputable lab. If you are using Kodak film, then we recommend that you either have the film processed by the Eastman Kodak company or by a custom lab that you have used before and whose work you have found reliable. If you have used Agfa or Fuji film, then have it processed by the manufacturer's lab. A lot of work has gone into making those photos and this is no time to take chances with cut-rate processing. This is also no time to be inviting theft, so we suggest you give a business rather than personal address when leaving your film.

Film left in a mailbox in warm weather can be ruined by the heat. When mailing film for processing, take it directly into the post office.

EDITING THE SLIDES

To review slides, you need a slide viewer, light box or slide projector. It does not matter which method you use as long as you keep the slides in order and don't mix up slides from one box with those from another.

Set up the slide boxes in the same order in which you exposed the rolls, beginning with the living room. Assign a letter to each box —A, B, C, and so on. A spot check of a couple of slides from each box will tell you which is which. Go through the box and write the box letter on each slide mount and put the slides in order using the numbers stamped on the mounts.

INVENTORY PROCEDURES

You are now ready to begin the final phase of the inventory process, which consists of filling in the inventory sheet and keying the entries to the photos. An example of the standard inventory sheet used by Photo Protection Services is shown here. You can make up your own using this sheet as a model.

In the left hand column, enter the roll (box) letter and photo number as you look at each slide. Then fill in the other columns to the best of your ability before going on to the next slide. If you have to look up information, such as a bill of sale, put a small asterisk or check mark in the margin next to that entry so that you can find it later. When you

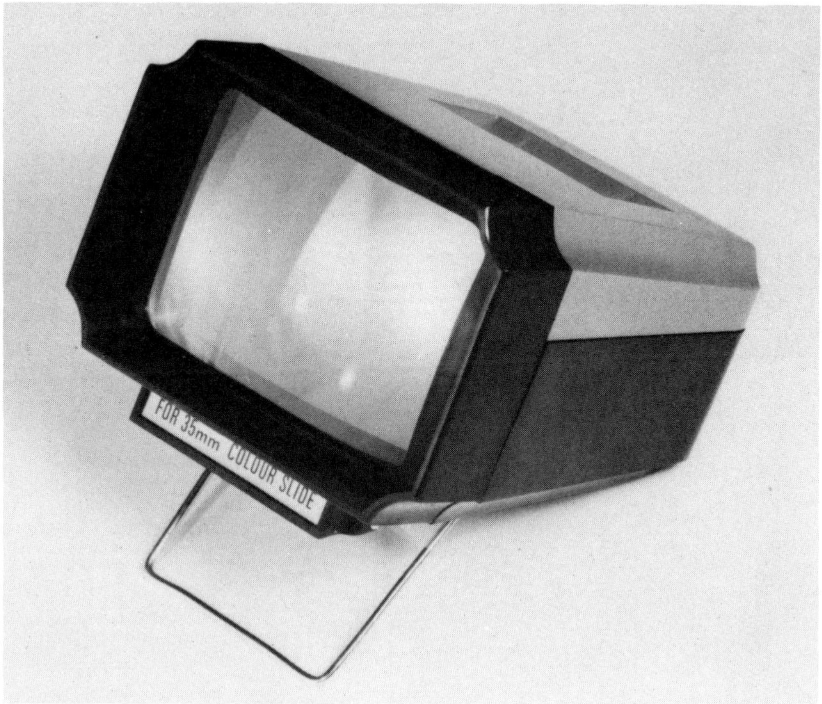

To edit your slides, use a slide viewer (above) or light box (below).

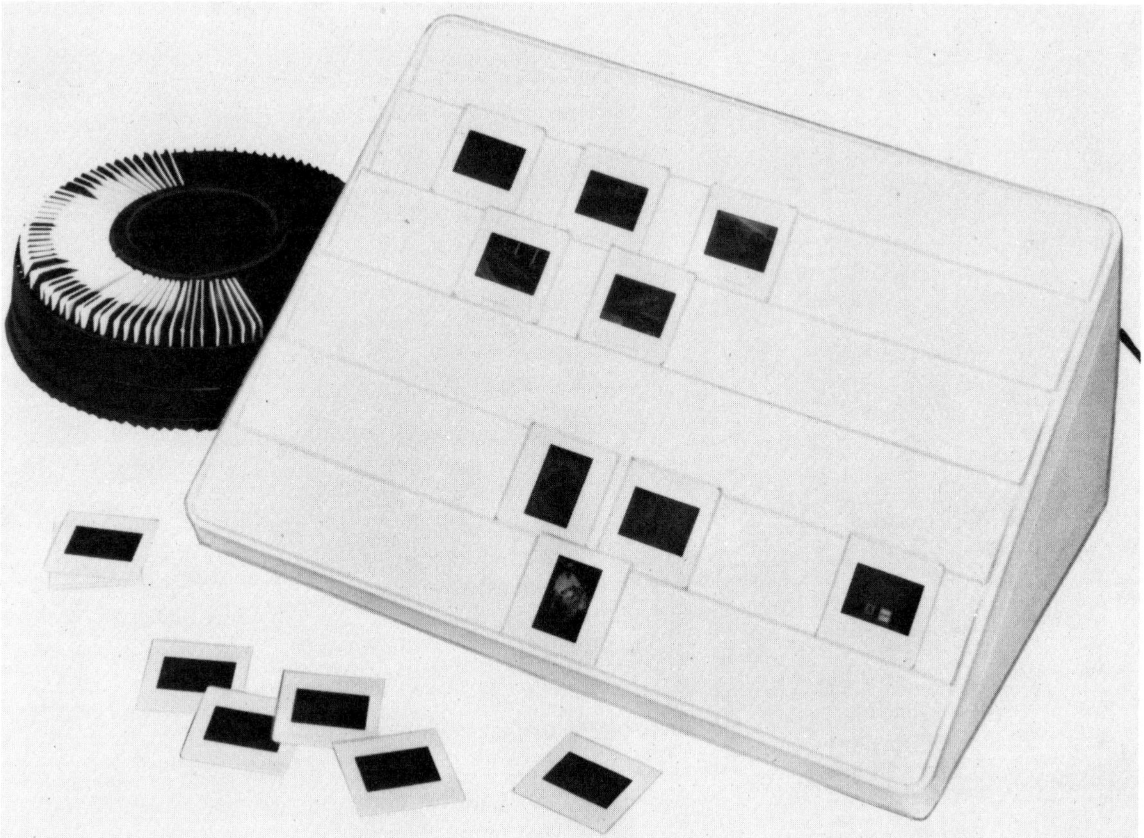

PHOTO PROTECTION SERVICE INC.

P. O. BOX 214, WALDWICK, N. J. 07463
(201) 797-8099

INVENTORY DATA

DATE:

PHOTO	PURCHASE DATE	ORIGINAL COST	PRESENT VALUE	REMARKS

have filled in all the columns, go on to the next slide.

The *purchase date* is the date you purchased the item photographed or the approximate date on which you acquired it. The *original cost* is the price you paid. If the item was a gift or inheritance, then leave this column blank.

The *present value* may be more difficult to determine. Machinery tends to depreciate. Glassware, silverware, jewelry and art often appreciate. A rough estimate of replacement value is usually okay. This estimate can always be changed if more accurate information becomes available. If you feel unsure of present value, just leave the column blank. This is not the time to get involved with complex appraisal procedures. Remember, the job at hand is to take the photo, fill in whatever inventory data you have at hand, and get on to the next shot.

Under *remarks,* list any important facts about the subject that may determine its worth and/or a short description that tells what the subject is. For example, the remarks column may contain notations such as "Meissen china," "solid oak," "oil by Prendergast, 1908," "cameo pin: family heirloom," "Ibo sculpture, 19th century," and so on. Avoid getting too detailed. The photo provides the necessary visual detail and saves you the proverbial thousand words.

STORAGE

After you have completed the written portion of your inventory, you can either store the slides in the box in which they come from the processor or put them in plastic, see-through pages with individual pockets for each slide. When you store slides in pages you can retrieve individual slides with a minimum of effort because you can hold the page up to any convenient light and quickly scan it to find the photo you want. When you store slides in boxes, you have to fumble with the entire box to find individual slides.

If you have done your inventory on color print film and had it processed by a large-volume photofinisher, the chances are it will be returned to you in a two-pouch envelope known to the trade as a "kangaroo." These paper envelopes are not suitable for long-term storage. We recommend that you purchase plastic, see-through negative storage pages. A typical storage page has sleeves for

The easiest way to store your slides is in plastic see-through pages.

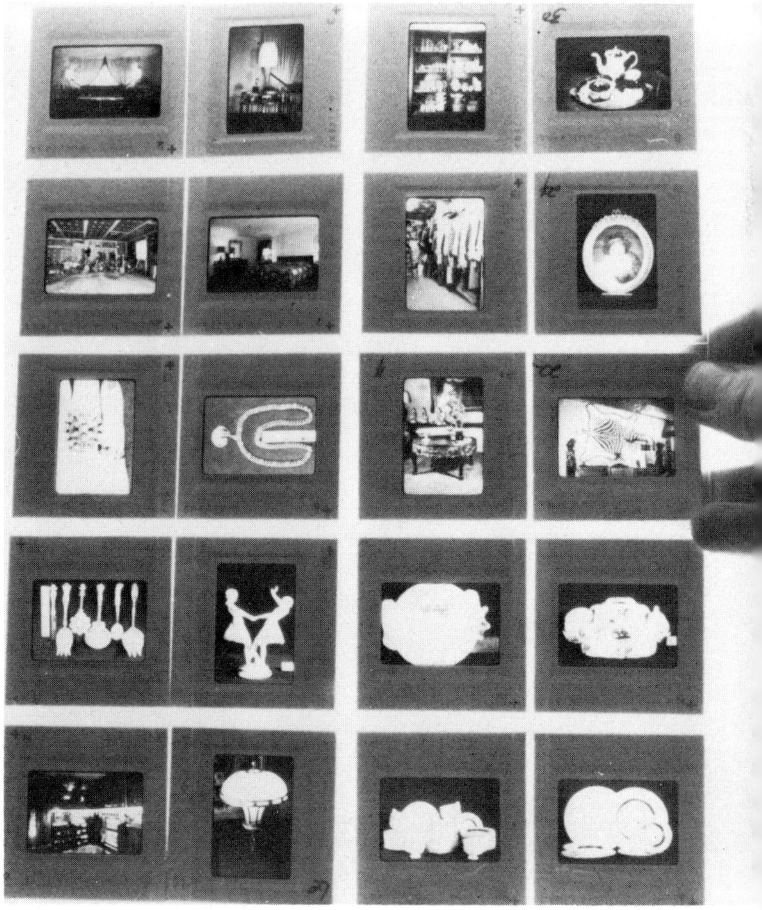

either six five-frame strips of 35mm film, or five six-frame 35mm strips. These storage pages preserve negative life and make it easier to find individual shots when you want reprints. You can also store negatives in glassine negative-storage envelopes, but this method is less convenient than see-through pages.

Do not keep the inventory slides or prints in your home. If you were to have a fire or theft, you could lose both your possessions and your insurance inventory. Instead, store the photos, a copy of your written inventory sheets and original bills of sale for major items in a bank vault box or other safe place.

HOW TO MAKE SLIDE DUPLICATES

You may want to have one or more duplicate sets of inventory photos, one to keep in your vault box, another to keep at home or with a relative or lawyer. There is no need to have duplicate slides made by a commercial lab that charges you an arm and a leg for each dupe. You can easily do it yourself if you have a 35mm SLR camera with a built-in meter.

Some photographers shy away from making slide dupes because they assume there must be something complicated about it. But in fact a duplicate is nothing more than a close-up shot of an illuminated slide, or a normal photograph of a slide projected on a screen or on a sheet of white paper.

The accompanying chart shows you how to match your light source to the film you have in your camera so that you get good color quality. For example, most projectors have a 3200 K bulb that is just about perfect for use with Ektachrome 160 tungsten film. Tungsten floods such as ECA and ECT bulbs also match tungsten film. Kodachrome 40 is a perfect match for No. 1 and No. 2 photofloods. Daylight films such as Kodachrome or Ektachrome 64 are a perfect match for electronic flash. If you use a light source that doesn't match the film you have in the camera, then you should use the filter recommended in the chart if you want to get duplicates that do not have a red, yellow or blue cast.

The easiest way to copy your slides is to project them on a matte surface screen and photograph the projected image. (Beaded and lenticular screens are okay but the results will appear a bit grainy. A piece of tempered hardboard painted with a couple of coats of matte white paint works very well.) Set up your camera on a tripod directly behind your projector. If you use Ektachrome 160 tungsten film, the color should be about right. You don't need filters. Meter the image on the screen just as you would any other subject. For best results, the room should be as dark as you can make it. If you do your copying at night, turning off all the room lights and closing the curtains or window shades will do the trick.

If you use daylight slide film such as Kodachrome, Fujichrome or Ektachrome 200 to copy a projected image, then use an 80A conversion filter on your lens. If you want color prints, you can put color print film in your camera. Again, an 80A filter will give you slightly better color quality.

Slide-copying attachments: Another way to make duplicate slides is to use a bellows with a slide duplicating attachment. The bellows goes between your camera body and the lens. The slide duplicating attachment goes in front of your lens. It's nothing more than a slide holder with a diffusing screen. Set up your camera with bellows and duplicator on a tripod and put a large sheet of white paper a couple of feet in front of the camera. Aim two photofloods at the paper, one on either side at about a 45° angle. This will give you

MATCHING FILM TO LIGHT SOURCE

FILM TYPE	LIGHT SOURCE		
	Electronic Flash or Daylight	*3400 K photo-floods (No's 1 & 2)*	*3200 K tungsten (ECA & ECT bulbs)*
	Filter	*Filter*	*Filter*
Daylight:			
Kodachrome 25 Agfachrome 64 Kodachrome 64 Ektachrome 64 Agfachrome 100 Fujichrome RD-100 Ektachrome 200 Ektachrome 400 Agfacolor CNS-2 Fujicolor F-II Fujicolor F-II 400 Kodacolor II Kodacolor 400	None: perfect match	80B	80A
Type A:			
Kodachrome 40	85	None: perfect match	82A
Type B (tungsten):			
Ektachrome 160	85B	81A	None: perfect match

brilliant, even illumination of the white paper, which becomes an ideal diffuse light source. Put a slide in the duplicating attachment, focus, take a through-the-lens reading or put your camera on automatic, and press the shutter. You should have a perfect slide duplicate.

Slide duplicating systems: If you have a large number of slide duplicates to make, at least several hundred each year, then you might want to consider a special set-up for slide duplicating. The simplest consists of a close-up lens and slide holder designed as one unit, such as the Spiratone Vario-Dupliscope. These units attach to your camera in place of your regular lens. You can use them with the lighting set-up described for a bellows with slide-duplicating attachment or purchase a special electronic flash with calibrated card that allows you to position the flash for precise exposures at several different *f/*stops.

Inexpensive slide duplicating illuminators consist of a box with a 3200 K light inside

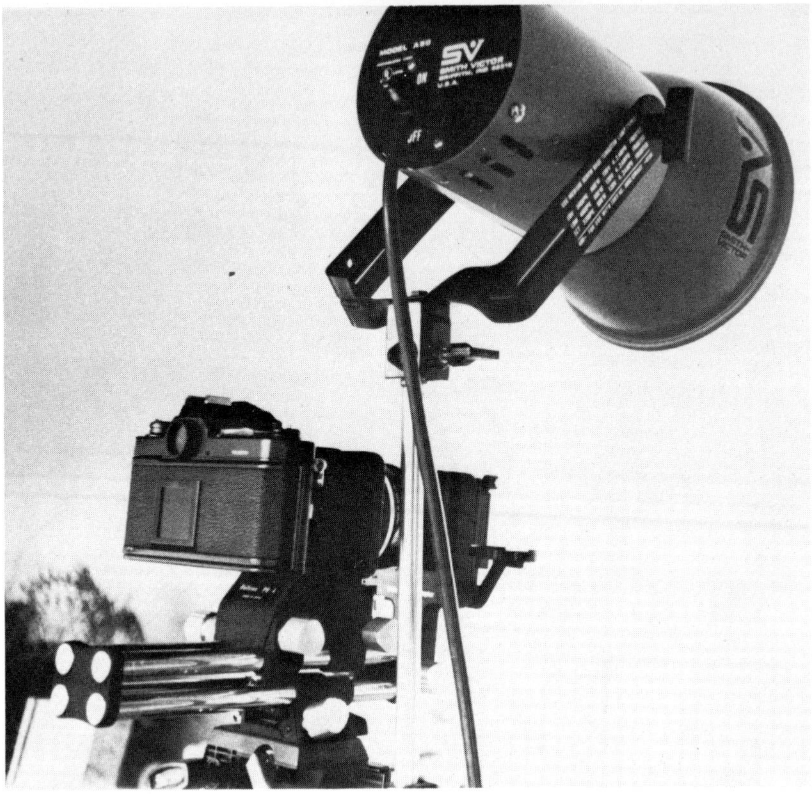

You can copy slides using bellows and a slide duplicating attachment. Set up your camera and equipment on a tripod, and point the lights at a sheet of white paper in front of the camera for diffuse but brilliant illumination.

and a diffusion screen on which you place the slide. These must be used in conjunction with a bellows and tripod or copy-stand mounted camera.

Audio-visual labs often use sophisticated duplicating systems such as the Bowens Illumitran, which has a built-in electronic flash light source and a copy stand that will handle any camera. These units are almost as easy to use as an office copy machine, but they are expensive. You do not need one to make good slide dupes.

AFTER THE DAMAGE IS DONE

If your property is vandalized or damaged by some disaster such as fire, flood, or windstorm, we recommend that you take camera in hand and make overall views plus close-ups of individual items to record the actual extent of damage. If a dispute arises after clean-up has begun or things have been repaired, these photos are documentary evidence of the original damage.

THE WRAP-UP

Once the written inventory is complete, you might want to reconsider your insurance coverage. Make a copy of the inventory sheets and discuss them with your insurance agent. You may be adequately insured, but then again, you may not be. It's surprising how the figures can add up. Either way, you will have the comfort of knowing exactly where you stand so far as the financial value of your possessions is concerned.

Once you have completed the photo inventory and put it away in a safe place, you can take satisfaction in knowing that you have created one more layer of security for yourself and your family.

The inventory procedures detailed in this book tell how to do the job as an amateur, do-it-yourself photographer. If you feel the need for more formal instruction or wish to know how to go about setting up a full-fledged photo protection service in your community, you can write or phone us to find out about our seminars. Our address is:

Photo Protection Service, Inc.
P.O. Box 214
Waldwick, N.J. 07463
(201) 797–8099

Glossary of Photographic Terms

This glossary is designed to help readers who are unsure of the meaning of some of the basic technical terms used in photography.

ASA: When photographers say ASA, they are referring to *film speed.*

Automatic camera: A camera with a built-in light meter and computer circuit that sets the correct exposure for you.

Automatic flash: A flash unit containing a light sensor and a special circuit that automatically provides correct exposure. Like any computer, it is up to you to program an autoflash correctly by setting film speed on the flash and using the calculator dial to find the right *f/*stop to set on your lens. Once set, the flash will give correct exposure over a wide range of flash-to-subject distances without further adjustment.

Dedicated flash: An electronic flash unit designed to work with a particular camera model. A dedicated unit gives you correct exposure over a wide range of conditions using circuitry inside both the flash unit and the camera.

Depth of field: The zone of sharp focus from near to far. Anything falling within this zone will appear sharp in a photograph. The extent of this zone of sharp focus depends on the focal length of your camera lens, the distance to which the lens is focused, and the *f/*stop you select. Small *f/*stops, such as *f/*11 or *f/*16, provide the greatest depth of field. Wide *f/*stops such as *f/*2.8 or *f/*4 give a very narrow depth of field. For photo inventory work, where sharpness is critical, you should use the smallest *f/*stop possible.

DIN: The German national standard for indicating *film speed.*

Electronic flash: A photographic lighting unit that produces a brilliant flash of light by means of a high-voltage spark inside a glass tube. Although we prefer floodlights for inventory work, a small, portable electronic flash, particularly an automatic or dedicated type, is a valuable accessory for general photography.

Exposure: The light required to produce a picture. A good exposure for an inventory photograph is one that yields the best color and detail rendition. Exposure depends on the *f/*stop and shutter speed that you set on your camera, and these will vary, depending on the speed of the film you are using, the strength of the light on your subject, and the lightness or darkness of the subject itself. The easiest way to get good exposures is to rely on a camera with a built-in light meter, such as an automatic camera, or to use an automatic or dedicated electronic flash unit. Hand-held light meters are a fine exposure measurement tool when used by a skilled photographer, but the average camera owner is better off using the metering system built into the camera.

F/stop: A lens opening. A normal 35mm camera lens contains a diaphragm with a hole in the middle that opens to admit more light and closes down to reduce the strength of light that hits the film. Many photographers find the *f/*stop scale on the lens confusing because the numbers used are unfamiliar. In fact, the numbers are fractions with the top part left off. A small number, such as *f/*4 indicates a larger opening (more light) than *f/*16 because 1/4 is larger than 1/16. This is fairly obvious when it comes to numbers such as *f/*2 (1/2), *f/*4 (1/4), *f/*8 (1/8) and *f/*16 (1/16). It is the numbers in between that most people stumble over. These numbers—*f/*2.8 (1/2.8), *f/*5.6 (1/5.6), *f/*11 (1/11) and so on—are based on the progression of the square root of 2 (1.41414), resulting in a number sequence that makes sense only to someone skilled in mathematics. Fortunately, you don't have to memorize the scale in order to use it. Just remember that the little numbers (1.8, 2, 2.8, and so on) give you more light and a smaller zone of sharp focus (see *depth of field*) and the big numbers (11, 16, and so on) give you less light and more depth of field.

The difference between adjacent numbers on the scale is one full stop. If you want to open up one full stop, click the *f/*stop (aperture) ring to the next smaller number, from *f/*11 to *f/*8 or *f/*8 to *f/*5.6 for example. To close down one stop, go to the next higher number, from *f/*11 to *f/*16 or from *f/*5.6 to *f/*8, for example.

*F/*stops bear an exact relationship to shutter speeds. Closing down one stop has the same effect as doubling the shutter speed: it reduces the amount of light entering the camera by one half. Opening up one stop has the same effect as dividing the shutter speed in half: it doubles the amount of light entering the camera. If you close down one *f/*stop and compensate by decreasing the shutter speed, say from 1/250 sec. to 1/125 sec., the amount of light entering the camera remains the same. In practice, this means that there is a whole range of *f/*stop-shutter-speed combinations that will give you the same exposure. For photo inventory work, your best bet is to use small *f/*stops (large numbers on the scale) such as *f/*11 or *f/*16 and whatever shutter speed will give the correct exposure at that *f/*stop.

Film speed: The speed with which a film reacts to light. Most films are marked in the ASA system, in which a doubling of the ASA number indicates a doubling of the film speed. For example, ASA 200 is twice as fast as ASA 100. Today, many film manufacturers also give their films ISO speed numbers, such as ISO 100/21°. The first part of the ISO number is the same as the familiar ASA number and is the one you should set on your meter. The second number, following the slash, has a degree sign to indicate that it is a log and is the same number found on the German DIN and British log scales, in which an increase of 3 indicates a doubling of the film speed. To find a correct exposure, you must set the right film speed on your camera, light meter or flash.

Flash bulb: A bulb containing foil that provides a brilliant burst of light when it burns. Technically, flashcubes, flashbars, and flipflash arrays are all variations on the old-fashioned flash bulb. If you have a lot of flash photos to take, flash bulb and its variations begin to get very expensive. On a shot-per-shot basis, electronic flash is significantly cheaper.

Floodlight: As used in this book, any lightbulb or lamp with a polished reflector designed for photographic use.

Focal length: The distance between the film and an optical point called the node of emission when the lens is focused to infinity. Most photographers prefer to think of it as the distance between the film and the middle of the lens. The shorter the focal length, the wider the view included in the picture. Short focal-length lenses are called *wide-angle lenses;* long focal-length lenses are telephotos. Wide-angle lenses for 35mm cameras run from about 18mm to 35mm, with 24mm and 28mm lenses preferred for inventory photography. Moderate telephoto lenses start at about about 85mm and the true telephoto range begins at about 200mm.

ISO: A standard for indicating *film speed* that has been developed by the International Standards Organization.

Manual flash: A fixed power electronic flash unit or a fixed-power (manual or "M") setting on an automatic flash. To calculate manual flash exposure, you must use the calculator dial or exposure table on the flash unit or use a guide number, as explained on page 64.

Photoflood: 1. Any screwbase lightbulb designed for photographic use. 2. A 3400 K lightbulb with a color quality that exactly matches the color response of Kodachrome 40 color slide film.

Normal lens: The lens supplied with most cameras. For 35mm cameras this is usually a 50mm or 55mm focal length, although some cameras designed for snapshot work have normal lenses in the 39 to 41mm range. (See *focal length.*)

Shutter speed: A camera contains a shutter that opens for a brief instant to let light in when you make an exposure. The length of time this shutter is open is called the *shutter speed.* To take consistently sharp photos with a normal lens when you hand-hold the camera, you should use a minimum speed of 1/125 sec. and for critical work, 1/250 sec. At slower speeds, use a camera support such as a tripod.

These restrictions do not apply when you use electronic flash, which is so fast it stops motion for you. The important thing to remember when you use flash is to set the correct flash synchronization speed on your camera. For 35mm single-lens reflex cameras, the synch speed is usually 1/60 sec., although some cameras have a special "X" setting, which is about 1/90 sec., and some will synchronize at 1/125 sec. If you are unsure, use 1/60 sec. If you forget and use too high a shutter speed, part of the picture will come out blank.

Tungsten light: 1. Any lightbulb containing a tungsten filament, such as a standard household lightbulb or a photoflood. 2. A 3200 K lightbulb with a color quality that exactly matches the color response of Ektachrome 160 tungsten color slide film.

Zoom lens: A lens that gives you a continuous range of focal lengths and will stay in focus while you zoom in or out. Wide-angle and normal-range zoom lenses are the most useful for inventory photography.

Index